THE
ANARCHISTS

James Joll

THE
ANARCHISTS

The Universal Library
GROSSET & DUNLAP
NEW YORK

Contents

Plates

Acknowledgements are due for the following plates: To the
National Portrait Gallery for no. 1; to the Musée du Petit Palais,
Paris, and Photographie Giraudon, Paris, for no. 2; to the
Staatliche Gemäldegalerie, Dresden, and Deutsche Fotothek,
Dresden, for no. 4; to the Radio Times Hulton Picture Library
for 3, 5, 6, 8(*a*); to the British Museum for no. 7; to Señora
Montseny for no. 8(*b*).

Acknowledgements

A work of synthesis of this kind necessarily owes much to the researches of others, and I should like to acknowledge my debt to all those authors cited in the notes and to apologize to them when I have used the facts they have discovered to support conclusions with which they may not agree.

I am most grateful to my friends Raymond Carr, Hugh Thomas, and David Footman, who have given me invaluable advice on the sections of the book dealing with Spain and Russia and who have saved me from many errors. I am additionally indebted to Mr Raymond Carr for allowing me to see parts of his forthcoming volume on Spain for the Oxford History of Modern Europe. Mr Marshall Shatz, of Columbia University, New York, was also kind enough to let me use an unpublished paper on anarchists in Russia.

I should also like to thank the many people who have helped me with their ideas and suggestions, and especially Mr Ivan Avakumovič, Professor Sir Isaiah Berlin, Dr C-P Clasen, Mr F. W. Deakin, Mr Arthur Lehning, M. Jean Maitron, Mme Federica Montseny, Mr Bertil Ollman, Dr Saul Rose, Mr Christopher Seton-Watson, and Dr Theodore Zeldin.

I am also very grateful to Miss Mary Worthington and Mrs Jane Wilson for valuable secretarial help.

Introduction

'You are miserable isolated individuals. You are bankrupt. You have played out your role. Go where you belong, to the dust-heap of history.' Trotsky's denunciation of his menshevik opponents in October 1917 is typical of a whole way of looking at history. According to this view, it is the causes which triumph that alone should interest the historian, and those movements and individuals which do not contribute to the forward march of the historical process are, it is held, rightly neglected and scorned, or dismissed as reactionary or blind. It is not the Marxists alone who have regarded history in this way; Christian historians have implied the same view about pagans, and liberal historians about conservatives. But it is unsuccessful revolutionaries who have been the chief victims of those historians who are only interested in success. When a revolution succeeds, historians are concerned to trace its roots and unravel its origins and development, so that, very often, the whole chain of events leading to it over many decades is represented as an inevitable process, and each idea or episode is judged by the extent to which it helped or hindered the final result. On the other hand, the revolutions which failed are treated as blind alleys, and the men and ideas that inspired them are rarely studied for their own inherent interest. As a consequence, much that is interesting and curious is neglected and forgotten, and the field of vision of the historian is deliberately restricted. Yet, if the aim of the historian, like that of the artist, is to enlarge our picture of the world, to give us a new way of looking at things, then the study of failure can often be as instructive and rewarding as the study of success. A recurrent type of failure and its causes may throw light both on the psychology of individuals and on the structure of societies.

The anarchists have suffered as much as any minority from

the historians' cult of success. They never made a successful revolution. Their political theories are full of logical flaws and
mistaken assumptions. The sympathy which one type of anarchist
doctrine might have won has been lost by the ruthless and sense-
less violence and terrorism which was characteristic of another
school of anarchist practice. Nevertheless, the theory and practice
of the anarchists over the last hundred years have raised a number
of questions about the nature of industrial society. They have
provided a continuous and fundamental criticism of the modern
concept of the state, and have challenged the assumptions of
nearly all schools of contemporary political thought. They have
attacked, often in the most brutal and direct manner, the values
and institutions of the established social and moral order. Much
of this has ended in futility, sometimes farcical, sometimes tragic.
Yet the protests which the anarchist movement has made express
a recurrent psychological need, and one which has by no means
disappeared with the apparent failure of anarchism as a serious
political and social force.

The anarchist movement is a product of the nineteenth century. It is, in part at least, the result of the impact of machines
and industry on a peasant or artisan society. It throve on the
myth of the revolution as it was developed after 1789; yet, at the
same time, it was the failure of political revolutions and constitutional reforms to satisfy economic and social needs which led the
anarchists to challenge the methods and the goals of the revolutionaries themselves. The values the anarchists attempted to
demolish were those of the increasingly powerful centralized,
industrialized state which, in the nineteenth and twentieth centuries, has seemed the model to which all societies are approaching. The anarchists were thus obliged to accumulate enemies: to
the landlords and priests of the old order were soon added the
revolutionary tyrants and bureaucrats who were being produced
by the movements that aimed at creating the new society. The
anarchists were always engaged on at least two fronts simultaneously.

Although the anarchist movement is a phenomenon of the past
century and a half, it represents a type of revolt that can be found

far earlier. The anarchists themselves are proud of this ancestry and have laid claims to many a forerunner who would have been surprised to find himself in their company. Zeno and the Stoics, the Gnostic heretics and the Anabaptists have all been hailed as ancestors of the modern anarchist movement. There is, indeed, a sense in which these movements of religious and social revolt or withdrawal do represent one of the important strands in anarchist thought and action. The anarchists combine a belief in the possibility of a violent and sudden transformation of society with a confidence in the reasonableness of men and in the possibility of human improvement and perfection. On the one hand, they are the heirs of all the utopian, millenarian religious movements which have believed that the end of the world is at hand and have confidently expected that 'the trumpet shall sound and we shall be changed, in a moment, in the twinkling of an eye'. On the other hand, they are also the children of the Age of Reason. (Metternich, indeed, once called Proudhon the illegitimate son of the Enlightenment.) They are the people who carry their belief in reason and progress and peaceful persuasion through to its logical limits. Anarchism is both a religious faith and a rational philosophy; and many of its anomalies are the product of the clash between the two, and of the tensions between the different kinds of temperament which they represent.

Part One

CHAPTER I
Heresy and Reason

I

There are movements in the history of all religions which reject all authority, whether temporal or spiritual, and claim complete liberty to act in accordance with an inner light. And, both because of persecution and as a mark of their complete turning away from the world, the devotees of many heretical sects were forced into clandestinity and conspiracy. In the Christian church movements of this kind are familiar enough. They have been studied by the sociologists who want to establish the laws of human social and political behaviour; they have been quoted by Marxist writers as examples of the first stirrings of proletarian revolt and as early stages in the class struggle. Other writers[1] have attempted to show the links between these ways of thought and action and the all-embracing totalitarian movements of our own time. Certain of these sects have undoubtedly attracted men and women of the same type as were later to be captivated by the ideas of the anarchist movement; and, before discussing the development of modern anarchism, it is perhaps worth briefly considering what recurrent human needs seem to be satisfied by these extreme beliefs and what kind of people are drawn to them.

All heresies are movements of revolt against established authority, but some of them are purely religious and doctrinal. Their attack is on the beliefs held by the established church and their criticism of the social order is implicit only. They do not have as their objective the changing of social conditions in this world, but rather withdrawal from it and a purification of religious beliefs in preparation for the next. Yet any heresy which demands a withdrawal from the world implies a criticism of the world's values. And, moreover, the very act of withdrawal, especially if it led to the establishment of a group of like-minded devotees, often involved those who practised it in measures which might seem dangerously subversive. Many sects, such as the Waldensians in north Italy and southern France in the early thirteenth century, made a cult of poverty – and thus implicitly condemned their fellow citizens who pursued riches. Others, as one of them told an ecclesiastical court near Turin about 1030, practised a kind of communism among themselves – '*omnem nostram possessionem cum omnibus hominibus communem habemus*'.[1] Such · movements of renunciation did not necessarily disturb the authorities; and the instincts which gave rise to them could be canalized into the service of the church and inspire the great orders of mendicant friars.[2] There were, however, sects of an even more subversive kind, which, without going so far as to provoke open political revolt, yet rejected the values of existing society so completely as to make the authorities regard them as inherently dangerous. These are the movements which are loosely grouped as the Gnostic heresies. In the Middle Ages the most famous of these was that of the Cathari or Albigensians, who won the support of the counts of Toulouse in the thirteenth century, and who were only suppressed after a bloody civil war and persecution.

The central belief of the Gnostic sects was that the existing world was totally corrupt, unreal, transient and of no importance. It was the world of the spirit that mattered, the spiritual values and exercises which kept the soul in touch with the eternity for which it was ultimately destined after it had escaped from the snares and delusions of this world. This was an attitude which could have very different results in practice. Some, like the Cathari of Languedoc themselves, practised an ascetic purity of life as a sign of their rejection of the world's values. But this austerity was not the only possible way of behaving once the current system of morality had been dismissed. If the world were viewed as transient, then one's conduct in it did not matter, as none of the accepted moral rules applied, and, indeed, actions which defied these rules could be held to be in the interests of the true faith. It is easy to see how sects which professed a disregard for accepted values could very quickly be suspected of every kind of immorality and debauchery. The propaganda against the Albigensians, for example, is full of accusations of every kind of vice, especially sexual. Any group of people which met in secret, which was reputed to have repudiated marriage, and which rejected as irrelevant the ties and standards of existing society, was almost inevitably bound to seem to the authorities to be an intolerable danger. And, even if it is true that, in the history of heretical sects, examples can be found of conduct that could be labelled immoral by the standards of contemporary society, it is also true that accusations of sexual misbehaviour are one of the easiest ways of inciting men to action against a minority. All doctrines, whether religious or anarchist, which wholly deny the value of the existing order of things may produce either puritans or libertines; and a single one of the latter quickly makes the public forget the far greater number of the former.

Men were attracted by the Gnostic heresies because they were stirred by a violent hatred of what seemed to be the false values of the existing order. By the circumstances of the time they were forced into small clandestine communities; and often the secrecy which was forced on them developed into a love of conspiracy for its own sake. The rejection of the world could lead to extremes of ascetic devotion; or occasionally it could lead to acts of shocking and violent defiance of existing morality. The reaction of the worldly authorities to movements of this kind has always been the same: fear of the subversive results which follow the denial of existing values leads to persecution, based on rumours of a widespread conspiracy to overthrow the whole social order; and in turn the rumours are turned into an effective propaganda campaign in which every sort of accusation, smear and innuendo is used against the victims, regardless of their actual behaviour or crimes.

However, while those religious sects whose doctrines and practice were based on a withdrawal from the world and a contempt for its values have obvious similarities with many later utopian and quietist beliefs, as well as with an extreme kind of anarchist individualist nonconformity, it is the sects that had an explicit programme of social change in this world which have

been claimed as the ancestors of later revolutionary movements
and which, indeed, do have many features in common with
them. The history of medieval heresies is full of movements like
that led by Tachelm in Flanders in the twelfth century, who persuaded his followers to withhold tithes on the grounds that
'sacraments were no better than pollutions, churches no better
than brothels'.[1] In cases of this kind resentment against the
worldliness and alleged corruption of the established church led
to action which was revolutionary in its implications. Sometimes
the leader and his followers set themselves up as an ideal community waiting for the Second Coming, in confident expectation
that it was imminent. Others limited their attack on the powers
and corruption of the church to a more general demand for social
justice: 'magistrates, provosts, beadles, mayors – nearly all live by
robbery . . . they all batten on the poor . . . the stronger robs
the weaker', one fourteenth-century pamphleteer wrote, in language which comes close to that of later movements of social
revolt.[2] And another agitator was already posing the question of
what happens to the surplus value of the goods produced by the
poor. 'I would like to strangle the nobles and the clergy, every one
of them . . . Good working men make the wheaten bread but
they never chew it; no, all they get is the sifting from the corn,
and from good wine they get nothing but the dregs and from
good cloth nothing but the chaff. Everything that is tasty and
good goes to the nobles and clergy.'[3]

Movements of this kind based their demand for social changes
on a belief in the immediate possibility of the millennium – a
combination of the Second Coming and a return to the Golden
Age of the Garden of Eden before the Fall. Some of these beliefs
survived and recurred over centuries; others were tacitly absorbed
into orthodox doctrines. Most of these sects, however, met the
fate that awaited the utopian groups of later centuries. The
leader would become increasingly megalomaniac; the group
would split into rival movements; or else it would provoke the
resentment of the authorities, and its chief members would be
burnt at the stake. It is easy to understand the type of temperament that was attracted to movements of this kind. There was

simultaneously a sense of desperation, a feeling that there was
something hopelessly wrong with the world, and at the same time
there was a firm belief in the possibility of putting things right,
if only the institutions which hindered the doing of God's will
could be destroyed. What is harder to discover is whether there
were any common social or economic factors which led to these
movements of revolt, and whether the historian would be justified in comparing these movements, sociologically as well as
psychologically, to some of the revolutionary movements of the
nineteenth and twentieth centuries. It is tempting to look for
similarities of external circumstances under which utopian or
millenarian sects flourished; and it is a temptation which not all
writers about heresies have resisted. One historian, for example,
boldly explains the success of the Cathar movement in Languedoc
by writing: 'With their lively taste for independence, for personal
liberty, the population of this region felt itself in harmony with
a doctrine which implied as its essence spiritual liberation and
the dignity of the individual.'[1] How convenient it would be to
the historian of anarchist movements to be able to accept this
view, and thus account for the success of Spanish anarchism by
applying it to the artisans of Catalonia, the land bordering on
Languedoc! However, he would then find it hard to explain the
continuous success of millenarian heresies among the less volatile
Dutch or Czechs. Nevertheless, it does seem that, although occasionally, as in the case of the Albigensians, the nobility joined
these movements for their own political ends, or even for that
matter from genuine conviction, the bulk of the support for them
came from the lower classes of society. Thus, as the Cathar movement declined and was driven deeper underground, its most
faithful adherents were to be found among the weavers and
butchers and, lower still in the social scale, the whores and the
strolling players.[2]

Many of these movements arose in periods of social and
economic change when the population was increasing fast and
urban industry growing. Thus the cloth cities of Flanders, and the
growing industrial centres in the west and south of Germany
were, as Professor Cohn has suggested, areas where these heretical

movements were especially frequent in the twelfth and thirteenth centuries. For the most part, however, the evidence about the background of these medieval heresies is too scanty to justify any generalization about the social and economic conditions which produced them. They spread from one country to another and from one class to another, and they naturally grew more rapidly when traditional ties were loosened by war or other disasters, when pestilence filled men with the fear of imminent dissolution, or when crop failure or the pressure of increased taxation made the economic basis of their lives uncertain. In such circumstances it was not surprising that the foundations of the social system should be shaken by waves of mass religious emotion.

It is in writing about the Reformation that historians have made more determined efforts to link heretical movements with economic and social change. This is mainly because it is in certain religious movements of the fifteenth, sixteenth and seventeenth centuries that modern revolutionary writers have seen their precursors, and because they are therefore anxious to interpret these revolts in terms of their own political and philosophical beliefs. Works about communism and anarchism by adherents of these doctrines devote much space to Thomas Müntzer and the Peasants' Revolt in Germany in the sixteenth century, and to the Anabaptists and especially to the group that controlled the city of Münster for a few months of desperate 'war communism' in 1535. This interpretation, by which religious reformers are made to appear primarily apostles of social revolution, has often been pressed too far, and it underestimates the extent to which men are moved by abstract ideas and the genuinely religious motives which prompt many of their actions. Nevertheless it is true that many of the religious movements of the Reformation had a revolutionary content and attacked not only the religious dogmas of the established church but also the social and political institutions of the established state.

Thomas Müntzer, who became a revolutionary leader after starting as a purely religious reformer like Luther, began as a priest in the church he was to attack so bitterly, and at the start was much influenced by Luther's doctrines. However, Luther's

criticism and, above all, Luther's doctrine of justification by faith
were too mild for Müntzer's turbulent and twisted nature, and,
from 1520 on, he plunged into the most violent agitation, de-
manding the immediate destruction of the existing order of things
in order to prepare the way, here and now, for the advent of the
Kingdom of God upon Earth. It was an appeal of a kind that
always finds a response in a time of change, when the hopes of a
rapid transformation of the world have been raised and then disappointed by the slow pace of reform; and it was an appeal to
which the peasants of Thuringia, as well as the silver miners of
Zwickau and the copper miners of Mansfeld, where Müntzer
preached his apocalyptic doctrine, responded eagerly. For a time
members of the ruling house of Saxony showed some interest in
his teaching, but, partly at Luther's prompting, they soon
realized that Müntzer's views implied a social as well as a religious
revolution, and over the next two or three years Müntzer's writings became more and more outspokenly and unequivocally revolutionary in content. In 1525 he became involved in events
which sealed his reputation as an apostle of social revolt; for in
March of that year the great Peasants' Revolt broke out all over
Germany. Its causes were many and complex; and how far
Müntzer was responsible for stirring it up is still a subject of
controversy. There is no doubt, however, that, at least in Thuringia, his doctrines exacerbated the state of unrest caused by the
establishment of strong princely power in the German states and
the consequent increase in taxation. And there is no doubt, too,
that Müntzer himself welcomed the upheaval as a step on the
way to the overthrow of the existing order. Müntzer joined the
peasant army, and, when it was easily defeated, he was captured and executed.

However, the historical problems of the causes of the Peasants'
Revolt and Müntzer's exact part in it are not what is important
for the study of later revolutionary movements. What gave
Müntzer his appeal to subsequent revolutionary writers, whether
Marxist or anarchist, was his association with a genuine attempt
at a social revolution and the revolutionary violence of the language in which he expressed himself. It is this above all that

brings him close to later anarchists. He insisted constantly that the wholesale overthrow of the existing system by force was a necessary preliminary to the new order. 'At them, at them while the fire is hot,' he exhorted his followers. 'Don't let your sword get cold! Don't let it go lame! Hammer cling-clang on Nimrod's anvil! Throw their tower to the ground! So long as they are alive you will never shake off the fear of men. . . .'[1] Müntzer is typical of one class of revolutionary in that it is the act of revolt that is more important to him than the nature of the post-revolutionary world. And in this, at least, he is the true precursor of many of the revolutionaries of a later age.

The Anabaptists are also claimed as precursors by the revolutionaries of the nineteenth century. Here again the similarities are perhaps more of temperament than of doctrine or circumstance; but there is at least one episode, the siege of Münster in 1535, which has achieved legendary importance in revolutionary historiography. In fact, it is a mistake to talk of the Anabaptists as if they were a single coherent movement. The various Anabaptist groups often had little in common except their belief that they belonged to the Community of Saints. They included a wide variety of doctrines and temperaments among their adherents. Some were violent revolutionaries, some tranquil and puritanical quietists. Some believed in practical revolutionary action; others preferred, like the Gnostic heretics in the Middle Ages, to withdraw from this world and its ways and to place their hopes in the next. All of them, however, agreed in denying the necessity of the state. Since the baptized were in direct contact with God, all further intermediaries between God and themselves were redundant. States and churches were unnecessary, indeed evil, since they stood between man and the divine light that was in him and which would direct him how to order his life. From this it was an easy step to demand the destruction of existing society and the substitution of a millenarian new order whose laws would be revealed to the faithful by the inner light of a prophet or leader: and, as so often in the history of revolutionary movements, what began as a movement of liberation could easily end as terrorist autocracy.

The Anabaptists were to be found in Switzerland, Germany and the Low Countries, and it was in the city of Münster in Westphalia – a state under the rule of its bishop – that the movement assumed its most extreme revolutionary form. Münster had become a Lutheran stronghold by 1533, but its inhabitants quickly became converts to the more exciting Anabaptist creed. The town and its neighbourhood had for the past few years suffered from a series of disasters and difficulties – plague, economic distress, heavy taxation, religious strife – and its people were in the mood to listen to prophets of doom and destruction, and to place their hopes in a cataclysmic and imminent change. Thus it was easy for the Anabaptist 'prophets', Jan Mathys of Harlem and his disciple and successor John Boeckeler, known as John of Leyden, to rouse them to a state of revolutionary fervour and excitement that lasted for about a year, during which they believed that Münster was about to become the New Jerusalem, while all outside it would perish. The Anabaptists took complete control of the town. Roman Catholics and Lutherans were expelled; and this led the bishop, still the nominal sovereign of the city, to take action. With an army of mercenaries, and later with the help of neighbouring rulers, the bishop laid siege to the city, and the Anabaptists' social revolution and reign of terror were carried out simultaneously with the fighting of a fierce war. First of all, to show their contempt for the existing laws of property, they destroyed all records of contracts and debts. (This destruction of the physical evidence of an unjust social structure was a feature of Italian and Spanish anarchist movements in the nineteenth century; and their revolts usually began by a ceremonial burning of the property and other registers at the Town Hall.) Then a kind of emergency communism was instituted, with communal stores of food, clothing and bedding. The movement was militantly anti-intellectual (again a feature of some later revolutionary movements) and books and manuscripts were destroyed as worldly and unchristian.

As might be expected, Anabaptist rule in Münster did not last long. Jan Mathys was killed leading a sortie; and John of

Leyden's rule soon turned into an insane megalomaniac terror –
accompanied by the polygamy that was so common a feature in
the lives of the 'prophets' of later utopian communities. In June
1535 the city was captured and early the following year John of
Leyden was tortured to death by his captors. The whole incident
has acquired a certain legendary character in the genealogy of
revolutions, and, like Müntzer, John of Leyden has been claimed
by later revolutionaries as one of themselves, although in fact his
rule in Münster exemplified only the blindest, maddest and most
negative aspects of anarchistic fanaticism and violence.

What emerges from any study of heretical religious movements is that certain kinds of people feel a recurrent need to
react violently against the existing order, to question the right
of the existing authorities to rule, and to assert instead that all
authority is unnecessary and evil. And this revolt against society
and its leaders is accompanied, according to the temperament
concerned, either by a belief in the healing properties of violent
destruction, the importance of revolution as an end in itself, or
else by a boundlessly optimistic belief in the possibilities of an
immediate and radical change for the better, the building of a
completely new social order on the ruins of the old. The total
rejection of the values of contemporary society, a hatred of
authority, a belief in the possibility and indeed the imminence of
a complete revolution – these characteristics are accompanied by
a sense of belonging to an elect and often secret group.

The temperament that once led men to adopt millenarian,
utopian religious beliefs may (as some writers have suggested)
have led them in our own time to support all-embracing, totalitarian revolutionary dogmas, but it can also lead to the rejection
of all authority and to the revolt against any sort of state.
Beliefs which lead one man to the acceptance of a totalitarian
dictatorship may lead another to the complete rejection of all
authority.

Although anarchism is also a product of the rationalism of the
eighteenth century, and anarchist political theory is based on
confidence in man's reasonable nature and belief in the possibility
of intellectual and moral progress, this is only one of its strands.

The other is a tendency which can only be described as religious, and which links the anarchists emotionally, if not doctrinally, with the extreme heretics of earlier centuries. It is the clash between these two types of temperament, the religious and the rationalist, the apocalyptic and the humanist, which has made so much of anarchist doctrine seem contradictory. It is also this double nature that gives anarchism a wide and universal appeal. The beliefs of anarchists cannot be understood without an understanding of the political ideas they inherited from the Enlightenment. But their actions can often be explained only in terms of the psychology of religious belief.

2

If it is the heretical religious temperament that drives men to become anarchists, many of the actual doctrines they have adopted are, like most other systems of modern political thought, derived from the philosophers of the eighteenth century. A belief in man's infinite possibilities of improvement, a confidence that societies can be reformed on rational principles, these are ideas that are common to Condorcet and Bentham, Montesquieu and Helvetius; and they form the basis of all subsequent liberal theory and practice. Yet, while anarchism presupposes the natural goodness of man, it is a doctrine that came to differ profoundly from the political ideas of the Enlightenment. The French philosophers of the eighteenth century were not by any means anarchists: they accepted the idea of the state, and of a state that might, in certain circumstances, have wide powers to coerce its citizens in their own interests. Moreover, even the most radical writings of the eighteenth century – Rousseau's *Discourse on Inequality*, for example – envisage that it is by political change that the social reforms that they advocate will come about, whereas the anarchists have always insisted on the necessity of social and economic change as opposed to political reforms, which they have constantly regarded as irrelevant and even harmful.

The only eighteenth-century thinkers who might be claimed as forerunners of the anarchists are one or two figures on the

fringe of the great philosophical movements of the day, shadowy
figures with cranky views such as the Abbé Jean Meslier, or the
mysterious Morelly, whose 'negation of government' Proudhon
was later to praise. Yet these writers were so obscure and so un-
influential that their very existence has sometimes been questioned. Meslier's *Testament*, for example, was first published by
Voltaire, who has sometimes been suspected of being the author,
using the name Meslier as a convenient pseudonym for the utterance of violently anti-clerical sentiments. Another work, *Le bon
sens du Curé Meslier*, is actually by d'Holbach. In fact, Meslier does
seem to have been a real person, a village priest enraged by his
ecclesiastical superiors and moving on from criticisms of the
established church to an attack on all religion and all authority
as such. The title of his *Testament* gives the gist of his message:
'Memoirs of the thoughts and sentiments of Jean Meslier concerning part of the errors and false conduct and government of
mankind, in which can be seen clear and evident demonstrations
of the vanity and falseness of all divinities and all religions. . . .'
What made Meslier a true if ineffective revolutionary, and has
earned him his place in anarchist history, is the violence of his
language and his insistence – in phrases that might be by that
other rebellious priest Thomas Müntzer – on the need for action:
'Let all the great ones of the earth and all the nobles hang and
strangle themselves with the priests' guts, the great men and
nobles who trample on the poor people and torment them and
make them miserable.'[1] Sometimes, too, he strikes the authentic
note of social revolt that is characteristic of anarchists: 'Your
salvation lies in your hands . . . keep for yourselves with your
own hands all the riches and goods you produce so abundantly
with the sweat of your brow; keep them for yourselves and your
fellows. Do not give anything to the proud and useless idlers who
do nothing useful in this world.'[2] In general, however, it is his
anti-clerical and anti-religious sentiments which appealed to men
like Voltaire and d'Holbach, who were pleased to discover this
eccentric and 'primitive' figure uttering, with sincerity and
naïveté, views which expressed some of their own feelings.

Morelly is an even more shadowy figure. Was he invented by

Diderot? Was he the same as the Morelli whom Rousseau knew in Geneva? There seems still to be considerable uncertainty about the answers. However, his *Code de la Nature*, published in 1755, shows how the accepted ideas of the eighteenth century could be given a radical and anarchistic tinge. 'From the sceptre to the shepherd's crook, from the tiara to the humblest smock, if one asks who governs men, the answer is easy; personal interest or the interest of another which is adopted as one's own for reasons of vanity and which always derives from the first. But what is the origin of these monstrosities? Property.'[1] Yet there is little that is truly anarchist in Morelly's crabbed book. If he is claimed as a forerunner by anarchist writers, it is simply because of his belief that institutions must somehow conform to the intentions of Nature, and because he saw that the question of property was the fundamental one for both morals and politics. In fact, Morelly is more accurately described as a forerunner of the most rigorous communism than of anarchism. The two doctrines, during the nineteenth century, are often close to each other; and, as will be seen, some later theorists, such as Kropotkin, called themselves anarcho-communists. Yet anarchists and communists are temperamentally far apart; all that they have in common is their view of property and their rejection of private ownership. The true anarchist tradition would reject the intense communal regulation of the individual's activities which Morelly suggested, for, although Morelly proclaimed the abolition of private property and the right of every citizen to be supported by the community, it was a community of spartan discipline which he envisaged: everyone was to do compulsory labour service between the age of twenty and twenty-five; marriage was compulsory at the age of puberty, and no divorce was allowed for at least ten years. Everyone was rigidly kept in his place in the family; families were organized into tribes, and tribes into cities, so that Morelly seems to have envisaged a hierarchy of authorities rather than the free association of independent communes which is characteristic of later anarchist thinking. Morelly had no immediate or, for that matter, long-term influence, and it is only because of the extreme nature of his communist doctrines and his attack on

private property that he has regularly found a place in the writings of communist and anarchist historians.

The true eighteenth-century ancestor of anarchism, as of
almost all other later political doctrines, is Jean-Jacques Rousseau. Although minor and forgotten figures like Meslier and
Morelly may have thought of specific ideas and institutions comparable to those of the later anarchists, it is Rousseau who
created the climate of ideas in which anarchism was possible.
It is Rousseau who changed the whole style of political discussion
and who fused the rationalism of the *philosophes* with the warmth,
enthusiasm and sensibility of the romantics. In some degree,
what he said is less important than the way he said it, and it is
for this reason that he finds a place in the history of all subsequent
political thought, so that he is seen by some as the forerunner of
'totalitarian democracy' and by others as the ancestor of the
most extreme libertarianism. As far as the anarchists were concerned, it was perhaps Rousseau's ideals of Nature and of education which were to have the most influence.

To the belief in the perfectibility of man and of human institutions, Rousseau added in particular the notion of the Noble
Savage, a figure dear to all anarchists' hearts. 'Man was born
free and is everywhere in chains' becomes, in fact, a first principle
of anarchist thought. The idea of a happy primitive world, a
state of nature in which, so far from being engaged in a struggle
of all against all, men lived in a state of mutual cooperation, was
to have a powerful appeal to anarchists of all kinds. And, even
if Rousseau himself was to contribute to the development of
political theories based on strong state power, the ideas of primitive simplicity and goodness which he propounded, the theories of
rational education which he advocated, are very similar to those
of Kropotkin or of Francisco Ferrer.

The fundamental idea that man is by nature good and that
it is institutions that corrupt him remains the basis of all anarchist thought; and almost all anarchists would agree with Rousseau's remark that '*On façonne des plantes par la culture et les hommes
par l'éducation*'.[1] And, just as in Emile's ideal education, the child's
latent qualities are drawn out by sincerity, simplicity, liberty

and natural behaviour, so in the anarchist society men's instincts for good will be brought out by much the same treatment.

While Condorcet or Rousseau contributed many of the ideas to the anarchist thinkers of the next century, and while figures like Meslier or Morelly provide the anarchist historian with ideological links between certain apostles of modern social revolt and their predecessors, there was one English writer who, starting from the commonplaces of eighteenth century philosophical belief, elaborated the most complete and worked-out statement of rational anarchist belief ever attempted, a philosophy of anarchism carried through to its logical conclusions, however surprising and absurd these might be. This was William Godwin. Godwin was born in 1756 and lived to the age of eighty. During his long life he was to be very famous – so much so that his second wife was able to introduce herself to him by asking: 'Is it possible that I behold the immortal Godwin?' – yet by the time he died he was almost forgotten.

Godwin was the son of a Calvinist minister and was himself first intended to be an Independent clergyman. His upbringing left a permanent mark on his thought, and although his reaction against it was what turned him into an anarchist ('To Godwin God was a tyrant to be dethroned', as H. N. Brailsford has put it),[1] the puritanism and asceticism of Calvinistic doctrine colour all his political beliefs. His utopia, like that of so many British political thinkers, is redolent of the nonconformist chapel, even though religion has been banished from it. Godwin had considerable success as a novelist, but his great work is the *Enquiry Concerning Political Justice*, published in the midst of the French Revolution in 1793. By this time Godwin was already disillusioned about the prospects of achieving any sort of reform within the existing political system. Five years earlier, at the time of the Westminster election of 1788, he had written: 'Scandal, pitiful mean mutual scandal, never was more plentifully displayed. Electioneering is a trade so despicably degrading, so eternally incompatible with moral and mental dignity that I can scarcely believe a truly great mind capable of the dirty drudgery of such vice.'[2] But the experiences of a direct revolution in France were

no more encouraging than the workings of the British constitution at home. Godwin, for all his sympathy with the Revolution
and its supporters in England, was a bitter opponent of Jacobin-
ism and the Terror. All his political thought was inspired by
beliefs and ideals very different from those of Robespierre, and
it is ironical, as well as being typical of the fate of many anarchists, that he was regarded at home as the most extreme kind
of revolutionary terrorist.

The fundamental principle of Godwin's political thought is
that justice and happiness are indissolubly linked. The practice
of virtue is the true road to individual happiness, he writes.[1]
Consequently, the society which is based on justice will be a
society whose members will necessarily be happy. It is a theory
which implies a profoundly optimistic view of human nature,
for Godwin does not seem to have doubted for a moment that his
ideal society could sooner or later be created. 'Perfectibility', he
wrote, 'is one of the most unequivocal characteristics of the
human species, so that the political as well as the intellectual
state of man may be presumed to be in a course of progressive
improvement.'[2] The perfectibility of man is the result of the fact
that he is, according to Godwin's extreme version of a doctrine
first held by Hume, born without any innate ideas. His mind
and character are therefore capable of being influenced to an
indefinite degree by suggestions from outside. This suggestibility,
the vulnerability of human beings to all forms of intellectual and
moral pressure, is both man's weakness and his strength. It is his
weakness because it gives governments an almost unlimited power
of controlling their subjects by all sorts of propaganda and education. But it is also man's strength, since, given an educational
system that inculcates the right ideas, he can learn to live peacefully with his neighbours in a community where force is unnecessary and the good of each is the happiness of all. Since it is
one of Godwin's fundamental, and most questionable, premises
that man is always amenable to reason and argument, all vice is
eradicable by explanation and an understanding of its causes.
'All vice', he says, 'is nothing more than error and mistake reduced into practice and adopted as the principle of our conduct.'[3]

There are moments when he goes further and suggests that not only man's moral vices but also his physical ills can be cured by the exercise of reason. He looked forward to a remote future when disease and even perhaps death itself might be removed by mental effort: 'We talk familiarly indeed of the limits of our faculties, but nothing is more difficult than to point them out. Mind, in a progressive view at least, is infinite.'[1]

Usually, in the world as it exists, it is the state which applies the pressure on individuals; and the present political, social and economic order only serves to keep man in ignorance of his true interests and to perpetuate his vices. 'Whips, axes and gibbets, dungeons, chains and racks are the most approved and established methods of persuading men to obedience and impressing upon their minds the lessons of reason. Hundreds of victims are annually sacrificed at the shrine of positive law and political institutions.'[2] The only possible way to improve human beings is to remove the causes of their vices. All crime must have a reason; if the reason is removed, the crime will vanish. In Godwin's view there is no crime without a motive, no act that has not a rational aim that can be explained and discussed. It is this that makes the question of property fundamental in any society, since the commonest cause of crime is the lack of the necessities of life. 'The subject of property', he says, 'is the keystone that completes the fabric of political justice.'[3]

The solution he put forward was simple enough. If property is the cause of all evil, it should be abolished. Men's needs, he thought, were in themselves few; and little would be required in a society where the motives of vanity and ambition, the desire to outshine one's neighbour, had been eradicated by the inculcation of a true scale of values. Moreover, since men would quickly learn to despise ostentation and luxury, the amount of labour required for the necessities of life would be far less than in existing society; and indeed machinery might soon enable manual labour to be abolished almost completely. 'It is by no means clear', Godwin thought, 'that the most extensive operations will not be within the reach of one man; or, to make use of a familiar instance, that a plough may not be turned into a field and perform its office without the need of superintendence.'[1] Such tasks as do need to be performed will quickly be allotted on a rational basis: 'Do you want my table? Make one for yourself; or, if I be more skilful in that respect than you, I will make one for you. Do you want it immediately? Let us compare the urgency of your wants and mine, and let justice decide.'[2]

Godwin is a true anarchist in that he does not envisage property being exploited in common but simply that it should be available for whoever needs it. In fact, he carries his dislike of coercion and of any infringement on the individual to its most extreme logical conclusions. 'Everything that is usually understood by the term cooperation is to some degree an evil. . . . If I be expected to eat and work in conjunction with my neighbour, it must either be at a time most convenient to me, or to him, or to neither of us. We cannot be reduced to clockwork uniformity. Hence, it follows that all supererogatory cooperation is to be carefully avoided.'[3] Even music is suspect, because it involves an intolerable subjection of the players' individuality: 'Shall we have concerts of music? The miserable state of mechanism of the majority of the performers is so conspicuous as to be even at this day a topic of mortification and ridicule. . . . Shall we have theatrical exhibitions? This seems to include an absurd and vicious cooperation. It may be doubted whether men will hereafter come forward in any mode gravely to repeat words and ideas not their own. It may be doubted whether any musical performer will habitually execute the compositions of others. . . . All formal repetition of other men's ideas seems to be a scheme for imprisoning for so long a time the operations of our own mind. It borders perhaps in this respect upon a breach of sincerity, which requires that we should give immediate utterance to every useful and valuable idea that occurs to our thoughts.'[4]

Other forms of communal activity are equally repugnant. 'Ought I to come at a certain hour', Godwin writes, 'from the museum where I am working, the recess where I am meditating or the observatory where I remark the phenomena of nature, to a certain hall appropriated to the office of eating, instead of eating, as reason bids me, at the time and place most suited to my avocations?'[1]

The same principles are rigorously applied to the family. Indeed, this is a doubly mistaken institution, for it not only involves unnecessary subordination of one personality to another but it is also based on property. Therefore there is no need of it: sex and reproduction are for Godwin, one cannot help feeling, unnecessary complications for a rational man in a rational society. 'It cannot be definitely affirmed whether it be known in such a state of society who is the father of each child.'[2] Children will be brought up on strictly rational principles, though even Godwin admits that in infancy this 'will frequently devolve upon the mother; unless by frequent parturition or by the very nature of these cares, that were found to render her share of the burden unequal; and then it would be amicably and willingly participated by others'.[3] Subsequent education will be on lines that go further than those practised by even the most advanced twentieth-century educational reformers. 'No creature in human form will be expected to learn anything, but because he desires it and has some conception of its utility and value; and every man, in proportion to his capacity, will be ready to furnish such general hints and comprehensive views as will suffice for the guidance and encouragement of him who studies from a principle of desire.'[4] There are indeed hints that the production of children, and therefore their upbringing and education, may become unnecessary, since reason may yet discover the secret of physical immortality and perpetual youth. Godwin's attitude to sex is, in fact, typical of his view of man's nature. In the ideal society, 'I shall', he writes, 'assiduously cultivate the intercourse of that woman whose accomplishment shall strike me in the most powerful manner. "But it may happen that other men will feel for her the same preference that I do?" This will create no difficulty. We may all enjoy her conversation and we shall all be wise enough to consider the sensual intercourse a very trivial object.'[5]

The rational ordering of our relations with each other is carried very far. Since promises create obligations which impinge

on us, and arouse expectations which we may not be able
to fulfil, they should be made as rarely as possible, in the interest
both of personal liberty and sincerity. Since dealing with un-
welcome visitors may involve one in the predicament of either
telling a lie or submitting to personal inconvenience, the section
of Godwin's book entitled 'Of the Mode of Excluding Visitors'
shows his morality at work in everyday life. 'Let us suppose that
we are ourselves destined . . . to give this answer that our father
or our wife is not at home', Godwin says, 'when they are really
in the house. Should we not feel our tongues contaminated with
the base plebeian lie?' Nor, if he is reasonable, will our visitor
mind being turned away: 'He must in reality be the weakest of
mankind who should conceive umbrage at a plain answer in
this case, when he was informed of the moral considerations that
induced me to employ it.' Even if our refusal to see him is due to
plain dislike, this is usually 'for some moral fault that we perceive
or think we perceive in him. Why should he be kept in ignorance
of our opinion respecting him, and prevented from the opportunity either of amendment or vindication?'[1] Sincerity, independence, a natural self-restraint, serious high-mindedness, these
are the intellectual virtues which Godwin's view of society demands.

The institutions of society, in so far as they are necessary at
all, follow logically from Godwin's view of man's nature and of
the evils of the existing system. 'The only legitimate object of
political institutions is the advantage of individuals.'[2] 'Government can have no more than two legitimate purposes, the suppression of injustice against individuals within the community,
and the common defence against external invasion.'[3] This presumably is only in the intervening period before education has
removed the causes of injustice by making man rational and
therefore virtuous. Godwin is a true anarchist in that, although
he accepts some degree of association for minimal administrative
purposes – 'an association of such extent as to afford room for the
institution of a jury to decide upon the offences of individuals
within the community which may chance to arise'[4] – such
associations must be as decentralized as possible. The parish is

the unit on which they must be based, and no central assembly is necessary. 'If once the unambitious and candid circles of in-quiring men be swallowed up in the insatiate gulf of noisy assem-blies, the opportunity of improvement is instantly annihilated.'[1]

Godwin was not a revolutionary in method, however startling his aims must have seemed; and he carefully and consistently avoided any appeal to violence. 'If the government of Great Britain were dissolved tomorrow, unless that dissolution were the result of consistent and digested views of political justice previ-ously disseminated among the inhabitants, it would be very far from leading to the abolition of violence',[2] he writes; and, once again, the experience of the French Revolution might be held to prove him right. 'I am bold and adventurous in opinions, not in life,' Godwin once said;[3] and it is easy to laugh at so remote and ineffectual a reformer. Nevertheless, he behaved bravely enough in 1794, when the founders of the radical London Cor-responding Society were accused of treason by Pitt's government, and Godwin conducted an active campaign in the press and in pamphlets so successfully that the accused were, in fact, ac-quitted. But his own revolutionary views tended to be more about the future than the present. In spite of his attacks on the family, he was twice married. His first wife was Mary Wollstonecraft, herself a remarkable pioneering reformer and one of the first champions of women's rights in England. She died after a few years of a marriage which brought out a tenderness in Godwin's nature that is unexpected in so cold a rationalist. Their only daughter, Mary, became the wife of Shelley, who was one of Godwin's first disciples. Godwin's second wife, Mrs Clairmont, was a woman of less distinction; and the marriage was not a particularly happy one.*

If by becoming a husband and father Godwin might seem to have violated his principles, in other respects he might be said to have behaved as if he were already a member of the ideal community in which each citizen had but to ask in order for his

---

* Her daughter by her previous husband was the Clare Clairmont who pursued Byron even more vigorously than her mother had pursued Godwin, and who became the mother of the poet's daughter, Allegra.

needs to be met. Godwin believed that property was of no importance; he believed that society owed a living to the wise; and,
in consequence, he became one of the most notorious and unashamed spongers of his time, constantly borrowing money which
he rarely repaid. Nevertheless, the familiar picture of the ageing,
impoverished, scrounging Godwin, as he appears in the literature about Shelley (one of his chief victims) and in the memoirs
of the early nineteenth century, should not obscure the merits of
the *Enquiry Concerning Political Justice*. In stately eighteenth-
century prose Godwin unfolds a vision of man and society that
remains the most complete statement of that type of anarchist
doctrine which is based on an unbounded confidence in the
rational nature of man and the possibilities of his improvement.
It is as a constructor of theories rather than as a practical revolutionary that Godwin is of interest. Not only was his temperament,
as we have seen, unrevolutionary, but his influence was extremely
limited. Although the *Enquiry* sold 4,000 copies and created some
stir in the England of the 1790s, where everyone was eager for
ammunition for and against the Revolution, there was some
truth in the comment Pitt is said to have made about the work:
'A three-guinea book could never do much harm among those
who had not three shillings to spare.'[1] Godwin's fame evaporated
fast and his work was forgotten, although it was translated into
German, and although Mme. de Stael and Benjamin Constant
devoted some attention to it. However, he was an influence on
Robert Owen, and through him on the early development of
British Trade Unionism, while he deeply affected the outlook of
both Coleridge and Shelley. There are passages in Shelley, especially in *Prometheus Unbound*, which are simply Godwin in
blank verse.*

---

* E.g.   The loathsome mask has fallen, the man remains,
              Sceptreless, free, uncircumscribed, but man
              Equal, unclassed, tribeless and nationless
              Exempt from cast, worship, degree, the king
              Over himself; just, gentle, wise; but man
              Passionless.

It was not until late in the nineteenth century that Godwin was rediscovered, when anarchists were looking for rational doctrines to justify their call to revolution. And, as there are always men who believe in progress and reason just as there are always others who believe in the necessity of violent change and the immediate transformation of the world, Godwin remains an admirable example of the philosophical anarchist, a reminder of what anarchism owes to the doctrines of the Enlightenment, just as other anarchists after him provide examples of the apocalyptic, millenarian temperament which makes anarchism so similar to the religious heresies of the Middle Ages and Reformation.

However, neither a revolutionary temperament nor a rational doctrine was enough to produce the anarchist as he emerged in the nineteenth century. It was the disruptive example of the French Revolution and the growing challenge of the new emerging industrial society that were to produce the circumstances in which both heretics and rationalists could join a movement that provided a fundamental criticism of the old society and a programme of violent action to remedy its defects.

CHAPTER II

The Myth of the Revolution

'The French Revolution is only the forerunner of a much bigger, much more solemn revolution, which will be the final one.'

Gracchus Babeuf

I

In 1909, Prince Peter Kropotkin, the leading anarchist theorist of his generation,[1] published a history of *The Great French Revolution*. 'What we learn today from the study of the Great Revolution', he wrote, 'is that it was the source and origin of all the present communist, anarchist and socialist conceptions.' And he ended his book with a fervent invocation of the spirit of the French Revolution. 'The one thing certain is, that whatsoever nation enters on the path of revolution in our own day, it will be heir to all our forefathers have done in France. The blood they shed was shed for humanity – the sufferings they endured were borne for the entire human race; the struggles, the ideas they gave to the world, the shock of those ideas, are all included in the heritage of mankind. All have borne fruit and will bear more, still finer, as we advance towards those wide horizons opening out before us, where, like some great beacon to point the way, flame the words – LIBERTY, EQUALITY, FRATERNITY.'[2]

By the end of the nineteenth century, indeed, the French Revolution was an established myth which historians of various schools were busy interpreting for their own ends; and, shortly before Kropotkin wrote his book, Jean Jaurès, the French socialist leader, had already embarked on a 'socialist' history of the Revolution. The events of 1830, 1848 and 1871 in France had all been consciously enacted as in some way imitations of 1789 or 1792. The great moments of the French Revolution had provided terms to describe certain types of revolutionary action, such as the Commune or the Eighteenth Brumaire. Like most major historical events, the French Revolution left its effects at two levels. It had immediate, irreversible and profound consequences in France and Europe; and it left a legend that has continued to operate in men's minds right down to the present. To understand the influence of the French Revolution on the origins and history of the anarchist movement, therefore, it is necessary to see how the French Revolution both started a belief in the possibility of successful insurrectionary movements against the established order and also provided legends to which subsequent anarchists were to look back for inspiration. In fact, of course, the French Revolution was not in the least anarchistic in aims, achievements or even methods. Neither decentralization nor the abolition of property – both prerequisites of all anarchist conceptions of society – followed. Instead the revolution resulted in a strong, centralized state and in the establishment in political power of an active middle class. While it freed the peasants from feudal ties, it created a nation of peasant proprietors. Nevertheless, it was the spectacle of the greatest political upheaval for centuries that was most impressive, the very fact that by revolutionary methods a powerful monarchy and an entrenched aristocracy had been overthrown, and the political and social structure of a great nation radically reformed. What had happened once might happen again, and consequently, even if the final results were not what were in fact required, there was always the possibility that the next revolution might have better success.

However, there were in the revolution certain movements which later anarchists and communists were perhaps justified in regarding as similar to their own, movements which seemed to be more concerned with social and economic problems than with political and constitutional ones. The great period of the revolution, in their view, was the spring and summer of 1793, when the *sans-culottes* were in the streets and when the constant pressure of their agitation contributed to the overthrow of the Girondins and to the establishment of the Jacobin dictatorship. The rise in food prices and the general scarcity encouraged popular agitation, and Robespierre knew how to use this against his opponents:

'*Pour vaincre les bourgeois, il faut rallier le peuple.*'[1] But the leaders
of the more extreme sections of the *sans-culottes* movement –
Hébert or Jacques-Roux – were soon disappointed at the results
of Robespierre's success, and, like Trotsky in a later revolution,
they fell victim to the reign of terror they themselves had helped
to instigate. The popular agitation of these months, though, was
prompted by the same basic human reactions which had led men
to follow the popular movements of the Middle Ages – a primitive desire for a more just distribution of the necessities of life.
'You have a pretty dress,' one woman was heard to say to another
in 1793. 'Be patient; before long, if you have two, you will give
me one and that's how we want it to be; it will be like that with
everything else.'[2] Or, as the *Sans-Culottes de Beaucaire* put it in
their address to the Convention in September 1793, 'We are
poor and virtuous *sans-culottes*; we have formed an association of
artisans and peasants . . . we know who our friends are: those
who have delivered us from the clergy and nobility, from the
feudal system, from tithes, from the monarchy and all the ills
which follow in its train; those whom the aristocrats have called
anarchists, followers of faction (*factieux*), Maratists.'[3] The epi-
thets were significant; 'anarchist' was the term adopted by
Robespierre to attack those people on the left whom he had used
for his own ends but whom he was determined to be rid of.
Marat, after his murder in 1793, became the hero of all the
extremists, each of whom claimed to be his true successor.

Among these 'anarchists' there were a few leaders who struck
the true note of social revolt that was to be characteristic of later
anarchists. Jacques-Roux, for example, the lapsed priest who
for a short time was an influential mob orator and journalist, is
mainly remembered as the man who escorted Louis XVI to his
execution and who refused the king's request to take charge of
his will with the words '*Je ne suis içi que pour vous mener à l'échafaud*'
– an example of brutal cold-heartedness or of revolutionary devotion to duty as you choose to look at it. Jacques-Roux was the
most violent of the extremists known as the *Enragés*, and it is the
violence and brutality of his speeches and action that have kept
him a place in the histories of anarchism and communism. More-

over, he insisted, more vigorously than any other revolutionary, on the fact that political freedom without economic freedom was meaningless, and that it was social revolution and not just political change that was important. 'Freedom', he said, 'is but an empty phantom if one class of men can starve another with impunity. Freedom is but an empty phantom when the rich man can through his monopoly exercise the right of life and death over his fellow men.'[1]

What Jacques-Roux contributed to later anarchist practice was a demonstration of the revolutionary power of the mob, an example of what could be done by direct action – in this case the seizure of goods in the grocers' shops – and of the way in which acts of pillage and robbery could be represented as acts of social justice. Jacques-Roux had soon served his purpose as a mob leader. Robespierre ordered his arrest, and he committed suicide in prison.

Among the other 'Enragés' and 'anarchists' of 1793, Jean Varlet was the most explicit and eloquent. A young man of good family, he was already, at the age of twenty, one of the most violent of the mob orators, and he coined slogans with a real anarchist ring – 'We cannot prevent ourselves being distrustful even of those who have won our votes'; 'Kings' palaces are not the only homes of despots.'[2] He, too, was arrested and imprisoned, but survived the terror to write an indictment of Jacobin government under the title of L'Explosion, which expresses the disgust of a man of revolutionary principles – who had exclaimed, 'Périsse le gouvernement révolutionnaire plutôt qu'un principe!' – when confronted with the practice of revolutionary government. 'What a social monstrosity, what a masterpiece of Machiavellism is this revolutionary government,' he wrote. 'For any rational being, government and revolution are incompatible – unless the people is willing to set up its delegates in a permanent state of insurrection against themselves – which is absurd.'[3]

Two other features of the Jacobin era were to leave their mark on anarchist thinking. First of all, there was the terror itself. Subsequent attitudes towards it were ambivalent, and reveal yet another of the clashes of temperament among anarchists.

On the one hand they disapproved of all dictatorship and its methods. Yet there was much in Robespierre's theory and practice that appealed to them. Many responded eagerly to the ruthlessness and violence of a régime whose supporters could talk enthusiastically of seeing 'the heads of despots fall like apples in Normandy in the autumn';[1] and, to many, terror seemed an indispensable, and indeed desirable, means of achieving the success of the revolution. Moreover, although the revolution was primarily political in its results, both Robespierre and Marat had had a social aspect to their thought. Robespierre dreamt of a community not entirely unlike that imagined by Proudhon, a society of peasants and artisans working to support themselves and voluntarily exchanging their products with one another. Marat, in a passage Kropotkin quoted with approval, wrote of the dangers of the betrayal of the revolution. 'Thus it is that the Revolution has been made and maintained only by the lowest classes of society – by the workers, the artisans, the little trades-men, the agriculturalists, by the plebs, by those luckless ones whom the shameless rich call *canaille* and whom Roman insolence called proletarians. But who would ever have imagined that it would be made only in favour of the small landowners, the lawyers, the supporters of fraud.'[2]

Moreover, the Jacobins had propounded ideals of genuine equality and of Republican virtue which were to find their echoes in the anarchist groups, particularly of Spain. The use of '*tu*' instead of '*vous*' and of '*citoyen*' instead of '*monsieur*' acquired a symbolic value. 'Under the happy reign of equality, familiarity is simply the image of the philanthropic virtues we carry in our soul', one revolutionary newspaper wrote in 1792.[3] In the eyes of the ever-optimistic anarchists these virtues were to remain more vivid than the brutality and meaningless violence which accompanied them. Even if the anarchists claimed descent from specific groups like the *Enragés*, it was the fact that the revolution had happened at all that was important. From now on revolution could go on working like a leaven below the surface of society until the next great outburst came. The prophecy which Marat – always the favourite revolutionary character among later extreme

revolutionaries – made at the end of 1789 could be extended to
cover a whole century. 'The lot of the poor, always downtrodden,
always subjugated and always oppressed can never be improved
by peaceful means. This is doubtless one of the striking proofs of
the influence of wealth on the legal code. Besides, laws only rule
as long as people are willing to submit to them; the people have
broken the yoke of the nobility; in the same way they will break
that of wealth. The great point is to enlighten them and make
them aware of their rights, and the revolution will function infallibly without any human power being able to oppose it.'[1]

The revolution, too, sanctified the act of conspiracy and, indeed, some of its heirs were to adopt conspiracy as a way of life.
The *'Conspiration des Égaux'* of Gracchus Babeuf and his friends in
1796 became a model to which all later revolutionaries felt
obliged to pay homage. In this way a comparatively unimportant
episode has been given more historical weight than it seemed to
have at the time. Babeuf had been a *commissaire à terrier*, a kind of
land-agent, working on behalf of feudal lords, and he wanted passionately to overthrow the society which made such a profession
necessary. Already in 1787 he had proposed to the Academy of
Arras an essay competition to discuss the following theme: 'With
the general accumulation of knowledge now achieved, what
would be the state of a people whose social institutions should be
such that the most perfect equality would reign among the individual members, and that the land on which they lived belonged to
no one – if, in short, everything was in common, including
the products of all kinds of industry.'[2] It was not a subject the
Academy of Arras was prepared to hear discussed. Once the
revolution had started, however, Babeuf was proclaiming his
views once more: 'Private property is the principal source of all
the ills which burden society . . . the sun shines on everyone and
the earth belongs to no one. Go on then, my friends, batter, upset,
overturn this society which does not suit you. Take what suits
you everywhere. What is superfluous belongs by right to him who
has nothing.' Violence alone could bring about the new order,
and, as passionately as Thomas Müntzer had done 250 years
earlier, he exhorted his hearers: 'Cut without pity the throats of

the tyrants, the patricians, the gilded million, all the immoral
beings who might oppose our common happiness.'[1] With the
coming of the Directory in 1795 and the end of any prospects of
a social revolution, Babeuf and his friends started a conspiracy
against the government. 'The moment has come', the conspirators
proclaimed in their *Manifeste des Égaux*, 'to found the Republic
of Equals, this great *hospice* open to all men. The days of general
restitution are at hand. Groaning families, come and seat yourselves at the table as it was laid by nature for all her children.'[2]

Babeuf came from the north-east of France, and it was the condition of the peasants in Picardy, and his own experiences of
poverty among them, that first inspired his political ideas. The
fundamental necessity, in his view, was a thoroughgoing land
reform – and he took the name of Gracchus to emphasize his
links with earlier agrarian reformers. From advocating land
reform, he went on, in an often confused and contradictory way,
to develop ideas which he had found in Mably, Morelly and
Rousseau, and turned them into a programme for revolutionary
political action. He was, in fact, never an anarchist, although
his insistence on the abolition of private property links him to
later anarchist thinkers. But the results which, for a true anarchist like Godwin, would come about through the free cooperation of individuals would, according to Babeuf, be brought about
by the state. 'The government', he wrote, 'will get rid of boundary
marks, hedges, walls, locks on the doors, quarrels, litigation, theft,
murder, every kind of crime; envy, jealousy, greed, pride, deceit,
duplicity, in short all the vices, as well as the worm of general,
individual and perpetual anxiety about tomorrow, next week,
next year, our old age, our children and grandchildren, which
gnaws at each of us.'[3] If the aims are those of the anarchists, the
means are not. Babeuf believed in a strong state, run by a kind of
revolutionary dictatorship, responsible for the organization of
economic life, with collective ownership of the means of production and wide powers to direct labour. Thus he is rightly claimed
as a predecessor by communist writers. He is, however, an important legendary figure for all later revolutionaries because of
his insistence on the necessity of turning a political revolution into

a social and economic one, and, above all, because of his belief in conspiracy as being the right way to achieve this.

His own *Conspiration des Égaux* was totally ineffective, in part because he and his friends, like many later conspirators, could not resist publicly discussing their aims and declaring their intentions, so that it was easy for the police to penetrate their organization, and the plot was quickly and easily suppressed. But although Babeuf was executed and many of his associates deported, the idea of a conspiracy to make the social revolution remained. There were, indeed, opponents of the revolution very ready to take up the idea that the whole thing was the result of a universal plot. 'In this French Revolution everything including its most terrible outrages was foreseen, premeditated, arranged, determined, decided; everything has been prepared and induced by the men who held the thread of conspiracies, long pondered in secret societies, men who knew how to choose and hurry on the moment favourable to their plots.'[1] These suspicions of an *émigré* priest in 1797 are typical of beliefs that were to be held throughout the nineteenth century by many conservatives; and, indeed, those people in our own time who are ready to attribute any untoward event to the international machinations of the communists (or the freemasons, or the Catholics or the Jews) are victims of the same illusion. As a result, it has been easy for conspirators both to overestimate their own importance and, in some cases, to lead historians to overestimate it, too.

In the generation after the Conspiracy of Equals the great prototype of the conspirator, the example to which many later professional revolutionaries looked back, was Filippo Michele Buonarroti, whom Bakunin was to call the 'greatest conspirator of the century'.[2] He was born in Tuscany and at the university acquired the revolutionary ideas of the *philosophes* as well as being influenced by the struggle for independence in Corsica. As soon as the revolution broke out in France he was there. He met Babeuf and became involved in his conspiracy, of which he later wrote the history. In exile in Switzerland and Belgium, and after his final return to France, he devoted the rest of his life to the foundation of innumerable, and often mythical, secret societies and the hatching of countless abortive plots. He believed that it was he who was to redeem the errors of his revolutionary predecessors: 'The infatuation of the atheists, the errors of the Hébertists, the immorality of the Dantonists, the humbled pride of the Girondists, the dark plots of the Royalists, the gold of England, disappointed on the Ninth Thermidor the hopes of the French people and the human race.'[1] The revolution, in fact, had still to be made.

In France, where he returned after the revolution of 1830, Buonarroti continued, totally without effect, to invent secret societies and carry out what, as a young man, he had called his 'deep conviction that it was the duty of a man of means to work towards the overthrow of the social system which oppresses civilized Europe, in order to substitute an order which would conserve the happiness and the dignity of all'.[2] He lived till 1837, embodying for younger revolutionaries the traditions and virtues of the great revolution, 'a brave and venerable old man', who, as the English Chartist leader Bronterre O'Brien noted, 'at the advanced age of seventy-eight shed tears like a child at the mention of Robespierre's name'.[3] Sometimes he was on the fringe of real conspiracies, in Belgium or in Italy. More often he was simply a conspiracy in himself, an indispensable patron of revolutionary gatherings, an unbending and argumentative member of all republican societies, such as the *Société des Droits de l'Homme*, which was – quite wrongly – held responsible for the attempts on the life of Louis-Philippe in 1835 and 1836.* Buonarroti was the first of a series of figures, such as Blanqui and Bakunin in the next generation, who seemed to their contemporaries, and still more to their successors, the embodiment of the spirit of revolution, the dedicated apostles of revolution for revolution's sake.

* The second of these was, in fact, an act of social protest, strangely like some of the anarchist crimes at the end of the nineteenth century. The assassin, Alibaud, stated: 'I wanted to kill the king because he is the enemy of the people. I was miserable through the fault of the government; and as the king is its chief, I decided to kill him.' When asked who his fellow conspirators were, he replied: 'The chief of the conspiracy was my head; the accomplices are my arms.' And on the scaffold he shouted: 'I die for liberty, for the good of humanity, for the extinction of the infamous monarchy.' (Thureau-Dangin, *Histoire de la Monarchie de Juillet*, vol. III (3rd ed., Paris 1892), p. 35.)

The French Revolution had left behind at least three myths which were to contribute to the revolutionary creeds of the nineteenth century and which became part of the beliefs of the anarchists. First there was the myth of the successful revolution. Henceforth violent revolution was possible; and, secondly, the next revolution would be a true social revolution and not just the substitution of one ruling class for another. '*La Révolution française*', as Babeuf put it, '*n'est que l'avant courrière d'une autre révolution plus grande, plus solennelle, et qui sera la dernière.*'[1] Finally, this revolution could only be brought about after existing society had been undermined by a conspiracy of devoted revolutionaries. These are doctrines which were to be shared by German Marxists, Russian populists and French and Spanish anarchists. From now on revolutions were to be made in the streets as much as in philosophers' studies.

2

The myth of the revolution satisfied the temperamental need for action of those who, in earlier ages, might have embarked on a crusade or a religious revolt. At the same time, however, the economic and social changes in Europe in the early nineteenth century were giving rise to new discussions about what society would be like after the revolution, and what kind of life men could hope for in a new industrial age. In the generation following the revolution new visionary utopias were developed, based on an awareness (which Godwin, as we have seen, also shared) of the productive capacities of industry and machines, and on a realization of the failure of the French Revolution to satisfy more than a small part of the economic and social aspirations of the poor. To the myth of the revolution were added new myths of a future society.

The utopian socialists, of whom Fourier and Saint-Simon are the most remarkable and the most influential, were, like Godwin, concerned with the future state of society rather than with the means by which the revolution could be made. They believed, and in this they were the true heirs of the eighteenth century, that reason and human progress would bring about the necessary changes without the need for violence. As Friedrich Engels put it, 'Socialism is for all of them the expression of absolute truth, reason and justice, and need only be discovered in order to conquer the world through its own power'.[1] There was much in their visions of a new society, however, that was to recur in future anarchist thought; and the beliefs of Saint-Simon and, especially, Fourier contributed much to the peaceful, rational, mild type of anarchist, just as the actions of the *Enragés* or Babeuf or Buonarroti provided examples for the violent, revolutionary apostles of anarchist terror.

Fourier, who died in 1837, the same year as Buonarroti, was a not very successful commercial traveller, a dim and quiet bachelor who lived a totally uneventful life. Like Godwin, he believed that a new society could be brought about by rational cooperation between men. His society, which he called Harmony, was in some ways very odd indeed, and it is made odder by the symbolism with which it is described, and the endless tables in which the human passions are somehow equated to colours or the notes of the scale. It is tempting, too, to remember only the most eccentric aspects of life in Harmony – the use, for example, of small children to clear the refuse, since, after all, it is well known that children like playing with dirt, or the picture of three-year-olds shelling and sorting peas for the kitchen (with the aid of a sort of bagatelle board with holes of different sizes) before going off to their breakfast of sugared cream, fruit, jam and light white wine. Behind all the fantasy, however, there are one or two fundamental ideas that account for Fourier's influence, and which later thinkers about social organization borrowed from him.

Fourier believed that the evils of society largely derived from the fact that men's natural instincts and their social environment were constantly opposed to each other. The solution therefore lay in adapting society and the natural world to men's natures and needs. A society which would satisfy men's desire for variety, for social life and intrigue, for good food and refined pleasures, could be made to run itself. By an advanced degree of division of labour, by making work in itself attractive and ensuring that no one worked at one task for more than two hours at a stretch, the bitter monotony of the new industrial society would be abolished. By a rationalization of agriculture and improved methods of transport there would be enough food for all, and industry would be reduced to a minimum necessary for men's simple requirements. (Commodities such as bread, which required a great many processes in their preparation – threshing, grinding, kneading, baking – would be dispensed with and simpler products substituted.) Production on a large scale would simplify life and reduce costs, while mass consumption would provide a stable market so that the anomalies of overproduction would be avoided. (Fourier had once worked for a merchant who had dumped a cargo of rice into the sea in order to keep the price up, and he had never forgotten it.)

Fourier's communities – the 'phalansteries' – were to be co-operative enterprises in which each member had a varying number of shares. For all the self-disciplined routine of the lives of the inhabitants of Harmony, it was not an egalitarian society and it was based on the ownership of capital. As Charles Gide pointed out, the phalansteries were something between a vast hotel and a vast cooperative department store. While they would have been a little more comfortable than Godwin's ideal society (at least there was central heating), they represent a similar extreme of selfless and impersonal cooperation. It is a world where children are taken away from their parents, all meals are in common, and a bedroom and dressing-room the only private accommodation its members require. Yet it is a truly anarchist society. Fourier at no point requires the intervention of a state to regulate the relations within and between the various phalansteries. He condemns the use of force: 'All that is founded upon force', he wrote of the Jesuit communities in Paraguay, 'is fragile and denotes the absence of genius.'[1] His communities are the ancestors of those attempts at cooperative utopian enterprise with which idealists in the nineteenth and twentieth centuries have tried to escape from the industrial world, sometimes directly inspired by him, like the famous settlement at Brook Farm, Massachusetts, sometimes reflecting similar beliefs and hopes, like the *kibbutzim* of contemporary Israel. His influence was by no means exclusively on anarchists: his insistence on large-scale production and on mass consumption by standardized associations foreshadowed the methods of later capitalism. In his emphasis on the possibility of changing the environment to suit man rather than changing (and perverting) man's nature, he is a forerunner of all who have believed in economic planning and social engineering, whether socialist or capitalist. Nevertheless, he is an essential part of the world of ideas from which true anarchism emerges. No social theorist of the 1840s and 1850s could ignore his ideas, even if many of them seemed too fantastic to be taken seriously. 'For six whole weeks I was the captive of this bizarre genius', Proudhon wrote.[1] He was at other times to deny Fourier's influence on him: 'I certainly read Fourier and I have talked of him more than once, but in the long run I don't think I owe him anything.'[2] Yet the ingenious, childlike vision of Fourier underlies much of Proudhon's picture of the world and, consequently, that of many of the anarchists who are Proudhon's intellectual descendants.

If Fourier, with his emphasis on the gregarious nature of man and his belief in what could be achieved by cooperation – so oddly contrasting with his own solitary, bachelor existence – provides a picture of what society might be like after the revolution, the other great utopian socialist thinker of the first quarter of the nineteenth century, Henri de Saint-Simon, though contributing much to the development of the concept of revolution, was never an anarchist. True, he believed that, in the ideal society, the state would become unnecessary and political action pointless. 'The men who brought about the revolution, the men who directed it, and the men who, since 1789 and up to the present day, have guided the nation, have committed a great political mistake. They have all sought to improve the governmental machines, whereas they should have subordinated it and put administration in the first place.'[3] This is an earlier version, in fact, of the phrase of Karl Marx about the 'government of men giving way to the administration of things'. However, the 'administration' which Saint-Simon so much admired was far removed from the spontaneous cooperation of Fourier's phalansteries or the workers' control of industry which later anarchists were to advocate. Saint-Simon's true heirs in this respect were indeed the bankers and capitalists who were among his first disciples. It is the great industrialists and financiers of the nineteenth century who should claim Saint-Simon as their ancestor, and not the revolutionary leaders.

Nevertheless, the influence of Saint-Simon on Marx was enormous. Saint-Simon was the first thinker to analyse historical change in terms of the struggle between social and economic classes. He also believed that the process of history was on the side of the revolution, a belief which, when given its Hegelian form by Marx, has been the biggest single psychological factor in the spread of Marxism. Saint-Simon's untidy, unsystematic, capricious teaching was diffused and discussed in the decades after his death in 1827. Some of his disciples turned Saint-Simonianism into a new religion: others developed his cult of science and originated the study of sociology: others became successful entrepreneurs, and indeed, such undertakings as the Suez Canal or the Paris–Lyon–Méditerranée railway were directly inspired by him. Although it cannot be claimed that he was an anarchist, his ideas, like those of Fourier, contributed much to the intellectual climate in which the two great anarchists of the nineteenth century, Proudhon and Bakunin, grew up.

If the utopian socialists in France supplement the work of the French Revolution by suggesting what society might be like after the next successful social revolution, it is the German philosophers who provide the other essential element in the thought of the new generation of practical as well as theoretical revolutionaries who were emerging in the thirties and forties. 'My true masters are three in number,' Proudhon wrote, 'the Bible first, Adam Smith second, and lastly Hegel'[1]: and his work shows more traces of the last than of the two former. About the same time, Bakunin was, like all the Russian intelligentsia of his generation, experiencing the impact of Hegel and responding to it with all the violence of his passionate nature. Through the study of Hegel he had, he wrote, 'risen never to fall again'.[2]

The French Revolution had shown that it was possible to destroy the old forms of government. The utopian socialists suggested idealized pictures of what the new world might look like. It was the Hegelians who provided the new generation of revolutionaries with the conviction that history was on their side, and with a philosophy of radical change. The successors of Hegel – the 'Young Hegelians' – took the master's doctrine and turned it to revolutionary ends. While Hegel himself had used his philosophy as a means of justifying the existing Prussian state, his successors, as Marx put it, stood the dialectic on its head, and turned it into a philosophy of revolution. Since, according to Hegel, all that was real was rational, it should, the Young Hegelians thought, be possible to remodel the existing world so that it corresponded to the demands of Reason. Since, again, history moved dialectically so that all conflicts contributed to a new synthesis, the clash of classes or the succession of revolutions must inevitably produce a new order. It was, of course, in this way that Marx elaborated the doctrine of the class struggle which would end in the dictatorship of the proletariat, but others who had fallen under Hegel's spell contributed to the development of purely anarchist doctrine. While Marx and others, such as Moses Hess, combined the doctrine of the class struggle with the Hegelian conception of the state, to produce the idea of state communism in which an all-powerful, all-rational state would finally abolish the various classes and weld all the citizens into a harmonious whole before ultimately withering away itself, some of those who were influenced by Hegel saw the final synthesis, as Proudhon did, as being the immediate disappearance of the state.

Of the revolutionaries of the 1830s and '40s who contributed directly to the anarchist doctrines of the next generation, Wilhelm Weitling is the most important. Weitling himself came from the humblest and poorest origins. He was born in 1808, the illegitimate son of a German housemaid and an officer in Napoleon's army. He became a tailor and moved to Zurich, where he met Bakunin, and later to Paris, where he was in touch with Marx. Bakunin and Marx did not really succeed in making him a Hegelian, and it was from Saint-Simon and Fourier that his ideas were mostly derived. He never lost, however, a kind of primitive Christianity, a belief that Christ was the first communist, who had preached against property and wealth, who had been a bastard like Weitling himself, and associated with whores and fishermen. He constantly referred to Thomas Müntzer and John of Leyden, and in some ways regarded himself as their successor in preaching that democratic ideas are 'an emanation of Christianity'.[1] In 1838 he published his *Humanity as it is and as it ought to be* (*Die Menschheit wie sie ist und wie sie sein sollte*), and in 1842 his *Guarantees of Harmony and Freedom* (*Garantien der Harmonie und Freiheit*). In those works he combined a belief in the class struggle leading to the inevitable revolution, with many ideas of a sketchy anarchist kind and in his *Gospel of a Poor Sinner*, published three years later, he linked these to his own version of Christian teaching. 'The perfect society', Bakunin quoted him as saying, 'has no government, but only an administration, no laws only obligations, no punishments only means of correction.'[2] Here, indeed, are ideas very near to those of Godwin, whom Weitling had almost certainly never read, as well as of Saint-Simon, whom he almost certainly had. From Hegel comes the belief in an ideal society whose laws are identical with the dictates of morality, so that there is no conflict between the individual and the community. Weitling's views can perhaps be better described as utopian communism rather than anarchism, for he thought of the state as being administered by a very Saint-Simonian committee of doctors, scientists and philosophers who would have powers to direct labour. At the same time, he disliked centralization and he hated the whole idea of the money economy – a very anarchist trait. He would have liked to have based the whole economy on barter, so that each man's labour could be directly related to what he produced, and the products directly exchanged within the community. It was an idea which haunted social reformers: Robert Owen had dreamed of a 'National Equitable Labour Exchange', and one of his American disciples, Josiah Warren, in 1826 opened a 'time store' in Cincinnati, where the customers obtained credit according to the amount of labour which they had put into the products which they delivered to the store. Proudhon was to develop the idea; and the abolition of money became a standard part of many anarchist programmes.

When they met in Switzerland, Bakunin had been impressed by Weitling's *Guarantees*. In the *Guarantees* Weitling had written that revolutions would come about 'either through harsh physical force or through spiritual power, or both. The sword has not yet wholly given way to the pen; but a time will come in which this will be the case. Then revolutions will no longer be bloody.'[1] In practice, however, time was short. It is only by appealing to people's material interests that the revolution will come about: 'to wait till everybody is patiently enlightened as is usually suggested means giving up the whole business'.[2] Soon after the meeting with Bakunin, indeed, Weitling's activities got him into trouble not only with the Zurich authorities, but also with some of his own friends. 'A time will come', he had said, 'when we shall not ask and beg, but *demand*. Then we shall light a vast fire with banknotes, bills of exchange, wills, tax registers, rent contracts and IOUs, and everyone will throw his purse into the fire. . . .' About the time of his meeting with Bakunin, Weitling was busy organizing a series of clubs, and he seems to have hoped that the means of revolution were already there, and that his followers would soon be ready to take what they wanted and to open the jails to receive help from the inmates.[3] Whatever specific ideas about the use of violence Weitling had at this period, there is no doubt that he was convinced – and here again Bakunin was to follow him – that true revolutions are made by those with nothing to lose. The new ethics of revolution, he wrote, 'can only be effectively taught among the bewildered masses swarming in our great cities and plunged in the utmost boundless misery'.[4]

It is the really poor, the *Lumpenproletariat* so despised by the Marxists, the people with no stake in society, and not the successful artisans who have made some sort of place for themselves in the world, who will be the revolutionaries. In fact, the successful anarchist movements of the nineteenth and early twentieth

centuries were based on a combination of men like Weitling himself – skilled, independent, self-educated artisans – and men in a
state of social and economic desperation, like, for example, the
landless labourers of Andalusia.

However, Weitling himself was not a violent revolutionary in
practice, although several times imprisoned because of the subversive nature of the ideas discussed in the Communist Workers
Clubs which he founded. After the revolution of 1848, when he
had hurried back to Germany, he left for the United States,
where he spent the rest of his life involved in a series of unsuccessful attempts to set up utopian communities.

It was not their often rather pathetic attempts to put their
ideas into immediate practice that made the utopian socialists
important in the development of the great revolutionary movements of the nineteenth and twentieth centuries, whether anarchist or communist. What they had achieved was to create the
belief that social and economic change must take precedence
over purely political reform, and that the discussion of the relations between producer and consumer, or between capital and
labour, was more important than argument about constitutional
forms and political institutions.

This awareness of the 'social question' had, of course, originated in the social and economic conditions of the early nineteenth
century, a time when new forms of industry and new technical
processes, together with an urban population which was increasing all over western Europe, were creating all sorts of new social
and political clashes and problems. The riots of the weavers of
Lyons in 1834 or of those of Silesia in 1841 had shown how
formidable the new working class could be. The outbursts of
violent radical working-class feeling in Paris or Berlin or Vienna
which disturbed the sedate course of the bourgeois revolutions of
1848 served to show what forces were now available to the
revolutionary leaders who knew how to organize them and to
canalize their vague aspirations into a true revolutionary philosophy. '*On a fait une révolution sans une idée*', Proudhon complained
in 1848. Revolutions were not to lack for ideas in the future. After
1848 Marx and Engels, Proudhon and Bakunin, were drawing

their respective lessons from what had happened. With them the modern revolutionary movement begins, and Marxists and anarchists start to teach rival views of what revolution might achieve and to issue rival instructions for its success.

Part Two

CHAPTER III
Reason and Revolution: Proudhon

'Mon malheur est que mes passions se confondent avec mes idées; la lumière qui éclaire les autres hommes, me brûle.'

Proudhon

I

'What is property? Property is theft.' The phrase appeared in a pamphlet by Pierre-Joseph Proudhon in 1840. It was to become one of the most effective revolutionary slogans of the nineteenth century and the pamphlet established the reputation of its author, who was thirty-one years old when it appeared. His background and early life are important for an understanding both of his doctrines and of their appeal to the French working class. Proudhon came from the neighbourhood of Besançon in the Franche-Comté, and, although he was to live and work in Lyons and Paris, his moral and political outlook remained that of a puritanical young man from the provinces, shocked and horrified by the luxury, extravagance, decadence and corruption of the metropolis, *centre de luxe et des lumières*, as he called it.[1] Proudhon's family were peasants by origin, but they were already becoming part of the lower middle class in the city. For once, Marx was right in describing Proudhon as a *petit-bourgeois*. His father was an artisan (he had worked as a cooper) who ended up as a brewer and innkeeper in Besançon. He was never very successful, and the family were often very poor indeed. The younger Proudhon liked to attribute this to his father's scrupulous refusal to accept the corrupt standards of contemporary commerce. 'He sold his beer almost at cost price; wanting nothing except a bare living, the poor man lost everything.'[2] At the same time, Proudhon's mother represented an ideal of the peasant virtues of frugality and independence which were to inspire much of his own view of an ideal society. He was passionately proud of his origins: 'My ancestors on both sides were all free labourers . . . famous for their boldness in resisting the claims of the nobility. . . . As for nobility of race, *I* am noble.'[1] As a child he worked as a cowherd, and all his life remembered the beauty of the countryside in his native province, the landscapes which his friend and compatriot Gustave Courbet was to evoke so vividly. Proudhon's view of the world remained rural and his ideal society one of sturdy, independent, self-supporting peasants. Throughout his writing, as in that of many later anarchists, runs a nostalgia for the vanished – and often imaginary – virtues of a simple agricultural society as it existed before it was corrupted by machines and by the false values of manufacturers and financiers.

Proudhon was entirely self-educated, and his writings are full of the odd and unexpected pieces of unsystematic knowledge of the autodidact. He was apprenticed as a printer (always a trade which was to produce serious, thoughtful anarchists); he taught himself Hebrew, Latin and Greek; he read a vast amount about religion and philosophy; he formulated amateur etymological theories. Finally, in 1838, he won a scholarship to Paris awarded by the Academy of Besançon, and it was to that body, somewhat ironically, that *What is Property?* was dedicated, although Proudhon's *Warning to Proprietors*, published two years later, was to be seized by the Public Prosecutor of Besançon. The success of *What is Property?* and the notoriety which Proudhon's controversies with the Besançon authorities brought him made him a famous man. For the rest of his life he was to be an unremitting propagandist and pamphleteer and a relentless critic of the whole of existing society. From now on he was to devote himself, as he put it in a famous phrase in *What is Property?*, to studying the 'means of improving the physical, intellectual and moral condition of the poorest and most numerous class (*la classe la plus nombreuse et la plus pauvre*)'.

However, although *What is Property?* and the other writings on the same theme which followed, to say nothing of Proudhon's prosecution and acquittal in Besançon, brought him considerable fame in radical circles both in France and abroad – by 1842 Karl

Marx knew his work – they did not bring him any money. During the next few years, therefore, he was earning his living by working for a river transport firm in Lyons, where he further considered, at first hand, the problems of the production and exchange of goods, and where he had his first experience of militant working-class groups. However, although he did not finally come to live in Paris till 1847, he paid several visits to the capital, and it was in these years that he first met the other great revolutionaries of his generation, especially Marx and Bakunin. Indeed, his writings on property had already established him as a radical thinker about economics, and his views were widely discussed, particularly after he had formulated them in an extensive philosophical work, the *Système de Contradictions Économiques ou Philosophie de la Misère.* It is very characteristic of Proudhon – rambling, discursive, all-embracing, ranging from discussions about the existence of God to detailed criticisms of methods of birth control. It is full of echoes of his eager reading of the classics and of history and philosophy as well as his puritanical moral views about marriage and the family. Above all, it reflects the exciting new philosophy of Hegel which Proudhon's Paris acquaintances Marx, Bakunin and Karl Grün were constantly discussing, and shows the ideas against which Proudhon was reacting. These were the ideas of Fourier, Saint-Simon and the other French 'utopians' who had recently made words like 'socialism' and 'communism' popular. Proudhon rejected any reorganization of society that merely tried to rearrange its existing components. There was no point in simply shifting power from one group to another or in taking the ownership of capital from the existing proprietors only to replace them by a new set of monopolistic exploiters of the poor. 'Whoever appeals to power and to capital for the organization of labour is lying, because organization of labour must be the overthrow of capital and power.'[1] Thus Proudhon was equally opposed to the vast industrial enterprises to which the Saint-Simonians looked for the abolition of poverty, and to the mass production and consumption of Fourier's phalansteries; but he also rejected the plans put forward by Etienne Cabet or Louis Blanc for utopian

communities in which all was common property, but where labour
was to be subjected to a rigorous central direction. Nor was he
any more favourable to the current doctrines of the liberals.
Although he had learnt his economics from the same sources as
they – Adam Smith, Ricardo, Say – he rejected their conclusion
that the abolition of tariffs and the introduction of international
free trade would solve all economic problems. Indeed, some of
the most eloquent pages of the *Système des Contradictions Économiques* are in favour of protection and against free trade, on
the grounds that the latter would merely allow the poor to be
exploited on an international scale by the same monopolists who
oppressed them at present.

Instead of societies based on the accumulation and circulation
of capital and on the exercise of central governmental power, it
was labour, the actual work performed by a man, that should be
the basis of all social organization. 'Work', he wrote, 'is the first
attribute, the essential characteristic of man.'[1] Once a man's
work was brought into direct relation with his needs, then the
problem of exploitation would vanish and everyone would
simply work to support himself and his family without producing
gains for the proprietor or employer who himself did nothing.
Property – and Proudhon always seems to mean either land or
capital by the word – is theft because the proprietor is appropri-
ating to himself what ought to be freely available to all. In place
of property, Proudhon maintains, 'there can only be possession
and use, on the permanent condition that a man works, leaving to
him for the time being the ownership of the things he produces'.[2]

To restore the direct relationship between what a man produces and what he consumes, the first condition for Proudhon
is the abolition of the whole existing structure of credit and exchange. Once financiers, banks and, indeed, money have gone,
then the economic relations between men will return to a healthy
natural simplicity. Proudhon was, in fact, in 1849 to make a
brief unsuccessful attempt to initiate this reform, by himself
founding a People's Bank which was to have no capital and to
make no profit, but in which the customers could accumulate
credit for the goods they had themselves actually produced and

thus exchange product for product without the need of money. 'We must destroy the royal rule of gold', he wrote after the collapse of his practical efforts to do this, 'by making each product of labour into current coin. . . .'[1] It was an idea which, for all its lack of success and for all its impracticability, Proudhon was never to abandon and it was an essential part of the view of social organization which he was to leave behind.

Before writing the *Système des Contradictions Économiques* and the other essays on property which preceded it, Proudhon had read the philosophy of Kant and Fichte, but it was his contacts with the German émigrés in Paris which taught him the way of thinking and the jargon of German philosophy, and which introduced him to the Hegelian school. Thus his writings of the 1840s are full of discussion about Subject and Object, the basis of morality and the dialectic. It was, indeed, Proudhon's rather clumsy attempts to organize the *Système des Contradictions Économiques* on a Hegelian pattern that particularly aroused Marx's scorn, and there is something in Marx's criticism that 'Herr Proudhon has taken only the way of speaking from the Hegelian dialectic'. (*Herr Proudhon hat von der Hegelschen Dialektik nur die Redeweise.*) Marx himself claimed to have introduced Proudhon to Hegelianism and wrote: 'I injected him with Hegelianism to his great disadvantage, since, as he did not know German, he could not study the subject deeply.'[2] Marx delivered an all-out attack on Proudhon's economic theories within a year of the publication of the *Système des Contradictions*, in a book which was called, by a parody of Proudhon's sub-title, the *Poverty of Philosophy*. In fact, however, as so often with Marx, the doctrinal differences masked a profound difference of personal approach. When Proudhon first met Marx in the winter of 1844–5, Proudhon was already a comparatively famous man whose writings and ideas were widely discussed, whereas Marx was still an unknown and struggling German radical journalist. Marx was quick to see how useful Proudhon could be to him and suggested that he should act as the Paris representative of an organization to link socialists of various countries together by correspondence – a first sign of the International which Marx was to dominate twenty years later. Proudhon

was not enthusiastic; perhaps, for all his admiration for Marx and
his excitement at the discovery of the new German philosophy,
he realized how difficult Marx would be to work with; and certainly there were already divergences which Proudhon's reply to
Marx clearly reveals. 'Let us seek together, if you wish, the laws
of society,' Proudhon wrote, 'the way in which they are realized,
the process according to which we succeed in discovering them;
but, for God's sake, after demolishing all *a priori* dogmatisms, do
not let us dream of indoctrinating the people in our turn; do not
let us fall into the contradiction of your compatriot Luther,
who, after overthrowing the Catholic theology, at once began,
armed with excommunications and anathemas, to found Protestant theology.'[1] It was the first time that the divergence of
attitude between the French and German working-class movements, which was to be a feature of later socialist history, had
been expressed, while the breach between Marx and Proudhon
set the pattern of the future breach between Marx and Bakunin,
which was to leave the international working-class movement
permanently divided. Marx followed up this attempt to win
Proudhon's cooperation with the all-out attack contained in the
Poverty of Philosophy. He was a better philosopher and a better
economist than Proudhon, and much of his criticism of Proudhon's theories was justified. Yet there is also something in the
remark with which Proudhon received Marx's attack: 'The true
meaning of Marx's work is that he regrets that I have thought
like him everywhere and that I was the first to say it.'[2]

Indeed, the importance of Proudhon's early works lies not so
much in their theoretical arguments, fascinating as these often
are, nor, on the other hand, just in the phrases like 'property is
theft' or 'the most numerous and the poorest class', which were
to become the commonplaces of revolutionary rhetoric. It lies in
his whole conception of the nature of man and society. For
Proudhon, as we have seen, work was the characteristic of man's
nature; not to work was not to be a true man leading a full life.
Consequently, labour was both a social necessity and a moral
virtue. It provided the basic element in economic and social life
and at the same time the basic ethical standard. And, although

Proudhon was himself an intellectual and admitted in his thinking the value of intellectual work, it is the manual work of the
peasant or craftsman which he has in mind. If for Marx the
proletariat was to be the class destined by the immutable laws of
history to triumph, for Proudhon the proletariat was to be the
class whose toil and sufferings were to make possible a new moral
as well as a new social order. The sense of the dignity of labour,
and the necessity of preserving it from the degradation imposed
by machines and the exploitation imposed by the capitalist
system, runs through all Proudhon's work, and this idea of the
worker's duty to himself and his mission to the world is the basis
of all subsequent anarchist thought.

However, Proudhon's doctrine that the working man must be
the basis of all society did not blind him to the weaknesses and
vices of the workers whom he knew. He saw the working class
with all their faults. For him, as for his friend and disciple, the
painter Gustave Courbet, they were individuals, and not simply
the anonymous symbol of the dignity of labour, as they are, for
instance, in the paintings of another contemporary, Jean Fran-
çois Millet. 'Man', according to Proudhon, 'is a tyrant or a slave
by his own will before he is made tyrant or slave by fortune; the
heart of the proletarian is like that of the rich, a cesspool of
babbling sensuality, a home of filth and hypocrisy.'[1] 'The greatest
obstacle which equality has to overcome is not the aristocratic
pride of the rich,' he wrote, 'but rather the undisciplined egoism
of the poor.' It was not sufficient to change the institutions of
society to change man's nature. Any real reform must also be a
moral reform in each individual. 'Man is by nature a sinner, that
is to say not essentially a wrongdoer (*malfaisant*) but rather
wrongly made (*malfait*), and his destiny is perpetually to re-
create his ideal in himself.'[2] Here again is a point of difference
both from the utopians, such as Saint-Simon and Fourier, for
whom it was sufficient if man's environment were changed for
his nature to change also, and also from Marx, for whom morality was totally conditioned by material circumstances. Proudhon's emphasis on the necessity of a voluntary effort by each
individual was something which was taken up by subsequent

anarchist ideas and practice, as well as by a whole school of French socialist thought.

Proudhon's sense of man's divided nature and of his original sin brings him far nearer to belief in God than most anarchists have been. For him God and man confront each other, and their struggle is the struggle of man with the better part of his own self: 'But God and man, in spite of the necessity which chains them together, are irreducible; what the moralists by a pious slander have called the war of man with himself, and which is ultimately only the war of man against God, the war of reflection against instinct, the war of reason, planning, choosing, temporizing, against impetuous or fatal passion, provides the irrefutable proof.'[1] If Proudhon's ideas about the organization of society are based on a belief in the possibility of rational economic and social laws, his conception of human nature is founded on a realization of the power of the irrational and the constant effort needed to make men behave reasonably. The new order of the future is no easy, immediately attainable utopia; when Proudhon wrote in his notebook, 'Liberty, Equality, Fraternity! I say rather Liberty, Equality, Severity',[2] he meant what he said.

The sense of the violence inherent in men, and of the importance of the irrational in their actions made later thinkers of the right, as well as the philosophers of anarchist violence, look to Proudhon as their master. It also produces some curious effects in Proudhon's own work and personality, so that the two conflicting aspects of human nature which he observed are reflected in his own character and writings. The violence of his own character did not impel him, however, to take a direct part in revolutions. Although he could exclaim during the Paris revolution of 1848 that he was 'listening to the sublime horror of the cannonade', he was not, as Bakunin was, irresistibly drawn to every centre of violent revolt. On the whole, indeed, he thought that the transformation of society might come about by peaceful means and he feared that revolution would bring with it its own dangers of a new tyranny. 'We must not suppose the *revolutionary* action is the means of social reform,' he wrote to Marx just before their breach, 'because this so-called means would simply be an appeal to force, to arbitrariness, in short a contradiction.'[1]

The violence in Proudhon's character is more personal and expresses itself in alarming outbursts against, for example, Jews and homosexuals or, for that matter, against the English nation; and although in his more reasonable moments he goes so far as even to question the right of society to punish at all, at other times he is calling for the death penalty and even for the use of torture.[2]

Towards the end of his life Proudhon tried to devise methods for utilizing and turning men's violent instincts to rational ends. It was these instincts which caused wars, and any system of law, domestic or international, was only effective in so far as it could canalize the natural human emotions of hatred and desire for revenge. War was inevitable in existing society because of its psychological origins: yet the attempts to keep it within bounds by means of conventions for its conduct were breaking down, and thus, since it could not be controlled, war must be abolished. 'The end of militarism is the mission of the nineteenth century on penalty of indefinite decadence.'[3] War would only end after the social revolution, which would provide an adequate method of diverting the instincts of hatred and revenge into support for a system of law which would be mutually respected.

Throughout his life and writing Proudhon's extreme puritanism, especially in sexual questions, comes from a sense of the violent, blind and destructive nature of men's instincts. One of the virtues of hard work, indeed, was that it would diminish sexual desire and provide a natural means of controlling the growth of population. Proudhon was consistently anti-feminist; the woman's place was in the home and there was no alternative for her but to be either a housewife or a courtesan. He had been deeply attached to his own mother, and her peasant virtues of frugality and abnegation remained for him the ideal qualities in a woman. He chose his own wife entirely on such grounds: after going up to a strange girl in the street because she seemed to him to have a suitable working-class appearance, he wrote to her: 'After the considerations of age, fortune, face, morals, come those of education. On this point you will permit me to say, Mademoiselle, that I have always felt an antipathy for the high-toned lady, the female artist or writer. . . . But the working woman, simple, gracious, naïve, devoted to work and to her duties, such, in short, as I believe I have seen exemplified in you, gains my homage and my admiration.'[1] (In the event, it turned out to be as good a way of choosing a wife as any other.)

It was the family that was necessarily the basis of Proudhon's society, and here again he differs from the communal schemes of the utopian socialists. '*Point de famille, point de cité, point de république*',[2] he wrote, and in the peasant-like simplicity of his own family life (admirably caught in a famous portrait by Courbet) he found for himself, as he preached to others, a release from some of the tensions of his own nature. It was his own instinctive passionate feelings that made him so effective a revolutionary thinker, and for all his miscellaneous learning and his attempts at systematic philosophy, it is this, as he himself realized, that gave him his strength, even if it also produced inconsistencies in his thought and outbreaks of violence and prejudice. He himself summed up this side of his life in a remark in his private note-books: 'Where do I get my passion for justice which torments me and irritates me and makes me angry? I cannot account for it. It is my God, my religion, my all: and if I try to justify it by philosophical reason, I cannot.'[3]

2

In his books and pamphlets of the 1840s, Proudhon had been concerned to work out his philosophical and economic beliefs, and had not said very much about the political organization of society after the achievement of the changes he advocated in the ownership of the means of production and in the system of exchange. From the start, however, it is clear that he rejected the idea of the state. 'What is government?' he asked in 1840; and produced the Saint-Simonian answer: 'Government is the public economy, the supreme administration of the labour and the assets of all the nation.'[4] Again, later on in *What is Property?* he already shows in what direction his political thought is moving: 'Free association, liberty, limited to maintaining equality in the means of production and equivalence in exchange, is the only possible form of society, the only just and the only true one. Politics is the science of freedom; the government of man by man, under whatever name it is disguised, is oppression: the high perfection of society consists in the union of order and anarchy.'[1] However, it was Proudhon's experiences in the Revolution of 1848 that turned his attention to questions of political as well as economic organization, and led him to elaborate the double programme which he summed up when he said: 'Our idea of anarchism is launched: non-government is developing as non-property did before.'[2] It is this negation of government and negation of property which makes Proudhon the first true and effective anarchist thinker.

Although by 1848 Proudhon was well known as a revolutionary pamphleteer, he had not, in fact, had much contact with practical political organizations. In Lyon, it is true, he had been in touch with one of the semi-secret radical organizations, the Mutualists, whose name was later to be revived by his own followers, and he had seen something of the revolutionary potentialities of the industrial proletariat. All his instincts, however, were against political action, and he was as sceptical about the aims, methods and motives of the middle-class liberal democrats as he was about those of the followers of Saint-Simon and Fourier. However, the Revolution of 1848 forced him into activity of which he really disapproved. He was excited by the situation, and was to be seen in the street helping to uproot a tree from which to make a barricade – the only practical revolutionary act he ever committed. He published a leaflet calling for the dethronement of Louis-Philippe, and finally even allowed himself to be elected to the National Assembly. All the time, however, he felt that the aims of the Revolution were the wrong ones. Instead of a social revolution and a reformation of the whole system of property, the leaders of the Second Republic were only interested in political and constitutional changes. Even the attempts at economic action, such as the national workshops

which Louis Blanc had been advocating, and which, in a modi-
fied form, the government introduced in a vain attempt to deal
with growing unemployment and distress, were based, according
to Proudhon, on the wrong principles, because they merely
substituted coercion by the state for coercion by the private
employer. Consequently, Proudhon's career in the National
Assembly was largely negative. 'I voted against the Constitution,' he said, 'not because it contains things of which I dis-
approve and does not contain things of which I approve. I
voted against the Constitution because it is a Constitution.'[1]
He was disappointed in his attempts to use the Assembly as a
means of economic reform: when he tried to introduce a bill
to reorganize the system of taxation in such a way as virtually
to confiscate a large part of all private fortunes in order to set
up credit banks and subsidies for peasants and workers, he was
greeted with incredulous laughter in a rapidly emptying chamber.
Nor, as we have seen, was his attempt in 1849 to set up a pri-
vately organized People's Bank any more successful.

The experience of 1848 left him disillusioned and his immediate
reaction was one of deep gloom: 'Yes, we are defeated and
humiliated; yes, thanks to our indiscipline, to our incapacity for
revolution, we are all dispersed, imprisoned, disarmed,
dumb. . . .'[2] From 1849 onwards he was to turn away from
politics and political reforms for good and to develop into a true
anarchist.

In January 1849, Proudhon published a violent attack on
Louis Napoleon, the recently elected President of the Republic,
and was tried for sedition. He succeeded in living in hiding for a
few months, but was arrested in June and imprisoned for three
years, although much of the time under conditions which enabled him to work as a journalist as well as to see his family and
friends. For the remainder of his life – he died in 1865 – he was
earning a precarious living as a pamphleteer and journalist, and
winning a reputation as a totally fearless and independent
thinker who was not to be silenced by spells of imprisonment or
exile. His relation to Louis Napoleon was an ambivalent one. At
the time of the *coup d'état* of 1851, Proudhon even welcomed

Louis Napoleon's dictatorship. His reasons were mixed, indeed confused. On the one hand – like the eighteenth-century *philosophes* looking for a benevolent despot – he had not entirely abandoned the hope that Louis Napoleon might take up some of his schemes for tax reform and free credit. At the same time Napoleon was, in Proudhon's eyes, at least a safeguard against the monarchist restoration which seemed the only alternative now that the attempt at a bourgeois democracy had failed. On the other hand, there seems to have been an element of *Schadenfreude* in Proudhon's acceptance of the *coup d'état*. Like the German communists in 1932 who were prepared to accept Hitler's rise to power rather than collaborate with their social democratic rivals, Proudhon seemed to regard dictatorship as a means of defeating his enemies and as a preliminary to revolution, a stage in the collapse of established society that might pave the way for true social and economic reform.

Proudhon's welcome to Louis Napoleon's dictatorship and his attacks on liberal democracy and universal suffrage were to have a strange effect on his reputation. In the twentieth century he has been hailed as a forerunner by members of the extreme right: he has been called an ancestor of Maurras and the *Action Française* and even, under the Vichy régime, hailed as a representative of true 'French' socialism in contrast to the Marxist Russian variety. It is certainly true that Proudhon is hard to fit into the tradition of 'progressive' liberal political thought. His sense of the irrational and violent nature of man, his puritanism, his contempt for elections and parliaments and all the phrase-making of democratic government, are enough to explain the sympathy sometimes felt for him by fascist thinkers. Yet it would be a mistake to regard this as the true trend of his thought, or to label him as a prophet of twentieth-century dictatorships on account of his reactions to Louis Napoleon's seizure of power.

The Social Revolution demonstrated by the Coup d'État of the Second of December – the work which did much to injure Proudhon's reputation with liberal democrats, both then and later – does, in fact, show how he got himself into a rather ambiguous position. What the events of the years 1848–51 had shown was the complete bankruptcy of conventional political and economic thought. None of the régimes since 1789 in France had been able to ensure the observance of the 'principles of '89', which Proudhon defined as freedom of property, freedom of labour and the natural, free and equal division of labour by aptitude and not by caste. The history of the previous sixty-four years had shown, he says, that despotic government is impossible. The way is therefore clear for a new organization of society which will be based not on a permanent central government but on the continuous but shifting interplay of interests: 'If there is a government, it can only result from a delegation, convention, federation, in a word from the free and spontaneous consent of all the individuals which make up the People, each one of them insisting on and canvassing for the guarantee of his own interests. Thus the government, if there is one, instead of being Authority as hitherto, will represent the relationship between all the interests created by free property, free labour, free trade, free credit and will itself only have a representative value, just as paper money only has value through what it represents.'[1] If society can be organized on the basis of the direct interplay of interests, and if such organization is based on the 'relation between liberties and interests', then, Proudhon goes on to say, the difference between economics and politics vanishes: 'For there to be a relationship between interests, the interests themselves must be present, answering for themselves, making their own demands and commitments, acting. . . . In the last analysis everyone is the government, so there is no government. Thus the system of government follows from its definition: to say representative government means to say relationship between interests; to say relationship between interests means absence of government.'[2]

Proudhon did not long retain any illusions that Napoleon III might usher in a new society where government would give way to a free interplay of decentralized economic and social groups. Instead, the monopolies he had attacked, the police and bureaucrats he had denounced, the economic and social ideas he had deplored, all seemed more firmly entrenched in French society than ever. However, the ideas which the failure of the

1848 Revolution and of the Second Republic had forced him to develop remained the foundation of his subsequent writings. The only hope of achieving the economic reforms for which he had hoped would lie in the complete reorganization of society so that economic interests, properly and equitably organized, would cooperate for their mutual advantage without the intervention of any central authority. 'What we put in place of the government is industrial organization,' Proudhon wrote in 1851, 'what we put in place of laws are contracts . . . what we put in place of political powers are economic forces.'[1]

In his voluminous writings in the seventeen years between 1848 and his death, Proudhon, when he was not just commenting on contemporary politics, was elaborating these themes. In fact, although he was to be forced into exile in Belgium between 1858 and 1862, in order to avoid a further period of imprisonment for his writings, he became less revolutionary. He was concerned to point out the contradictions of existing society and to preach the inevitability of change, but not to lay down what society would be like in detail after the revolution. This saves him from the fascinating, if often ludicrous, precise planning of a Godwin or a Fourier, but it also means – and it is something from which all anarchist thought suffers – that he never really explains how the obvious difficulties of his system are to be overcome. In his most extensive work, *Justice in the Revolution and the Church*,[2] Proudhon falls back on man's own nature as the only guarantee that his anarchism would ever work. Justice, the fundamental principle of society, is neither revealed by God nor inherent in nature: it is a 'faculty of the soul' which requires careful nurturing. 'Justice,' Proudhon writes, 'as we can see from the example of children and savages, is the last and slowest to grow of all the faculties of the soul; it needs an energetic education in struggle and adversity.'[3] Once men have developed the sense of justice, then their relations will be governed by the 'respect, spontaneously felt and mutually guaranteed, of human dignity, in whatever person and in whatever circumstances it is threatened, and whatever risks we are exposed to in its defence'.[4] And later he writes: 'What guarantees the observance of justice? The same thing that guarantees that the merchant will respect the coin – faith in reciprocity, that is to say justice itself. Justice is for intelligent and free beings the supreme cause of their decisions.'[1] Proudhon, in fact, falls back on his early reading of Kant's moral philosophy, and his society rests on the categorical imperative and on the maxim, 'Do as you would be done by'.

Proudhon envisaged a society in which men's products would be directly exchanged for the other goods they needed, and in which such institutions as might be required for this purpose would be provided by negotiations between the groups concerned. Sometimes he writes as though there will be some minimal permanent central government consisting of delegations from the communes which form the state. Elsewhere he suggests that a central government is only needed for such purposes as the initial reorganization of the economy and reconstitution of society. In any case, however, the key to the new organization is federalism, and it was this idea that Proudhon was most concerned to develop in the last years of his life and which was to have an important political influence after his death. Society must be based on small units: 'If the family was the basic element of feudal society, the workshop is the basic element of the new society.'[2] These small units will be loosely associated in the commune, which will be all that is needed to provide most of the administrative functions required. The communes will need to join a federation for certain purposes, but the delegation of power to any central authority must be very strictly limited and controlled: for example, the control of the militia necessary for defence against foreign invasion must be left with the local authorities except in actual time of war, and there need be no central budget or administration. Proudhon never faces the problem that in practice confronts all federal systems, namely how to keep some sort of equality of living standards between communes with differing resources. This is in part because, like all anarchists, he envisaged men as living an extremely austere life with few needs. He never forgot his own origins, and tended to equate all men with the peasants of the Franche-Comté or with the self-respecting, self-improving printers among whom his apprenticeship had been served. However much he may have realized that 'the workshop is the basis of the new society', it was a workshop in rural surroundings, and the artisans were smallholders at heart. After the Revolution, he wrote, 'Humanity will do as in Genesis, it will concern itself with the tilling and caring for the soil which will provide it with a life of delights – as recommended by the philosopher Martin in *Candide*, man will cultivate his garden. Agriculture, once the lot of the slave, will be one of the first of the fine arts,* and human life will be passed in innocence, freed of all the seduction of the ideal.'[1]

The groups out of which the new society is to be formed must be rational and natural ones. 'Every time that men with their wives and children assemble in one place, live and till the soil side by side, develop in their midst different industries, create neighbourly relations among themselves and, whether they like it or not, impose on themselves a state of solidarity, they form what I call a natural group, which soon sets itself up as a political organism, affirming its identity in its unity, its independence, its life, its own movement (*autokinesis*) and its autonomy.'[2]

Proudhon's enthusiasm for federalism and for the small group led him into some strange positions. He found himself defending the Jesuits for their stand in favour of cantonal independence in the Swiss Civil War of 1846, and in the American Civil War he was a firm supporter of the South, pointing out that the sacrifice of the Southern states' rights in return for the Union's anti-slavery policy simply meant that the Negroes would become proletarians instead of slaves, which was not, in Proudhon's eyes, much of a change for the better. He incurred the anger of all liberals by his violent attacks on Mazzini and Garibaldi for wanting to impose an artificial national unity on the varied and heterogeneous population of Italy. He was in favour of multinational states and – although he at times shows a touch of French chauvinism in the Jacobin tradition – he had no sympathy with demands for 'natural frontiers' and national self-determination. Almost alone among the radical writers of his day, he was

---

* This is a direct echo of the love of flower gardens which is so notable a feature of Fourier's phalansteries.

opposed to Polish claims for independence, on the grounds that
the independent Polish state would be entirely in the hands of a
reactionary aristocracy. (It was one of the few topics on which he
held the same views as Richard Cobden, in strong contrast to
Bakunin, who actually hired a ship to carry an abortive expedi-
tion to assist the Polish rising in 1863.)

Proudhon was not a philosopher who erected a consistent
rational structure like that of William Godwin. He is rather a
writer whose influence was due to a few striking slogans – 'Property is theft', 'God is evil' – and to a few reiterated fundamental
ideas about the nature of man and the future organization of
society. At the same time, the passion of his own temperament,
his stubborn refusal to conform or compromise, his wide range
of odd knowledge, all made him a first-rate popular journalist
and pamphleteer. The *'trois gros volumes'* of *Justice* sold some 6,000
copies on publication, and even if Proudhon's own claim of
10,000 readers of the articles written during his exile in Belgium
is exaggerated, his influence by the time he died was widespread,
not only among the French working-class movements which
were developing in the 1860s, but also abroad, especially in
Spain and Italy.

While it is perhaps Proudhon's understanding of the irrational side of man's nature and his awareness of the violence of
which human beings are capable that have led to a revival of
interest in his work in the twentieth century, his message to his
contemporaries was a simpler one. The abolition of the financier
and the *rentier*, the securing to the worker of the full value of the
goods he produced, the development of small, mutually supporting groups in place of the dehumanized factories, the constant reminder of the virtues of the peasant's life, all these had an
obvious and positive appeal. And Proudhon's negative message
was even more telling and contains the essence of anarchism, or
at least one side of it. 'To be governed is to be watched over,
inspected, spied on, directed, legislated at, regulated, docketed,
indoctrinated, preached at, controlled, assessed, weighed, cen-
sored, ordered about, by men who have neither the right nor the
knowledge nor the virtue. To be governed means to be, at each

operation, at each transaction, at each movement, noted, regis-
tered, controlled, taxed, stamped, measured, valued, assessed,
patented, licensed, authorized, endorsed, admonished, hampered,
reformed, rebuked, arrested. It is to be, on the pretext of the
general interest, taxed, drilled, held to ransom, exploited, mono-
polized, extorted, squeezed, hoaxed, robbed; then at the least
resistance, at the first word of complaint, to be repressed, fined,
abused, annoyed, followed, bullied, beaten, disarmed, garotted,
imprisoned, machine-gunned, judged, condemned, deported,
flayed, sold, betrayed and finally mocked, ridiculed, insulted,
dishonoured. That's government, that's its justice, that's its
morality!'[1] In both his positive and negative doctrines Proudhon
is the first and most important anarchist philosopher; and later
anarchist writers have not added very much to what he said.
What remained was to see how far these ideas could be put into
practice.

3

In September 1864 the International Working Men's Association
was founded in London. Although Karl Marx had not taken the
initiative in organizing the meeting, he was, from the start of the
First International, determined that it should be under his direction and control. However, the French delegates at the opening
meeting were, in fact, disciples of Proudhon. At the end of his
life, therefore, Proudhon found himself, for the first time since
1848, faced with the problem of what his attitude should be to the
practical politics of the working-class movements which had been
growing up in France over the past few years. In 1863 a group
of Parisian workers had announced that they would put forward
candidates for the elections for the *Corps Législatif*. Their leader
was Henri Tolain, a bronze-worker, and just the sort of worker
of whom Proudhon most approved – sober, thrifty, dignified,
with a passion for reading and learning. In 1862 Tolain had successfully organized a delegation of French workers to the Great
Exhibition in London, and he had used the opportunity to state
his principle that one must say to the workers: 'You are free,

organize yourselves, do your own business for yourselves.'[1] In spite of failing to win any seats in the Paris constituencies for which he and his friends had stood, Tolain persisted in his attempts at political action, and in 1864 he drafted a manifesto, known as the *Manifeste des Soixante*, in which he pointed out the necessity for the workers to have their own political organization so as not to be any longer dependent on the *bourgeoisie* for their representation.

Proudhon disagreed profoundly. For the past few years he had been preaching abstention from all elections as a demonstration of disapproval of the sham constitutionalism of the Second Empire. It was only by a mass expression of disapproval, he thought, and by a refusal to make the system work that the hypocrisy of the imperial régime could be exposed. Proudhon's campaign against voting was not very successful, and it was clear that many of those who, like Tolain, were his most devoted disciples, were not going to be content with the purely negative policy of complete abstention. It was in response to the Manifesto of the Sixty that Proudhon, a year before his death, felt obliged to define and revise his position. *On the Political Capacity of the Working Classes*, which was still in proof when Proudhon died, repeats most of his previous teaching. However, he now realized that working-class organization might really achieve something by political means: 'A social fact of incalculable importance is occurring in the heart of society; it is [and here he takes up one of the Saint-Simonian phrases he had used nearly thirty years before] the arrival in political life of the most numerous and poorest class.'[2] In effect, Proudhon was prepared to accept this new political development; but he was insistent that any political action must be based on the principle of mutuality. It was only, he repeated, through the action of small groups cooperating practically in day-to-day economic and social life and living on terms of mutual respect that any progress could come about. Otherwise – and it was of the dangers of political action rather than its advantages that Proudhon remained aware – the kind of politics which many socialists were advocating could only end in disaster. 'The political system', he

1. William Godwin: a portrait by H. W. Pickersgill

2. *Pierre Joseph Proudhon and his Children* by Gustave Courbet

wrote, 'can be defined as follows: A compact democracy founded in appearance on the dictatorship of the masses, but in which the masses only have so much power as is needed to secure universal servitude.'[1]

Proudhon's doctrines had a particular appeal for the intelligent working-class man in the Second Empire, if only because of the contradictions and anomalies in the social and economic life of France in the mid-nineteenth century. It was a period of expansion and change, of the building of railways, the construction of vast new factories, the growth of the banks and the foundation of the first great department stores, of the creation of the replanned and glittering Paris of Baron Haussmann (which Proudhon himself so much disliked). At a time when the real wages of the workers were stationary this only increased the distance and antagonism between classes, especially in Paris. Yet, while some workers were being uprooted and absorbed into the all-embracing world of the industrial town, others were still working at home or in small workshops and often tilled a small plot of land, so that they were still half-peasants in outlook.[2] The new working-class leaders, such as Tolain, who wanted to put Proudhon's teaching into practice, were the men who were aware of these contrasts and changes. 'The working-class leader', a French social historian has written of this period, 'is neither an artisan nor a proletarian: he is in general a man who has passed his childhood in the country and has not forgotten it; he is above all a man who is familiar with the small workshop but who follows attentively the development of the large factory ... he is a well-informed man who tries to anticipate and form a picture of the future. ... Half peasant, half worker, who mixes realism and utopia in a subtle blend.'[3] It might be a description of Proudhon himself or of his disciples such as Tolain (though he came from the old Paris artisan class and not from the country), or Eugène Varlin, the young bookbinder who became one of the leaders of the French section of the International and of the Commune of 1871.

In the sixties Proudhon's disciples practised his principles of self-improvement and mutual assistance. Varlin, for example,

founded a large cooperative kitchen in Paris to supply meals for
working men. At the same time they talked increasingly of the
necessity of revolution. The younger generation, of whom Varlin
was the most prominent, were often impatient of the limited aims
of Tolain and the older men. At the same time, from their committee room in the rue des Grandvilliers – the same street, as
their historians like to recall, where Jacques-Roux preached
social revolution in 1793 – they provided a stream of Proudhonian
ideas which were to bring the French section of the International
into conflict with Marx.

However, Proudhon's influence on the French working-class
movement was a long-term rather than an immediate one. In
the sixties men like Tolain and Varlin did not have many followers, and it was only with the Commune of 1871 that Proudhonian ideas became indissolubly part of revolutionary practice
in France. Proudhon lived just long enough to know and approve
of the founding of the International; but in fact his disciples soon
found their beliefs at odds with the centralized discipline which
Marx was trying to impose. Not all of them remained anarchists,
but the ideas of cooperation and decentralization which they
derived from Proudhon became an important element in French
socialist thought, and the differences between Marx and Proudhon were reflected later in the differences between the French
and German socialist movements at the beginning of the
twentieth century.

It was nevertheless in the 1860s that the anarchist movement
began to be a practical political force. Proudhon's own acquain-
tance with Marx and Bakunin linked him to the main traditions
of contemporary European socialist and radical thought. For all
his own political inaction, he inspired a large section of the
French working-class movement down to our own day. Finally,
the formation of the International, even though its immediate
practical importance was not as great as either its members or
its historians have believed, provided a stage on which took place
the clash of temperament and doctrine between Marx and his
supporters on the one hand and Bakunin and the followers of

Proudhon on the other. This clash was to split the European working-class movement irreparably and to offer two alternative ways of achieving the revolution and two alternative visions of what the world would be like once the revolution had succeeded.

CHAPTER IV

Bakunin and the Great Schism

'Pour soulever les hommes, il faut avoir le diable au corps.'
Bakunin

I

Proudhon provided most of the ideas which inspired the anarchist movement. It was Bakunin who gave later anarchists an example of anarchist fervour in action; and it was Bakunin who showed how great was the difference in theory and practice between anarchist doctrine and the communism of Marx, and thus made explicit the split in the international revolutionary movement which had already been implicit in the divergence between Proudhon and Marx in the 1840s. Bakunin, too, more than any of his contemporaries, linked the revolutionary movement in Russia with that of the rest of Europe, and derived from it a belief in the virtues of violence for its own sake and a confidence in the technique of terrorism which was to influence many other revolutionaries besides anarchists.

Michael Bakunin was born in 1814 about 150 miles from Moscow, in the province of Tver;[1] and in spite of a happy country childhood – his father was a conservative but comparatively enlightened member of the provincial nobility – he grew up to be a violently rebellious young man, with a love of stirring up dramas, which he never lost. 'Michael tells me', one of his friends wrote, 'that every time he returns home from anywhere, he expects to find something unusual.'[2] Certainly, if he did not find anything unusual, he set about remedying the situation. He himself 'attributed his passion for destruction to the influence of his mother, whose despotic character inspired him with an insensate hatred of every restriction on liberty.'[3] His later revolutionary activity seems to be the direct expression of a complex and turbulent temperament. (Some writers have seen in his career a compensation for the sexual impotence from which he appears to have suffered.) His character changed little during his life, and it was well summed up quite early in his career by his friend, the critic Vissarion Belinsky, who wrote: 'A marvellous man, a deep, primitive, leonine nature – this cannot be denied him. But his demands, his childishness, his braggadocio, his unscrupulousness, his disingenuousness – all this makes friendship with him impossible. He loves ideas not men. He wants to dominate with his personality, not to love.'[1]

Bakunin's love of ideas had already developed in the 1830s when, after a short and unsuccessful period as an officer, he had become involved in the Moscow world of literature and philosophy and become a friend of Belinsky. Like Belinsky, he was immediately swept away by the intoxication of German philosophy – first Fichte, and then Hegel, both of whom to him seemed to preach above all the cult of individual freedom and of revolt. In 1840, at the age of twenty-six, he travelled to Paris, and, like Proudhon, at once came into contact with the international radical intellectuals living there; and it was then that he first met Proudhon and Marx, and read and discussed the writings of the Young Hegelians and of Weitling. Just as Proudhon's contacts with Marx at this period revealed the difference between their temperaments as well as their doctrinal divergences, so Bakunin's first meetings with Marx gave some idea of the great schism of twenty years later. Marx, Bakunin later recalled, 'called me a sentimental idealist, and he was right. I called him morose, vain and treacherous; and I too was right.'[2]

Although Bakunin during his travels in Germany and France wrote a certain number of articles, his violent nature really wanted action; and it was the revolutions of 1848 which established his reputation as one of the foremost revolutionary figures of Europe. Just before the outbreak of the revolution in Paris, Bakunin had already been in trouble through his association with the Polish refugee organizations. In December 1847 he was expelled from Paris after a rousing speech in which he had offered the Poles his support in overthrowing the tsarist government.

(He was to show a lifelong devotion to the cause of the Polish national revolution.) Then he hurried back to Paris the moment the revolution broke out in February 1848, although he left again a month later to try to stir up trouble in Poland. He never reached Poland, however, as he was arrested in Berlin on the way, and was only released on condition that he did not continue his journey. Instead, he attended the Pan-Slav Congress organized at Prague; and this provided him with the first opportunity of addressing a large audience and of putting forward some of his basic ideas.

Bakunin's thought was never very subtle or very original; and, indeed, in all his lifelong devotion to the cause of revolution, it was in the acts of conspiracy and revolt that he expressed his passion, rather than in theories about social or economic change. His complaint that Marx was 'ruining the workers by making theorists of them' is characteristic. However, in the *Foundations of Slav Policy*, which he wrote for the Prague Congress, and in his *Appeal to the Slavs*, published at the end of the year, he put forward ideas which were to remain his stock in trade. The Slavs should form a federation, so that 'the new policy will not be a state policy, but a policy of peoples, of independent, free individuals'. Thus not only must the Austrian Empire be destroyed, but also the whole system of liberal bourgeois values which many people thought the revolutions of 1848 were aiming at establishing. 'We must overthrow from top to bottom this effete social world which has become impotent and sterile. . . . We must first purify our atmosphere and transform completely the milieu in which we live; for it corrupts our instincts and our wills and contracts our heart and our intelligence. The social question takes the form primarily of the overthrow of society.'[1] And at the same time he wrote to the German poet and radical politician, Herwegh: 'The epoch of parliamentary life, of Constituent and National Assemblies and so forth is over. Anyone who squarely asks himself the question must confess that he no longer feels any interest, only forced and unreal interest, in these ancient forms. I do not believe in constitutions and laws; the best constitution in the world would not be able to satisfy me.

We need something different; inspiration, life, a new lawless and therefore free world.'[1]

Proudhon had taken as his motto '*Destruam et aedificabo*'. For Bakunin, on the other hand, the act of destruction was sufficient in itself, for there was in his view a fundamental goodness in man and a fundamental soundness in human institutions which would automatically be released once the existing system was overthrown; and the initial act of revolutionary violence would reveal the natural virtues of man without much further preparation. Bakunin believed that these virtues were especially to be found in the Russian peasantry, and it was they who were somehow to take the lead in the redemption of Europe. Bakunin's Slavophil enthusiasm, as expressed at the Prague Congress, included a strong anti-German feeling which his quarrel with Marx was later to reinforce, so that for many years in the history of the European socialist movement, German Marxism seemed to represent the type of centralized, disciplined and bureaucratic political creed to which the anarchists in Russia and France or Spain or Italy were irrevocably opposed.

At the Pan-Slav Congress at Prague, Bakunin revealed another characteristic passion – that for establishing largely imaginary secret societies. All his life he was to see himself as the great conspirator, at the centre of a web of clandestine organizations controlled by himself and organized, in theory, on the basis of a 'strict hierarchy and unconditional obedience'. He was always planning central committees of which, as often as not, no other members except himself were ever appointed. Yet such was Bakunin's charm and conviction that young men willingly went off on a wild-goose chase to contact other cells of a conspiracy which often existed only in Bakunin's imagination. The first of such recruits was a young Czech journalist recruited at the time of the Prague Congress; and years later Bakunin was still issuing membership cards of non-existent organizations, such as the one which ran: 'The bearer of this is one of the accredited representatives of the Russian Section of the World Revolutionary Alliance no. 2771.'[2] However, Bakunin's make-believe undoubtedly helped him to put across his own view of the nature of the revolution and of his own place in it, and by the end of his life the police of several countries took Bakunin's conspiracies as seriously as he did himself.

During the winter of 1848–9, Bakunin was in Saxony; and in the spring of 1849 he was caught up in the brief but violent revolution in Dresden which was the last radical outburst in Germany before the counter-revolution triumphed. In fact, he had little sympathy with its aims, which were to protest against the king's dissolution of the Diet, a body of which Bakunin thoroughly disapproved. But the excitement of being actually present at a real revolution was too much for him, and he fought on the barricades, along with another revolutionary figure whose impact on nineteenth-century Europe was in a different way to be at least as great as his own – Richard Wagner. With the collapse of the revolution Bakunin was arrested and there began the long period of imprisonment which was to contribute much to his later reputation as the great revolutionary. The Saxon authorities eventually handed him over to the Austrians, who wanted to punish him for his activities at Prague and his advocacy of the destruction of the Empire. They, in turn, yielded to the Russian government's request that it was as a rebellious and actually condemned Russian subject that Bakunin should be punished. From 1851 to 1857 he was in prison in Russia; and in 1857 his sentence was commuted to one of banishment in Siberia. In 1861 he escaped with remarkable ease, after being released on parole, using his family connexions and his own social position, and made his way, via Japan and the United States, to London. His escape was so simple, and had even been helped by various Russian officials in Siberia, that it was sometimes rumoured that Bakunin was actually a tsarist agent. There was no truth in these reports; but they were typical of the sort of attack which many subsequent anarchist leaders had to meet from their Marxist rivals, and they were often revived in the struggle between Bakunin and Marx a decade later. Moreover, just as Proudhon had aroused the suspicion of other radicals by his brief flirtation with Bonapartism, so Bakunin, too, had in the first stages of his imprisonment produced a curious document, a

Confession to the Tsar, in which, speaking as 'a prodigal, estranged and perverted son before an indulgent father', he narrated the story of his life, and then went on to express his deep patriotic Slav feelings and his even deeper detestation of the Germans. The *Confession* was not published for seventy years; and not many people seem to have known about it at the time. It is a reflection of Bakunin's Russian nationalism as much as of any subservience to the tsar, and its interest lies more in the light it throws on the Dostoievskian side of Bakunin's nature than in its political significance. Yet, as in Proudhon's case, there is perhaps also a touch of the impatience and exasperation of the anarchist who, when confronted with more conventional revolutionaries and reformers, turns in desperation to authority in the hope of achieving his aims.

Bakunin's arrival in London brought him right into the centre of the international revolutionary movement. He went to live with the Russian exiles, Herzen and Ogarev, and, indeed, was to depend largely on Herzen for his financial support. Bakunin's prestige among the revolutionary groups was very great; and the malicious rumours about the circumstances of his escape could not dim the reputation which his revolutionary acts in 1848–9 and his subsequent long imprisonment had brought him. His appearance, too, was most impressive. He was immensely tall, immensely energetic, with at times an almost childlike simplicity. 'His activity, his leisure, his appetite,' Herzen wrote, 'like all his other characteristics – even his gigantic size and continual sweat – were of superhuman proportions, and he himself remained, as of old, a giant with leonine head and tousled mane.'[1] In comparison with the force of his character and his charm, Bakunin's defects – his complete fecklessness about money, his impetuosity, his childish petulance – hardly showed except to his intimate friends, such as Herzen, who was tolerant and ironical enough to put up with him.

Bakunin remained in London for some three years; and, although he met Marx, whom he suspected of encouraging the rumours that he was a tsarist agent, at Marx's request and discussed the International with him, he played no part in the founding of the organization. In 1864, the year of the foundation

of the International, Bakunin settled in Italy and lived there for
the next three years, first in Florence and then in and around
Naples. It was in Naples that he was to find his first disciples, and
Italy has remained one of the countries from which anarchist
ideas have never entirely vanished. The appeal of Bakunin's
revolutionary anarchism in the Italy of the 1860s was considerable. He arrived there just at the moment when Mazzini, for a
generation the hero of all the radical republicans in Italy, was
beginning to lose some of his influence over the young. Although
Mazzini had been one of the great prophets of Italian unification,
that unification had been accomplished in 1860 without his aid,
and in a constitutional form – the Monarchy – to which he was
bitterly opposed. There were some among the younger republicans who thought that Mazzini's liberalism was sterile and
old-fashioned, and who saw in Bakunin a new and more exciting
revolutionary leader preaching a social revolution at a moment
when it appeared that the political revolution of the previous
years had not solved many of Italy's social problems.[1] Moreover,
the young radicals of Naples, with whom Bakunin quickly
became friendly, were already much influenced by Proudhon's
ideas. Carlo Pisacane, who had been defeated and killed when he
tried to raise a republican rebellion against the Bourbons in
1857, had spread ideas of federalism and mutualism among his
followers, and they were ideas which seemed even more attractive
after 1860 when republicans in the south felt that the centralized
monarchy of the House of Savoy might be as dangerous to liberty
as their own local Bourbon dynasty which they had just overthrown.

Bakunin himself, too, found in Italy just the sort of situation
which appealed to him. Whereas Marx had become convinced
that the revolution could only take place in industrial societies
and by means of the class-conscious industrial proletariat,
Bakunin saw the possibility of revolution in non-industrial
societies, such as Italy or his native Russia. Soon after his arrival
in Italy he was writing as follows: 'The advent of the social
revolution is in no country nearer than in Italy. In Italy there
does not exist as in other countries of Europe a privileged class

of workers who, thanks to their considerable wages, pride themselves on the literary education they have acquired; they are dominated by the principles of the bourgeois, by their ambition and vanity, to such an extent that they are only different from the bourgeois by their situation and not in their way of thinking.'[1] The contrast between Bakunin's belief in the revolutionary potentiality of those with nothing to lose (an idea which, as we have seen, he may well have derived from Weitling) and Proudhon's ideal of the self-educated, self-improving peasant or craftsman cooperating with his neighbour to build a new society, is an obvious one and has remained a dichotomy in the anarchist movement. In fact, however, Bakunin was to find his disciples from both types of worker. For all his belief in the *Lumpenproletariat*, it was among the watchmakers of the Swiss Jura – some of the most skilled and best-educated artisans of Europe – that his most devoted followers were to be found. At the same time he was to recruit in Italy a band of loyal anarchists who were to be among the leaders of European anarchism in the next generation, and whose following lay among the ignorant and oppressed workers of the Italian cities and countryside, so that even in our time it was possible to find Roman or Sicilian children called 'Bakunin' or the three daughters of an anarchist father bearing the truly anarchist names of Hunger, Poverty and Revolution.*

While Bakunin was in Italy he founded the first of the international revolutionary organizations to which he was to devote the rest of his life. This was called the International Brotherhood and, although Marx had already launched the International Working Men's Association in London, he did not yet regard Bakunin as a serious rival and indeed welcomed his activity in Italy as a means of lessening Mazzini's influence. However, before his activities in Italy had become very important, Bakunin, whose movements were always largely determined by his perpetual financial difficulties, had settled in Switzerland, and it was there, from 1867 on, that the most influential phase of his life was passed.

* *Fame, Miseria, Rivoluzione.*

2

Once in Switzerland, Bakunin soon became the centre of innumerable plots, intrigues, projects, hopes and fears. His exuberant temperament, his love of conspiracy, his faith in the revolutionary potentialities of Russia, Italy and Spain, his feckless Bohemian way of life and his desire to surround himself with friends and disciples, all involved him in a series of difficult situations, and all produced consequences, which, by their very inconsistency, illustrate the internal conflicts from which the anarchist movement has constantly suffered. Bakunin's deep hostility to tsarist Russia was matched by an equally deep faith in the power of Russia not only to redeem herself but also to point the way towards a European revolution. For Bakunin, the oppressed were naturally revolutionary, and only needed leadership to make them rise in revolt. 'We are talking', he wrote, 'about the great mass of the working class, which, worn out by its daily labour, is ignorant and wretched. Whatever political and religious prejudices people have tried and even partly succeeded to implant in its consciousness, it remains *socialist without knowing it*; it is basically and instinctively and by the very force of its position more seriously and more really socialist than all the bourgeois and scientific socialists put together. It is socialist through all the conditions of its material existence, through all the needs of its being, while the others are only socialist through the needs of their thoughts; and in real life, the needs of a man's being always exert a much stronger influence than those of his thought, thought being here, as everywhere and always, the expression of being, the reflections of its successive developments, but never its moving principle.'[1]

This being so, it was in the backward countries that revolution was most likely, even if the oppressed classes themselves did not realize it. 'The Russian people', Bakunin says, 'are socialist by instinct and revolutionary by nature.'[2] The same is true of Italy, where 'the workers are socialist and revolutionary by circumstance and by instinct . . . but they are still in almost complete ignorance of the true causes of their miserable situation'.[3] 'The mass of Italian peasants', he wrote in 1871, 'already constitutes an immense and all-powerful army for the social revolution. Led by the proletariat of the towns and organized by the young socialist revolutionaries that army will be invincible.'[1] However, it is no use waiting for the slow processes of education to make the people aware of their own interests. 'We must not teach the people, but lead them to revolt.'[2] The act of revolution would be sufficiently educational in itself. 'Many of the good bourgeois socialists', Bakunin once wrote, 'are always telling us, "Let us instruct the people first and then emancipate them." We say on the contrary, "Let them emancipate themselves first and they will instruct themselves of their own accord."'[3] The Russian peasants were, in Bakunin's eyes, in a particularly strong position, since they had traditional forms of organization, village communes and the like, so that they might well be in a position to set an example to the working class in more advanced countries, if only they could be given vigorous revolutionary leadership. 'If the workers of the West delay too long,' he wrote in 1869, 'it will be the Russian peasant who will set them an example.'[4]

With his deep feelings for Russia and his faith in its revolutionary future, Bakunin was particularly anxious to feel himself in touch with the younger generation inside Russia. He thus welcomed enthusiastically in 1869 a twenty-two-year-old Russian, Sergei Gennadevich Nechaev, who appeared in Switzerland claiming to have escaped from a Russian prison. 'I have with me', Bakunin wrote to a Swiss friend, 'one of those fanatical young men who know no doubts, who fear nothing and who have decided in an absolute way that many, very many of them, must perish at the hands of the government, but who will not stop because of that until the Russian people rise. They are magnificent, these young fanatics, believers without gods, heroes without phrases.'[5] Bakunin's friendship with Nechaev was to cause him personal pain and political trouble, but nevertheless it was important for the development of anarchist concepts, since it was under the influence of Nechaev's truly terrorist temperament that Bakunin, for a time at least, came to advocate terror as the most effective way of challenging the values and the power of the state.

Nechaev was a self-made revolutionary, a dark, lonely tortuous man, part *poseur*, part fanatic, part idealist, part criminal. He had been born in very humble circumstances in the developing textile centre of Ivanovo, north-east of Moscow, but he soon succeeded in getting away to Moscow and attending classes at the university there. The revolutionary students whom he met there had been much impressed by the attempt to assassinate the tsar, Alexander II, in 1866; they read and admired the writings of Buonarroti and were devoted to the idea of the conspiratorial life. In Moscow, Nechaev had met Peter Nikitich Tkachev, the most consistent and thoroughgoing of these neo-Jacobins. He was a man whose doctrine of the professional dedicated revolutionary elite was to have considerable influence on Lenin and, although he had, like all his generation, fallen under the spell of the Bakunin legend, he was to end up by advocating a rigorously organized revolutionary movement and completely rejecting Bakunin's anarchist ideas. Nechaev and Tkachev produced in 1868 a *Programme of Revolutionary Action* which contained elements both of Bakuninist anarchism and of Tkachev's later centralized discipline. The leaders of the revolutionary insurrection would be men of a new stamp, dedicated wholly to the revolutionary cause and finding in their activity the full freedom and development of their personality. The revolutionary groups were to be decentralized and members were to change places, so that no one should be corrupted by the exercise of too much authority. Above all, the revolutionary must have no loyalties except to the revolution: 'Those who join the organization must give up every possession, occupation or family ties, because families and occupations might distract members from their activity.'[1]

When Nechaev arrived in Geneva in the spring of 1869, with all sorts of largely invented tales about his revolutionary past, he found Bakunin eager to cooperate with him and to place himself at the head of the new revolutionary generation in Russia. Together they drafted a *Revolutionary Catechism*, a set of *Principles of Revolution*, and other manifestoes, which proclaimed the necessity of ruthless terror in the fight against the state. Anyone who flouted and despised the values of existing society was an ally in the revolutionary cause: 'Brigandage is one of the most honoured aspects of the people's life in Russia. . . . The brigand in Russia is the true and only revolutionary, without phrase-making, without bookish rhetoric. Popular revolution is born from the merging of the revolt of the brigand with that of the peasant. . . . Even today this is still the world of the Russian revolution; the world of brigands and the world of brigands alone has always been in harmony with the revolution. The man who wants to make a serious conspiracy in Russia, who wants a popular revolution, must turn to that world and fling himself into it.'[1]

'The revolutionary despises and hates present-day social morality in all its forms . . . he regards everything as moral which helps the triumph of revolution. . . . All soft and enervating feelings of friendship, relationship, love, gratitude, even honour, must be stifled in him by a cold passion for the revolutionary cause. . . . Day and night he must have one thought, one aim – merciless destruction.

'We recognize no other activity but the work of extermination, but we admit that the forms in which this activity will show itself will be extremely varied – poison, the knife, the rope, etc. In this struggle, revolution sanctifies everything alike.'[2]

This passionate praise of terror, in which violence is almost accepted as an end for its own sake, is something which is not found elsewhere in Bakunin's writings, and is a sign of the extent to which he had come under Nechaev's influence. Nevertheless, it was sufficient to introduce into the anarchist movement an element which it never lost, and to suggest the doctrine of *le propagande par le fait* which was to be the impetus of so much anarchist action over the next thirty years. Nechaev, before returning to Russia, was calling for immediate, personal, violent action. 'Without respect for lives, without hesitating before any threat, fear or danger, we must – with a series of personal acts and sacrifices succeeding each other according to a predetermined established plan, with a series of bold, not to say rash, attempts – throw ourselves into the life of the people, from which to stir up faith in itself and us, faith in its own power, to shake it, unite it and urge it towards the triumph of the cause. . . . We have a uniquely negative plan that no one can modify: complete destruction.'[1]

Nechaev's career as a revolutionary ended in a sordid and mysterious fashion. After his return to Moscow, he murdered a student who was a member of his organization, perhaps because he feared treachery, or perhaps simply to demonstrate his own power over his followers, and then fled back to Geneva. Here he not only tried to seduce Herzen's daughter for her money, but also started to intrigue against Bakunin. In 1872 he was arrested and extradited to Russia, where he died in prison ten years later. Bakunin sadly admitted that he had been taken in by a crooked, dubious adventurer, and wrote: 'We were fools, and how Herzen would have had the laugh of us if he had been alive and how right he would have been to scold us. Well, there is nothing to be done. Let us swallow the bitter pill, and we shall be wiser in future.'[2]

The brief association of Bakunin and Nechaev had openly linked the doctrine of anarchism with the practice of individual terrorism, and with far-reaching results. From 1870 on there was always to be a section of the anarchist movement ready to commit acts of terrorism, if not for their own sake at least to symbolize a total revolt against society. Criminals and brigands were often able to claim that they were carrying out anarchist principles and that their crimes served to expose the hypocrisy and greed of the order they were attacking. There was to be a series of terrorist actions in Russia which, even if their aim was not the anarchist one of abolishing the state, derived their technique from the movements with which Bakunin and Nechaev had been associated. All over Europe and elsewhere, terrorism was to become an accepted political weapon; and in some cases, as in that of the conspiracy which led to the murder of the Archduke Francis Ferdinand in 1914, it was directly inspired by the anarchist example.

3. Prince Peter Alexeivich Kropotkin

4. *The Stonebreakers* by Gustave Courbet

This picture, formerly in the Staatliche Gemäldegalerie, Dresden, was destroyed by fire.

3

The Nechaev affair, although it absorbed much of Bakunin's energies in 1869 and 1870, and although it left its mark on his teaching, was not the most important episode in his years in Switzerland. As soon as he arrived there he was involved in the politics of the local radical groups, both Swiss and foreign, and, more important, through them with the politics of the International. At the same time, it was in these years that his influence in Italy was being consolidated and that the foundations were being laid in Spain of what was to be the most important section of the anarchist movement anywhere.

When Bakunin arrived in Geneva in 1867 there was already a vigorous revolutionary movement in the neighbouring districts, especially among the watchmakers in the mountains of the Jura. If his experiences in Italy had convinced him of the revolutionary potentialities of the landless peasant and of those workers with no stake in society, it was in Switzerland that he found another type of working man, the skilled artisan, thoughtful and self-improving, who was trying to create in the conditions of his working life something of the atmosphere of the society of the future. Bakunin himself told them: 'Working in small groups in your workshops or often working at home in your houses, you earn much more than you would in the great industrial factories which employ hundreds of workers; your work is intelligent and artistic, it does not brutalize you as working with machines does. Your skill and intelligence contribute much to it. And in addition you have more leisure and relative freedom; that is why you are better educated, freer and happier than others.'[1] Bakunin was perhaps overimpressed by the enthusiasm with which he was greeted, for the watchmakers of Saint-Imier and La Chaux-de-Fonds were often underpaid and exploited, forced to depend on others for the marketing of their products and the supply of raw materials. Nevertheless, the freedom and the possibilities of education and discussion which their work allowed were real enough; and, under the influence of Dr Coullery, a radical doctor, who was soon joined by an anarchist schoolmaster,

James Guillaume, they were already sufficiently well organized to have got in touch with the General Council of the International as early as 1865. When Bakunin appeared among them they at once responded to his teaching and to the warmth and exuberance of his personality, and 'Michel', as he soon became known in the Swiss Jura, became a familiar figure at their meetings.

Bakunin was thus directly involved in local working-class politics in Switzerland as well as maintaining contact with anarchists and revolutionaries in Russia, Italy, Spain and elsewhere. He was accordingly both caught up in purely Swiss disputes – for instance in the rivalry in Geneva between skilled workers in the watch trade and the unskilled building labourers – and, more important, in the politics of the International.

Bakunin had not hitherto been directly involved with the International, though his relations with Marx had been superficially quite friendly. His first public appearance at an international gathering after his arrival in Switzerland was, in fact, at a meeting in September 1867 of a heterogeneous liberal organization called the League for Peace and Freedom, of which the star was Garibaldi and which was also attended by Victor Hugo and John Stuart Mill. Bakunin, however, was already sufficiently famous a European figure to appear side by side with the Italian hero, and indeed the two men seem to have felt an instinctive liking for each other, as though their simplicity and directness and their dedication to revolutionary causes enabled them to transcend wider differences of belief and tactics. 'As with heavy, awkward gait', so an eyewitness described Bakunin's entry into the congress hall, 'he mounted the steps leading to the platform where the bureau sat, dressed as carelessly as ever in a sort of grey blouse, beneath which was visible not a shirt but a flannel vest, the cry passed from mouth to mouth, "Bakounine". Garibaldi, who was in the chair, stood up, advanced a few steps and embraced him. This solemn meeting of two old and tried warriors of revolution produced an astonishing impression. . . . Everyone rose, and there was prolonged and enthusiastic clapping of hands.'[1]

Bakunin never regarded membership of one revolutionary body as incompatible with membership of another. His Revolutionary Brotherhood, which he had founded while in Italy, was still nominally in existence, and in September 1868 he was to start yet another organization, the International Social Democratic Alliance. Consequently, it did not seem to him to be contradictory to try and make the League of Peace and Freedom more revolutionary by taking it bodily into the International, which had just shown its concern for the revolutionary cause in Switzerland by supporting a strike by the building workers of Geneva. Bakunin therefore used the congress of the League of Peace and Freedom at Berne as an opportunity for expressing his own revolutionary views and for opposing the mild bourgeois liberalism of most of the delegates, and he declared: 'In order to become a beneficial active force, our League ought to become the purely political expression of the great social-economic interests and principles which are now being so triumphantly developed and disseminated by the great International Association of Working Men of Europe and America.'[1] There was little chance of the League's becoming a truly revolutionary body, and Bakunin's proposals were defeated. Immediately afterwards Bakunin broke with the League of Peace and Freedom and decided to join the International. 'Once opposing ideas and tendencies of a bourgeois-sentimental kind were found to be in a majority,' he said, 'there was no place in it for a serious and sincere revolutionary. The tool had been tried, it had been found unsuitable, it had to be thrown away; it only remained to seek another. The International Working Men's Association presents itself as such.'[2]

Bakunin apparently did not wholly realize what joining the International involved. His Swiss friends already belonged; his relations with Marx had been distant, but mostly not unfriendly, while his admiration for Marx as a thinker was very great. Marx, he wrote in 1870, was a man 'of great intelligence, equipped with profound learning, whose whole life, one can say without flattery, has been solely devoted to the greatest cause which exists today, that of the emancipation of the workers.'[3] Marx himself described

Bakunin as 'a man devoid of all theoretical knowledge',[1] but in
so far as Bakunin had any general theoretical convictions he
shared most of them with Marx. He was a convinced materialist;
he believed deeply that the world could be understood in terms
of scientific laws and that there was no need for any metaphysical
or theological explanation of social, economic, political or ethical
behaviour, and indeed that such explanations only served to
obscure men's knowledge of their own interest. It was, he wrote,
Marx's materialism that made him superior to Proudhon, whose
great misfortune was 'never to have studied the natural sciences
and taken over their method'. Marx, on the other hand, 'is on
the right track. He has established the principle that all religious,
political and juridical developments are not the causes but the
results of economic developments.'[2] Yet the two men were too
different in temperament ever to cooperate happily. Their clash
of temperament was to develop into a conflict of doctrine, and
differences about revolutionary tactics were to result in the
division of the international working-class movement, a division
from which it has never wholly recovered.

Marx's attitude to the International was always an ambivalent
one. He believed in the importance of an international organization for the propagation of his own ideas and for maintaining
control over the growing working-class movements of Europe.
At the same time, however, he was often sceptical about the
congresses of the International which did not directly serve these
ends and which might give opportunities for the spread of
doctrines which, in his view, would prevent the working class
from seeing what the correct course of action was. In fact, at the
early congresses of the International, Marx's followers were out-
numbered by those of Proudhon, and, since these were most
numerous in France and Switzerland, they were particularly
strong at the congress held at Geneva in the late summer of
1866 – the first since the founding of the International. Marx
had already expressed doubts about the congress before it met:
'Although I am spending much time on the preparations for the
Geneva Congress,' he wrote on 23rd August, 'I am neither able
nor willing to attend, because it is impossible for me to leave my

work for a time. I expect thanks to it [my work] to do something more important for the working class than anything I can do personally in any congress.'[1]

Most of the Proudhonian members of the congress were by now comparatively mild and unrevolutionary. The purely anarchist side of Proudhon's doctrine was neglected in favour of his 'mutualist' ideas about credit and economic organization. Many of his disciples now even envisaged some forms of state action, in the field of education, for instance; and the attempt by Tolain to get the Geneva Congress to adopt a strong class-conscious revolutionary and anti-intellectual line was defeated. 'We hate no one,' he said, 'but in present conditions we are bound to consider as our adversaries all the members of classes which are privileged whether as capitalists or by virtue of a college degree.'[2] This dislike of intellectuals was often to recur among later anarchists – '*Pas de mains blanches, seulement les mains calleuses*' was a popular slogan – and it was an emotion which Bakunin often shared. The defeat of Tolain's motion and the confusion of the ideas of most of the delegates to the 1866 congress may well have contributed to Bakunin's willingness, after his own adherence to the International two years later, to accept the Marxists' attempts to make the organization more efficient and to give it a more class-conscious basis. Bakunin's own idea after joining the International was to create an organization which would train 'propagandists, apostles and finally organizers' and produce, as it were, the shock troops of the revolution to evangelize the workers all over Europe. The body that was to do this was called by Bakunin the International Social-Democratic Alliance. He did not apparently think of this as outside the International or in any way contrary to its purposes, but rather as an elite organization inside the International which would inspire its members with continuous revolutionary fervour.

The Alliance was the most effective of the many organizations invented by Bakunin, and by the end of 1868 it had branches in Lyon and Marseilles, had taken up again Bakunin's Neapolitan contacts and had dispatched Giuseppe Fanelli to Madrid and Barcelona to launch the Spanish anarchist movement on its

remarkable course. It is not surprising that these activities were
looked on with the deepest suspicion by Marx and Engels in
London, and, however loyal Bakunin was to the International in
intention, the Social Democratic Alliance must have appeared to
be a rival organization which aimed at taking over its functions.
Bakunin was puzzled by Marx's hostile attitude. In a letter in
December 1868 he wrote to Marx, after receiving complaints
from him in a letter from Marx to one of his associates in Geneva:
'You ask him if I am still your friend. Yes, more than ever, my
dear Marx, because I now understand better than ever how
right you have been in following and inviting us all to tread the
high road of economic revolution and in attacking those among
us who were about to get lost in undertakings which were either
nationalist or exclusively political. I am now doing what you
started to do more than twenty years ago. Since the solemn and
public farewell I addressed to the bourgeois at the Berne Congress,
I know no other society, no other milieu than the world of the
workers. My fatherland is now the International, of which you
are one of the main founders. You see then, dear friend, that I
am your disciple, and I am proud to be so. . . .'[1] This letter confirmed Bakunin's rejection of the League of Peace and Freedom,
even if it did not say anything specifically about the Alliance.
But in any case, however conciliatory it was meant to be, it
arrived too late. On the day on which it was written the General
Council of the International, which three months earlier had
formally condemned the League of Peace and Freedom, now
pronounced against the International Social Democratic Alliance: 'The presence of a second international body operating
inside or outside the International Working Men's Association
would be the surest way of disorganizing the latter.'[2]

Again Bakunin was prepared to cooperate: he suggested that
the Alliance should be dissolved and that its sections should
become directly sections of the International. The questions of
organization and control which were so important to Marx
meant little to Bakunin: but Marx, once he felt his authority
challenged, was determined to destroy Bakunin's influence in
the International. The crisis came at the congress of the Inter-

national at Basle in September 1869. Whereas previously Bakunin had seemed to Marx and his supporters to be threatening the jurisdiction of the General Council of the International, at Basle he questioned their position on matters of policy and doctrine. Neither Marx nor Engels attended the congress, while Bakunin's Swiss supporters were naturally there in some strength. Bakunin actually gave yet another demonstration of his willingness to accept the authority of the General Council and supported their proposal that their own executive powers should be extended and that they should have the right to suspend from membership any section acting against the spirit of the International.[1] Nor was there any immediate major quarrel about doctrine in the discussions on property and the collective ownership of land, which took up much of the congress's time. Bakunin opposed the General Council's views, however, on the comparatively minor question of including the abolition of the right of inheritance in the immediate programme of the International. The Marxists argued, with some justification, that this was something which would look after itself after the revolution, and that there was no need to make a specific point of it at this stage. However, it was a matter on which Bakunin had long held strong views. For him, hereditary property, far from being one of the many comparatively unimportant evils that would vanish with the transformation of society, was the basis on which the whole of existing society rested. The abolition of hereditary property, therefore, was an essential step towards the dissolution of the state, and any state which could be persuaded or forced to abolish inherited wealth would have taken a first and crucial step towards abolishing itself. Moreover, in Bakunin's view, it is only hereditary fortunes which prevent all men being equal: he denied that there was any inequality of natural gifts, and believed that it was only environment which produced the inequities of present society. 'The immense majority of men are not identical, but equivalent and consequently equal.'[2] Take away the inherited wealth from the rich man, and with it all the privileges of good nourishment, good education, good housing that it has brought him, and he will be no better than anyone else.

Bakunin's insistence on this point at the Basle congress may have been tactically mistaken and brought him little practical advantage. However, he carried his point, and the General Council's resolution was defeated by Bakunin and his Swiss, French and Belgian friends. When the result was known Eccarius, the German tailor from London who was Marx's representative at the congress, exclaimed: 'Marx will be extremely displeased.'[1] Marx's immediate reaction was that things might have gone worse at the congress. 'I am glad the Basle congress is now over,' he wrote to his daughter on 25th September, 'and that its results have been comparatively good. Such open displays of the party and all its sores always worry me.'[2] During the next six months, however, Marx and Engels, egged on by some of Bakunin's personal enemies among the refugees in Geneva, launched an all-out attack on Bakunin, both politically and personally. While the sections of the International in Switzerland became involved in increasingly bitter quarrels between the followers of Marx and those of Bakunin, all the personal grievances and complaints against Bakunin's behaviour were revived. The rumours that he was a Russian agent – a charge from which he had been formally cleared at the Basle congress – were repeated; Marx remembered that Bakunin had omitted to thank him for the presentation copy of the first volume of *Capital*; there were suggestions that Bakunin, who was supposed to be preparing the Russian translation of the book, had pocketed the advance and not done the work – though Mehring, the official German socialist historian of the Marxist movement, remarks understandingly: 'How many others, including many of the most famous, have not at some time or other found themselves in the position of having spent their advance and being unable to perform the promised work?'[3]

Throughout the next two years, against the dramatic background of the Franco-Prussian War and the Paris Commune, the dispute dragged on in a war of letters, circulars and pamphlets repeating the same accusations and rebuttals. Marx had come to believe, as firmly as the police of most of Europe, that Bakunin was leading a vast secret conspiracy. Bakunin and his friends were more and more convinced that Marx's attempts to organize the working-class movement on a centralized basis would frustrate the revolutionary aims which the movement was meant to serve. As the Jura anarchists put it in their 'Sonvillier Circular' of November 1871, after Marx's attack had been launched: 'How can you expect an egalitarian and a free society to emerge from an authoritarian organization? It is impossible. The International, embryo of future human society, must be from this moment the faithful image of our principles of liberty and federation, and reject from its midst any principle leading to authority and dictatorship.'[1]

Bakunin was slow to take up Marx's personal and political challenge himself, and left it to his Swiss friends to represent his views, partly from a genuine respect for Marx, partly from tactical considerations and partly from other preoccupations – his relations with Nechaev and his personal financial difficulties, as well as his growing interest in the anarchist movements in Spain and Italy and the shock of the war of 1870. Moreover, he was conscious that the breach with Marx, when it did come, should come on a clear question of principle. 'The situation might arise,' he wrote to Herzen in October 1869, 'and indeed quite soon, in which I would engage in a struggle with him, not because of his personal insults, but for a question of principle, the question of State Communism, of which he himself and the English and German parties he controls are the warmest partisans. Then it will be a struggle to the death. But there is a time for everything and the hour for this struggle has not yet struck.'[2]

It was Marx who decided when the hour had come. In the summer of 1871 he summoned a private conference of the International in London. This was both an attempt to take stock of the situation of the International after the collapse and repression of the Paris Commune and a means, Marx hoped, of finally eliminating Bakunin's influence. None of Bakunin's close supporters attended the conference, although some of his views were supported by some of the delegates even though they were always in a minority. At the London conference, Marx came out openly in favour of the formation of a working-class political party which was to be the organ of the emancipation of the

proletariat: 'Against the power of the propertied classes, the proletariat can only act as a class by turning itself into a political
party.'¹ This was, of course, directly aimed at Bakunin and his
complete rejection of political action; and another resolution
declared that 'the incident of the Alliance of Social Democracy'
was now considered closed. Marx was, as it turned out, to be
disappointed with the results of the London conference. Except
in Germany, the proletariat did not seem eager to constitute
itself into a political party under the direction of Marx and the
International, while Bakunin's influence remained as great as
ever in Spain, Italy and Switzerland, and over a considerable
number of the International's supporters in France and Belgium.

By 1872 Marx had made up his mind that the International
had in any case served its purpose, and indeed the repression
which everywhere followed the Paris Commune made its activities extremely difficult. Marx began by sending out a so-called
Private Circular of the General Council of the International –
largely the work of Engels – on *The Alleged Scissions in the International* in which the old charges, personal and political, against
Bakunin were repeated and which ended with the clearest statement yet to appear of the doctrinal differences between Marxists
and anarchists: 'Anarchism, that's the great warhorse of their
master Bakunin, who has taken nothing but the labels from socialist systems. All socialists understand by anarchism the following:
once the goal of the proletarian movement, the abolition of
classes, is attained, then the power of the state which serves to
maintain the great productive majority under the yoke of a
small exploiting minority, disappears, and the governmental
functions are transformed into simple administrative functions.
The Alliance looks at things the other way round. They proclaim
anarchy in the ranks of the proletariat as the most infallible
means of breaking the powerful concentration of political and
social forces in the hands of the exploiters. On this pretext, they
demand of the International, at the moment when the old world
is trying to break it, to replace its organization by anarchy. . . .'²

This final violent attack was not unexpected by Bakunin:
'The Damocles sword with which they have threatened us for so

long has at last fallen on our heads. It is not exactly a sword, but Mr Marx's usual weapon, a heap of filth.'[1] Soon after, Marx summoned a congress of the International at the Hague, sufficiently far from Switzerland, Spain and Italy to make it difficult and expensive for Bakunin's supporters to attend in any numbers. Bakunin was represented by the Swiss, James Guillaume: Marx was there in person. The proceedings were squalid and undignified. The usual accusations against Bakunin were repeated, including the one of financial dishonesty over the translation of *Capital*. The right of Bakunin's followers to attend was challenged, and Guillaume and his friends were expelled; and it was decided to move the seat of the General Council to the United States. Marx had scored his victory over Bakunin, but it was, in fact, the end of the International.

The immediate causes of the split in the international working-class movement were comparatively unimportant; a misunderstanding about the relations between the International Social Democratic Alliance and the International Working Men's Association, an argument about the abolition of hereditary property, local differences among the workers in the Geneva neighbourhood and allegations against Bakunin's personal integrity. Inevitably, however, since both sides needed a grander issue of principle on which to take their stand, the differences of approach and doctrine were formalized and magnified. The state communism based on a centralized disciplined party which the Marxists proposed was attacked by the anarchists, who offered instead a vision of a free federation of independent communes in which 'capital, factories, tools and raw materials belong to associations, and land to those who cultivate it'. Bakunin, however, was always more interested in the making of the revolution and in the preservation of liberty than in the economic organization of society. 'I detest communism,' Bakunin had declared to the League of Peace and Freedom in 1868, 'because it is the negation of liberty and because I can conceive nothing human without liberty. I am not a communist because communism concentrates and absorbs all the powers of society into the state; because it necessarily ends in the centralization of property in

the hands of the state, while I want the abolition of the state –
the radical extirpation of the principle of authority and the tute-
lage of the state, which, on the pretext of making men moral and
civilized, has up to now enslaved, oppressed, exploited and de-
praved them.'[1] And again, although he realized that Proudhon
lacked Marx's intellectual grasp of the world and his systematic
philosophical intelligence, nevertheless it was to Proudhon that
he felt himself most drawn temperamentally and instinctively:
'Proudhon understood and felt liberty much better than Marx;
Proudhon, when he was not dealing with doctrine and meta-
physics, had the true instinct of the revolutionary – he wor-
shipped Satan and proclaimed anarchy. It is possible that Marx
might theoretically reach an even more rational system of liberty
than that of Proudhon – but he lacks Proudhon's instincts. As a
German and a Jew he is authoritarian from head to foot. Hence
come the two systems: the anarchist system of Proudhon broad-
ened and developed by us and freed from all its metaphysical,
idealist and doctrinaire baggage, accepting matter and social
economy as the basis of all development in science and history.
And the system of Marx, head of the German school of authoritarian communists.'[2]

The difference of temperament between Marx and Bakunin
also led to a fundamental difference in the methods by which
they believed the revolution could be achieved. For Marx the
revolution would come through the ineluctable processes of
history and through the gradual realization by the proletariat of
their place in the inevitable class struggle. For Bakunin, on the
other hand, the revolution could be provoked by a handful of
devoted and fanatical leaders who would exploit the potentialities for revolution already existing. 'Three men alone if they
stand united already form an important beginning of strength',
he wrote to his Italian followers. 'Now what will happen when
you organize your country to the extent of some hundreds. . . .
A few hundred young men of good will are certainly not enough
to create a revolutionary power without the people . . . but they
will be enough to reorganize the revolutionary power of the
people.'[3] 'You want a popular revolution,' he told an Italian

disciple on another occasion, 'consequently there is no need to recruit an army, since your army is the people. What you must form are *general staffs*, a network well organized and inspired by the leaders of the popular movement. For this purpose you do not, in fact, need to have available a large number of people initiated into the secret organization.'[1]

This preference for loosely organized secret societies over the mass political parties which Marx's followers were organizing, especially in Germany, led to a radical difference in the tactics and organization of the revolution. As Bakunin put it: 'Their aim is the same: both parties want equally to create a new social order founded on the organization of collective labour. . . . Only the communists imagine that they can attain it by the development and by the political power of the working class and mainly of the urban proletariat with the assistance of bourgeois radicalism, while the social revolutionaries . . . think, on the contrary, that they can only attain this power by the organization of non-political power – power which is social and consequently anti-political – of the working masses in the towns and countryside. . . . Hence there are two different methods. The communists believe that they must organize the working-class forces to seize political power in states. Revolutionary socialists organize in order to destroy, or, if you want a politer word, liquidate states. . . .'[2] While Bakunin admitted that discipline would be necessary in a revolution (though it was not a quality for which he had any natural respect), the discipline of the revolutionary movement would not be the dictatorial, dogmatic discipline of the communists, but rather 'the voluntary and considered agreement of individual efforts towards a common aim. At the moment of action, in the midst of the struggle, there is a natural division of roles according to the aptitude of each, assessed and judged by the collective whole: some direct and command, others execute orders. But no function must be allowed to petrify or become fixed, and it will not remain irrevocably attached to any one person. Hierarchical order and promotion do not exist, so that the commander of yesterday can become a subordinate tomorrow. No one rises above the others, or if he does rise, it is only to fall back again a moment later, like the waves of the sea for ever returning to the salutary level of equality.'[1]

Bakunin realized clearly that the methods used to make the revolution were bound to affect the nature of society after the revolution had been made, and therefore insisted that the organization of the revolutionary movement should resemble the type of social organization which the revolution aimed at establishing. This was perhaps the most fundamental difference from Marx. Although Marx and Engels believed that the state would eventually wither away, they were less interested in this than in the analysis of existing society and in the methods of transforming it. Engels expressed the difference between the two viewpoints as follows: 'All socialists are agreed that the political state and with it political authority will disappear as a result of the coming social revolution, that is, that public functions will lose their political character and be transformed into the simple administrative functions of watching over the true interests of society. But the anti-authoritarians demand that the authoritarian political state be abolished at one stroke, even before the social conditions which give rise to it have been destroyed. They demand that the first act of the social revolution shall be the abolition of authority. Have these gentlemen ever seen a revolution? A revolution is certainly the most authoritarian thing there is; it is the act whereby one part of the population imposes its will on the other part by means of rifles, bayonets and cannon – authoritarian means if such there be at all; and if the victorious party does not wish to have fought in vain, it must maintain this rule by means of the terror which its arms inspire in the reactionaries.'[2]

The tragedy of the revolutionary movement has been that Engels was right, and that, while still proclaiming – as Khrushchev came near to doing at the 22nd Congress of the Communist Party of the Soviet Union – that the disappearance of the state is the ultimate goal, the communists have owed their effectiveness to the ruthless discipline of their organization; while those revolutionaries, such as the anarchists in the Spanish Civil War, who have put Bakunin's organizational doctrines into practice, have failed to survive.

Bakunin's quarrel with Marx led him to formulate many of his beliefs about the libertarian society and the nature of the revolution more clearly than he had done before. Moreover, during the years of his association with the International he was nearer than before to realizing his dream of an international revolutionary movement with himself as its centre. He was making new contacts in Italy, and anarchist groups and periodicals were appearing in a number of places, organized by young lawyers and students, such as the medical student Errico Malatesta, who first got in touch with the anarchists in Naples in 1871, and who was to continue stoutly to maintain his anarchist beliefs well into the fascist era. Most of these groups did not last long, but new anarchist sections were soon formed again. The idea of anarchism as a doctrine peculiarly suited to Italian social circumstances never wholly died; and, although the movement never became the force it was in Spain, anarchism long remained a living creed in Italy and was to influence much Italian political practice and to produce recurrent disturbances, while Italian immigrants to the United States took their ideas with them and found them appropriate to the crude, violent class struggle characteristic of industrial life in many parts of America at the end of the nineteenth century. As late as the 1920s two Italian anarchists, Sacco and Vanzetti, were to provide a *cause célèbre* in which a whole generation of American liberals came of age.

The most remarkable of Bakunin's successes was in Spain. In 1868, Elie Reclus, one of two brothers who were eminent intellectual leaders of the anarchist movement, went to Spain at the moment of the proclamation of the First Republic, and in October Bakunin's Geneva committee published an address to the Spanish workers, proclaiming that the demand for provincial autonomy, which the liberal leader Pi y Margall had long been pressing, would prepare the way for anarchism: 'The Spanish people will proclaim the republic based on the federation of autonomous provinces, the only form of government which, temporarily and as a means of arriving at a social organization in conformity with justice, offers real guarantees of popular freedom.'[1] In mid-November, 1868 another disciple of Bakunin was sent to Spain and laid the foundation of an organized anarchist movement there. This was Giuseppe Fanelli. Fanelli was a young architect and engineer who had given up his profession to devote himself to politics. He was first a follower of Mazzini and was elected a deputy (and made full use of the privilege of free rail travel attached to the office, since it is said that he spent every night on the train to save the cost of lodging). In 1865 he met Bakunin, and, like so many young followers of Mazzini, at once switched his allegiance to him as the representative of the true revolution. Fanelli's mission to Spain was surprisingly successful. He did not know Spanish; he failed to find the companion who was supposed to be making the journey with him; he had been given the wrong address in Madrid; he was short of money. Nevertheless, he succeeded in making contact with a group of young intellectuals who were already familiar with the doctrines of Fourier and Proudhon, and who were anxious to use the overthrow of the monarchy and the creation of a new republic as an opportunity for social revolution. They were naturally excited to hear of the existence of the International, and Fanelli made an immediate impression on them. 'He was a man of about forty years old,' Anselmo Lorenzo, one of the group, wrote many years later, 'tall with a serious and pleasant face, a thick black beard, large expressive black eyes which shone like torches or took on an aspect of affectionate compassion according to the emotion he was feeling. His voice had a metallic ring and could take on all the inflections suitable to what he was expressing, passing rapidly from accents of rage and threats against exploiters and tyrants to those of suffering, pity and consolation. . . .'[1] Talking in French, which his hearers scarcely understood, Fanelli all the same succeeded in forming a section of the International or of Bakunin's Alliance; and indeed the anarchists in Spain, like those of Italy, were often scarcely aware of the divisions, schisms and controversies of London or Geneva. The movement was launched and soon struck root; and the demand of the first followers of Bakunin in Barcelona: 'We want the end of the reign of capital, of the state and the church, to construct on their ruins anarchy, the free federation of free associations of workers'[1] – this demand became over the next sixty years the creed of millions of Spaniards.

Bakunin's hopes of becoming the centre of a European movement for social revolution were disappointed by 1871. He had been very excited by the Franco-Prussian War, and all his anti-German sentiments, inflamed as they had been by his differences with Marx, made him passionately pro-French, so that the French defeat made him afraid that France would become a German province and that 'instead of living socialism, we will have the doctrinaire socialism of the Germans'.[2] At first, it is true, the fall of Napoleon III gave Bakunin hopes of taking part in a real revolution for the first time since 1849. He hurried to Lyon in September 1870 and plunged into republican politics there. However, his passionate pleas for immediate revolutionary action met with little response, and by the end of September Bakunin was forced to leave the city for Marseilles, and then to return to Switzerland in disillusionment and poverty. Even the Paris Commune of March 1871 did little to encourage him, although some of his friends, associates or admirers – Varlin, Benoit Malon, Elisée Reclus – were actively involved. In fact, after 1871, Bakunin, feeling old, ill and disillusioned, withdrew to Switzerland. In 1874 he went briefly to Italy with the intention of joining a rising at Bologna, which the Italian anarchists hoped would be part of a general spontaneous revolt throughout the peninsula. The attempt, like so many of Bakunin's projects, ended in disaster; plans were betrayed to the police, many of the conspirators lost their nerve, and Bakunin, after contemplating suicide (his personal and financial situation was more disastrous than it had ever been), escaped disguised as a priest and retired once more to Switzerland, where he died on 1st July 1876.

The year before he died Bakunin wrote to Elisée Reclus: 'Yes, you are right, the revolution for the moment has returned to its bed, we have fallen back into a period of evolution, that is to say one of subterranean revolutions, insensible and even often imperceptible.'[3] The repression of the Paris Commune and the measures taken by the other governments of Europe, while they succeeded in giving the impression that the International had been far more effective than in fact it was, made most revolutionary activity impossible. The International would have hardly been able to survive even if Marx had not decided that it had served its purpose and even if it had not been badly split between Marxists and anarchists. However, it soon acquired a legendary status and was to serve as an ideal for the working class of Europe for fifty years or more. At the same time, the Commune, too, provided a myth which both Marxists and anarchists were to exploit. For the Marxists, the Commune was a classic example of a proletarian revolution directed by the International. For the anarchists, it was a pattern of a future anarchist society; it was 'simply the City of Paris administering itself. . . . Oh! how splendid it would be, Paris running its own business, having the same aim for each, the same scale, the same justice, the same fraternity!'[1] It was Bakunin's achievement that the idea of the libertarian revolution was now as strongly launched as Marx's doctrine of a disciplined class struggle and a centralized revolutionary movement. In Professor Franco Venturi's words: 'Bakunin succeeded in making a revolutionary mentality rather than a revolutionary organization.'[2] As, during the next twenty years, revolutionaries began to think of new methods of effective action, the revolutionary mentality often seemed in some places and circumstances more effective than a revolutionary organization.

Part Three

CHAPTER V

Terrorism and Propaganda by the Deed

'Let us arise, let us arise against the oppressors of humanity; all kings, emperors, presidents of republics, priests of all religions are the true enemies of the people; let us destroy along with them all juridical, political, civil and religious institutions.'

Manifesto of anarchists in the Romagna, 1878

'Je ne frapperai pas un innocent en frappant le premier bourgeois venu.'

Léon-Jules Léauthier, 1894

I

The Paris Commune left its mark on European politics for thirty years. For the revolutionaries it was yet another revolution that had failed, but which had at least revived hopes that a complete social revolution might be made some day, and that, when it came, it would be thorough and bloody. For the moderates, it was a lesson in the danger of the mob, and reinforced their fear of violence and their desire for peaceful and constitutional reform. For the conservatives, it was an event which revived all their fears and inherited memories of the Jacobin Terror and convinced them that a nineteenth-century revolution, complete with the incendiarism of the *'pétroleuses'* who were supposed to have set fire to Paris, would be far worse than that of 1792. Moreover, the fact that a few Communard leaders had been members of the International, together with the eagerness with which all sections of that body proclaimed their solidarity with the imprisoned and exiled Communards, convinced the governments and police of Europe that the International had to be taken seriously, so that, at the moment of its dissolution, it inspired more fear than it had in its lifetime. The vigilance of the authorities all over Europe, and the internal divisions in the International, also made revolutionaries think again about their methods. Above all, the experience of the Commune seemed to show how difficult it was for an old-style urban insurrection, complete with barricades and citizen volunteers, to succeed in a modern city when faced with modern weapons. In the industrial states of Northern Europe, the workers were led, over the next twenty-five years, to look increasingly to well-organized political parties or disciplined trade unions for an improvement in their conditions. In more backward countries, however, such as Italy and Spain, where endemic agrarian distress was reinforced by the impact of the new industrial processes on an old artisan class, the belief in direct action, in insurrection and acts of terrorism, never wholly died.

In Italy the strains resulting from the struggle for unification and from the eviction of the Austrians produced considerable economic distress in the early 1870s. The government had been obliged to introduce unpopular taxes – especially the tax on milling flour, the *macinato*. In the south the disruption of the feudal economy and the overthrow of the Bourbon monarchy seemed to many Calabrians or Sicilians simply to have introduced a new set of exploiters alongside the landlords of the old régime. Throughout the nineteenth century there had been local acts of social protest in Italy, when peasants and landless labourers seized on anything which seemed to offer a way out of their desperate situation. In the 1870s these protests varied from the apocalyptic religious sectarianism of the Lazzaretti in Tuscany[1] to more ordinary acts of spontaneous peasant revolt and brigandage. The general atmosphere of unrest, increased by bad harvests in 1873 and by the European financial crisis of the mid-seventies, which was eventually felt in one way or another by the Italian peasant and artisan, encouraged those followers of Bakunin who still hoped for a general insurrection. Indeed, just as the International was inclined to claim to have inspired the Commune, so the Italian anarchists tended to take the credit for any act of violent social protest in Italy, and hoped to use the unsettled situation, as Bakunin himself had preached, to further their cause. This sometimes led to disappointment; it seems, for example, that in 1873 Malatesta went to Sicily in the hope of recruiting the brigands to the anarchist cause, only to be told that 'the brigands were too religious and honest to take part in a rising in which the example of the Commune might be followed, where they shot the archbishop'.[1]

In this atmosphere it is not surprising that the doctrines of Bakunin were more popular than those of Marx, and that, in the 1870s, adherence to the International meant in Italy embracing the anarchist cause. The leaders of the movement in Italy were Carlo Cafiero, Andrea Costa and Errico Malatesta. Cafiero was a wealthy young Neapolitan who had inherited considerable estates in Apulia. He was originally Marx's and Engels' most trusted agent in Italy, but soon became an adherent of Bakunin, both because he believed in the correctness of Bakunin's analysis of the Italian situation, and because, like so many others, he succumbed to Bakunin's personal fascination. (Cafiero, indeed, spent much of his fortune in supporting Bakunin and his household, ruining himself and quarrelling with Bakunin through becoming involved in plans for developing an estate on Lake Maggiore.) Costa was one of the students who, disillusioned with Mazzini's republicanism, turned eagerly to the doctrines of the International. While at the University of Bologna, where he was a favourite student of the poet Giosué Carducci, he became involved in the anarchist movement, and the news of the Commune in Paris convinced him of the possibility of revolution at home in Italy. Cafiero's career as an anarchist agitator ended sadly in the 1880s, when the conspiratorial zeal of his youth turned to psychopathic persecution mania and his romantic egalitarianism to a pathetic fear that he was consuming more than his fair share of the sunshine.[2] Andrea Costa and Errico Malatesta later became leaders of the two rival branches of the Italian revolutionary movement, for Costa early in the 1880s became convinced of the impossibility of an immediate insurrection and realized the necessity of constructing an effective constitutional political party, while Malatesta remained until his death in 1932, through all the vicissitudes of prison and exile and the fascist régime, the most consistent of the Italian anarchists, a kind of Mazzini of the anarchist movement.

In the early seventies these anarchist leaders hoped that a general rising in Italy might be possible and that Bakunin's ideas could be put into practice. Mazzini had lost most of his influence because of his criticisms of the Commune; Marx's belief in a strong centralized industrial state as a preliminary condition for a proletarian revolution did not seem to apply to Italy. So, in an atmosphere and tradition of social revolt, the way was open for Bakunin's doctrines. As Costa later recalled: 'The rapidity with which the new spirit was propagated in Italy was marvellous. . . . We threw ourselves into the movement, compelled much more by the desire to break with a past that oppressed us and did not correspond to our aspirations than by conscious reflection on what we wanted. We felt that the future was there: time would determine by which ideas we would be inspired.'[1] It was in this mood of vague enthusiasm and total optimism that the Bologna rising of 1874 was planned, in which, as we have seen, the ageing and ailing Bakunin made a last rather pathetic revolutionary appearance.

Costa himself, the chief organizer of the movement in Bologna, was arrested before the revolt started, and elsewhere in Italy the insurrection petered out as completely as it did in Bologna. The leaders who were arrested were treated with surprising leniency. Their trials gave them the opportunity for spectacular rhetorical appeals and denunciations, while their defence lawyers (among them a rising young anarchist intellectual, Dr Saverio Merlino) seem to have been as clever as the prosecution was inept: the government was unpopular in the country and the jurors not unsympathetic to the plight of the poor so vividly described by young men of the fire and charm of Costa and Malatesta.[2] Malatesta, who had been in Apulia during the risings, was acquitted; Costa, too, after Carducci had given evidence on his behalf, was found not guilty; Cafiero was safe in Switzerland.

Even if their hopes of a general insurrection had been disappointed, the events of 1874 had gained considerable publicity for the anarchists, whose strength was estimated by the government as being around 30,000. At the same time, the experience made them think that they had been too public and not suffi-

ciently conspiratorial in their methods. However, they realized
that there was no immediate possibility of widespread revolution,
and as a result they developed what was to become a key idea in
anarchist tactics over the next twenty years. This was the idea of
'propaganda by the deed'. It was only violent action that would
impress on the world both the desperate nature of the social situation and the ruthless determination of those who wanted to change
it. Thus – and this, of course, had been Bakunin's idea – a small
body of determined men could point the way to revolution and
encourage revolt. A small armed band could, as one of Malatesta's
associates put it, 'move about in the countryside as long as
possible, preaching war, inciting to social brigandage, occupying
the small communes and then leaving them after having performed there those revolutionary acts that were possible and
advancing to those localities where our presence would be mani-
fested most usefully'.[1]

When this was written in April 1881, Malatesta and his friends
had already had one disastrous experience of these tactics, and
it was, in fact, never repeated. In the latter part of 1876, Malatesta and Cafiero had decided to plan an operation for the spring
of 1877, in the province of Benevento, north-east of Naples. They
were joined in this enterprise by a Russian revolutionary, Sergei
Kravchinski, who a year after was to kill the chief of the Russian
secret police with a dagger in the streets of St Petersburg and
was later well known in London revolutionary circles under the
name of Stepniak. Stepniak had joined the rising against the
Turks in Bosnia the previous year and used his experiences in
order to write a manual of guerrilla warfare, and he now happened
to be in Naples. Accordingly, Malatesta, Stepniak and a Russian
lady rented a house in the village of San Lupo on the pretext that
the Russian lady needed the mountain air for her health. There
they unloaded several cases of ammunition disguised as her
luggage. Unfortunately, by this time one of Malatesta's associates
had betrayed the plans to the police and San Lupo was under
observation as the members of the anarchist band began to
gather there. Several of them, including Stepniak, were arrested
on the way; in the village itself shots were exchanged between

anarchists and police, and one policeman died of his wounds. Malatesta, Cafiero and some twenty-five others then decided to take to the mountains and try to raise a revolt in the outlying villages. Instead, that is to say, of building up a base of operations and from there trying to evangelize the surrounding countryside, they set off in a haphazard manner at a time (it was early April) when the weather in the mountains was still cold and wet.

However, at first they were remarkably successful. At the village of Lentino the column arrived on a Sunday morning, declared King Victor Emanuel deposed and carried out the anarchist ritual of burning the archives which contained the record of property holdings, debts and taxes. The revolution in Lentino was greeted with some enthusiasm by the peasants, and even the village priest joined the insurgents. Then the column marched off to the next village, leaving the local innkeeper with a scrap of paper which read: 'In the name of the Social Revolution, the Mayor of Lentino is ordered to pay twenty-eight lire to Ferdinando Orso for food furnished to the band that entered Lentino on April 8, 1877.'[1] At Gallo, the next stop, much the same occurred, but by this time the villagers showed less enthusiasm, as government troops were now on their way to round up the insurgents. For two days Malatesta and his followers tramped through the mountains looking in vain for food and shelter. Then finally, hungry and cold, they were surrounded and taken off to prison.

Once again, however, the treatment of the rebels was surprisingly lenient, although they were kept in prison for sixteen months awaiting trial. They were accused of causing the death of a policeman; and, although the crime technically lay outside the scope of the amnesty granted in February 1878 on the accession of the new king of Italy, Umberto I, they were able to profit from the general atmosphere of clemency and from the jury's sympathy. In August 1878 they were acquitted.

The effects of the failure of the rising in Benevento were considerable. Although Malatesta and some of his followers persisted in thinking that they could achieve something by propaganda by deeds and by continuing to set an example of insurrection to the peasants of southern Italy, others, and notably Andrea Costa, began to think that such gestures were futile, and that any progress in dealing with the social question in Italy must, after all, come through better organization and even through political action. 'By means of a conspiracy,' Costa had already written even before the Benevento affair, 'a change in the form of government can be obtained; a principle can be dispossessed or punctured and another put in its place, but it cannot achieve social revolution. . . . To do this is a matter of widely diffusing the new principles in the masses, or rather, to awaken them in them, since they already have them instinctively, and to organize the workers of the whole world, so that the revolution occurs by itself from the bottom to the top and not vice versa, either by means of laws and decrees or by force. And this necessarily involves publicity, since it is impossible to reconcile the idea of such a vast propaganda within the necessarily restricted circle of a conspiracy.'[1] This belief in mass propaganda and wide publicity to show the oppressed classes where their interest lay was quite different from the action by small conspiratorial bands setting the example of direct revolt which Malatesta and Cafiero envisaged; and in the next few years Costa moved still further towards accepting the idea of mass organization and political action. By 1882 he was prepared to run for parliament and to claim that, as a deputy, he was carrying on the struggle as effectively as he had done in prison.[2] He soon became one of the most respected leaders of the Italian socialist party.

On 9th February 1878 a young man threw a bomb into a parade which was being held at Florence in memory of King Victor Emanuel II, who had just died. No one was killed, and the Italian anarchists disclaimed all connexion with the attack. Nine months later a twenty-nine-year-old cook, Giovanni Passanante, who had acquired a knife inscribed with the words 'Long live the international republic!' attacked the new king, Umberto I, as he drove through Naples. The king was only scratched, but the Prime Minister, who was with him, was slightly wounded. Once again, no connexion was established between the would-be assassin and the anarchists in the International. However, when a group of monarchist sympathizers in Florence organized a parade to celebrate the king's escape a bomb was thrown which killed four people and injured ten. Two days later another bomb was thrown into a crowd of people at Pisa who were celebrating the queen's birthday.

These episodes meant the end of the comparative leniency with which the anarchist attempts at insurrection had been treated in 1874 and 1877. From now on anarchist leaders were kept under strict supervision and were liable to arrest, detention and expulsion. Towards the end of 1878, Malatesta left the country to start the first of his long periods of exile. The International had been formally dissolved in 1876, and the anarchist members of it were forced to abandon any pretence that they still constituted an international organization. The last meeting of Bakunin's most loyal supporters in the old International, the *Fédération Jurassienne*, was held in 1880. One of the Italian anarchists sadly summed up the position in July 1879: 'The International . . . no longer exists, either as a Marxist association or as a Bakuninist sect. There are revolutionary and anarchist socialists in every part of the world, but there is no longer any contact, public or secret, between them.'[1]

2

The attempt to murder King Umberto occurred within a few months of two attempts on the life of the German emperor and also one to murder the king of Spain. The phrase 'propaganda by the deed' was taking on a more sinister meaning. The two would-be assassins of the Kaiser, Hoedel and Nobiling, do not seem to have had any anarchist connexions, but it was obvious that the police were bound to say that they were inspired by the socialist International, just as the Spanish police claimed that Juan Oliva Moncasi, who tried to kill Alfonso XII, was a disciple of Fanelli. And, just as Passanante's attempt on King Umberto was followed by persecution of the Italian revolutionary leaders, so in Germany, after the attack on the Kaiser, Bismarck passed anti-socialist legislation, while in Spain all trade-union and working-class political activity was made almost impossible. It is not surprising that the authorities in these countries genuinely believed, as Bismarck certainly did, in the existence of an international conspiracy to further social revolution. From the time of the Commune socialists and anarchists had claimed responsibility even for actions with which they had nothing to do, and hurried to express their sympathy with the would-be regicides. One of the anarchist papers in the Jura, for instance, saluted the author of one of the attempts on the Kaiser with the words: 'Humanity will preserve the memory of the tinsmith Hoedel, who was prepared to sacrifice his life to make a superb act of defiance against society, and, as his blood spurted beneath the executioner's axe, was able to inscribe his name on the long list of martyrs who have shown the people the way to a better future, towards the abolition of all economic and political slavery.'[1]

The belief in widespread international plots inevitably enhanced the reputation of those revolutionaries who were admired or feared for their uncompromising fervour and who appeared to be inspiring rebellion everywhere. Bakunin, the most important of these potent legendary figures, had died in 1876, but among the next generation there were others who occupied a similar position in the eyes of the police and of their own followers. Malatesta, in his long years of exile, was to acquire a reputation of this kind and was still able in 1920, after some fifty years as a revolutionary, to bring the police of Italy out in pursuit of him. At the end of the nineteenth century, however, the man with the strongest claim to occupy the position left vacant on Bakunin's death was another Russian, Prince Peter Alexeivitch Kropotkin.

Kropotkin was born in 1842 and was the son of a family of the highest Russian nobility.[2] He showed literary and intellectual interests as a boy, and in his *Memoirs of a Revolutionist* he gives a touching picture of an evening when his brother stole out of his cadet school to see him and they sat up till midnight 'talking about nebulae and Laplace's hypothesis, the structure of matter, the struggles of the papacy under Boniface VIII with the imperial

power, and so on'. However, he was given a conventional
education and became a member of the elite Corps of Pages on
the personal recommendation of the Emperor Nicholas I. He
soon revolted against the discipline and conventionality of court
life and, to the disgust of his family, joined an unfashionable
regiment in Siberia. Here, with time to read and reflect, he
began to think about social and philosophical problems. He read
Proudhon; he became interested in questions of prison reform.
At the same time he used the opportunity of his stay in a remote
area of Central Asia to turn himself into a serious, scientific
geographer and explorer. His wide reading, his scientific activity
and his experience, as a member of the landowning class, of
agrarian problems in the years after the emancipation of the
serfs, as well as his anger at the treatment of Polish prisoners
after the Polish revolt of 1863, all reinforced the independence
of his character and drove him in the direction of political
radicalism.

In 1872 Kropotkin paid his first decisive visit to the west, and
met James Guillaume and the watchmakers of the Jura. (He did
not call on Bakunin, who was, it seems, reluctant to see him
because of his friendship with another Russian radical, Peter
Lavrov, of whose comparatively mild reformist views Bakunin
disapproved.) Kropotkin was at once attracted by the Swiss
anarchist workers and was only dissuaded from remaining in the
Jura as a worker by Guillaume's arguments that he would be
more useful to the anarchist cause elsewhere. When he returned
to Russia, smuggling a number of subversive books and pamphlets
into the country, he formally resigned from the government service and plunged into revolutionary activity. This soon led to his
arrest, for his friends in St Petersburg belonged to the circle
round N. V. Tchaikovsky, the leader of the populist movement
there, and they spent much of their efforts in publishing and
circulating forbidden literature and in direct educational experiments among the workers and peasants. Kropotkin himself was
now advocating the formation of armed peasant bands, and was
already rejecting any piecemeal reforms such as many of his
associates were prepared to accept. 'Any temporary improve-

ment in the life of a small group of people in our present society only helps to keep the conservative spirit intact,' he wrote in 1873.[1]

The activities of the Tchaikovsky circle had already aroused the suspicion of the authorities by the end of 1873, and a number of its members were arrested for their propaganda and educational work among the workers. Kropotkin himself was arrested a few weeks later and in March 1874 imprisoned in the fortress of Ss. Peter and Paul. After two years his health was failing and he was removed to the prison attached to the military hospital in St Petersburg. Here friends to whom he had been able to smuggle letters managed to organize one of the most famous and dramatic escapes of the nineteenth century. A violin playing in the window of a house down the street gave the signal; a carriage was waiting; Kropotkin ran past the guard at the gate and was soon on his way abroad.[2] In August 1876 he landed in England, which was eventually to be his home until 1917, when he returned to Russia, where he died in 1921.

Kropotkin's life in England after 1886, when he finally settled there permanently, was quiet, respectable and scholarly and did little to justify the alarm in which his ideas were held. However, for the next forty years he was the adviser and philosopher of the whole anarchist movement. From being a conspirator and agitator he became a philosopher and prophet. Nevertheless, when he first arrived in the west, he played a part in encouraging violence. Thus a leading article in *Le Révolté*, the paper which he founded in Switzerland in 1879, sets the tone of anarchist action in the last twenty years of the nineteenth century: 'Permanent revolt by word of mouth, in writing, by the dagger, the rifle, dynamite. . . . Everything is good for us which falls outside legality.'[3]

Moreover, the murder of the Tsar Alexander II on 1st March 1881 by a group called the People's Will (*Narodnaya Volya*) gave an enormous impetus to the idea of revolution by assassination, and raised hopes that the self-immolating gesture of the young terrorists would have an instantaneous moral effect. Kropotkin wrote after the execution of Sophie Perovskaya, one of the five

who were hanged for their part in the murder: 'By the attitude
of the crowd she understood that she had dealt a mortal blow to
the autocracy. And she read in the sad looks which were directed
sympathetically towards her, that by her death she was dealing
an even more terrible blow from which the autocracy will never
recover.'[1]

In 1881 a number of leading revolutionaries, including Kropotkin and Malatesta, met in London and asserted their faith in
the policy that illegality alone would lead to revolution, while
many of them, in spite of Kropotkin's own scepticism – he was
too good a professional scientist to have much faith in amateurs
– called for the study of the technical sciences such as chemistry,
to make bombs which could be used for 'offensive and defensive
purposes'. Those anarchists who had not, like Costa, gone over
to the idea of legal political action were now committed to the
tactics of 'propaganda by the deed' in its most extreme form. It
is from anarchist actions over the next twenty years that the
traditional picture of the anarchist is derived – a slinking figure
with his hat pulled over his eyes and a smoking bomb in his
pocket. It is a picture to which many writers contributed, so that
anarchists make an unlikely appearance even in the pages of
Henry James (in *The Princess Casamassima*) as well as in the classic
description of the relations between anarchists and police in
Joseph Conrad's *The Secret Agent*.[2]

During this period the anarchist movement existed on two
levels. The leaders – such as Kropotkin, Malatesta, Elie and
Elisée Reclus – produced articles and philosophical works, held
congresses and discussed methods of social organization or the
problems of ownership in a future society. At the same time, all
over Europe and America small groups were set up, without
offices or secretaries or club rooms, often consisting of only two
or three people, determined to demonstrate their contempt for
society by an act of ultimate defiance. Thus it is often hard to
distinguish the devoted anarchist militant, moved by a deep
passion for justice, from the psychopath whose shadowy voices
prompt him to take his private revenge on society by means of
actions of which the anarchists had given him the example.

Inevitably, prominent anarchists were suspected of inspiring outrages of which they knew nothing; and both Kropotkin and Malatesta suffered in this way. Often police *agents provocateurs* deliberately formed 'anarchist' groups to trap unwary anarchists; the French police even ran an anarchist newspaper for a time and sent a representative to the London meeting in 1881. The Italian government kept two agents in Paris in the early 1900s, known as Dante and Virgil, who 'possessed a far from superficial revolutionary culture' and who reported to their shocked and fascinated superiors lurid details of anarchist orgies devoted to the practice of free love, and anarchist plots improbably centred on the villa at Neuilly of the ex-queen of Naples, Maria Sofia.[1] It is often impossible to tell whether some anarchist groups, like the famous *Mano Negra* in Andalusia, ever existed at all outside the imagination of the police, while some of the terrorist acts of the eighties and nineties have been attributed to policemen wanting to make arrests rather than to anarchist militants.

Terrorism is infectious; and it is striking how frequently attacks on prominent people took place in the years between 1880 and 1914. Some of these attacks were, of course, not anarchist at all, even if the technique was borrowed from the anarchists, but served different political purposes – the assassination of the Tsar Alexander II in 1881 or of the Archduke Francis Ferdinand in 1914 are examples. Yet the murder of President Sadi Carnot of France and of President William McKinley of the United States, the assassinations of the empress of Austria, the king of Italy and the Prime Minister of Spain, as well as the numerous unsuccessful attempts on other sovereigns, princes and statesmen – all these were in one way or another the result of the anarchist belief in the immediate, apocalyptic value of an act of self-immolation which would also remove the symbol of the existing social order. The attempt to murder a king or a minister at least had a direct practical significance; with the removal of a person of this kind, it could be argued, the state might start to wither away. Even so, such acts were often misplaced. When, for example, the Empress Elisabeth of Austria was stabbed by a young Italian as she walked up the gangway on to a steamer on the

Lake of Geneva, the assassin paid no attention to the fact that his victim had lived apart from her husband for years and that her one aim was somehow to escape from her royal destiny into private life. Sometimes, too, the courage of the monarch equalled that of the assassin and increased his own popularity, as when King Umberto I remarked that episodes of this kind were 'professional risks', and commuted the death penalty on his assailant and arranged a pension for his mother.

Very often anarchist acts of violence were acts of symbolic revenge against the state for the execution of a comrade. Thus, for example, in Spain in 1892 a young anarchist, Pallás, threw a bomb at General Martinez Campos, in revenge for the execution of four anarchists who had taken part in a rising at Jerez the previous year. And, in turn, Pallás's friend Santiago Salvador took revenge on society with an act of frightening impersonality, when he threw a bomb into a fashionable theatre in Barcelona, killing twenty men and women. Again, shortly afterwards a bomb was dropped from a window on a Corpus Christi procession, wounding only humble people and thus giving rise to suspicions that it had been dropped by the police themselves, who at once used the excuse to imprison, execute and torture many anarchists and even liberals. An Italian anarchist, Angiolillo, who was in London when he heard the news, was so upset that he at once went to Spain and murdered Canovas del Castillo, the Prime Minister.

Attacks were not only directed at the heads of states and their executives or used as symbolic acts of vengeance. Other outrages were committed against institutions which seemed to symbolize the false values of bourgeois society. When, for example, in 1882 there was a bomb thrown in the early hours of the morning in a notoriously *louche* music hall in Lyon, there were some people, including the police, who regarded this as the direct fulfilment of an article in an anarchist paper some months earlier which said: 'You can see there, especially after midnight, the fine flower of the bourgeoisie and of commerce. . . . The first act of the social revolution must be to destroy this den.'[1] A young anarchist called Cyvogt was later arrested and condemned to imprisonment, though it was by no means certain that he was guilty, and he was long regarded as an innocent martyr in the anarchist cause. At the same time a number of well-known anarchists were rounded up and imprisoned, including Kropotkin. He was in France at the time and the government believed that he had inspired strikes which had led to a riot in the mining district of Montceau; as a result he served three years in prison.

Two other incidents in France were typical of anarchist attacks on the institutions of bourgeois government and society. In 1886 Charles Gallo threw a bottle of vitriol from one of the galleries of the Paris stock exchange into the midst of the brokers and their clerks; he followed this up with three random revolver shots which did not hit anybody. At his trial – where he insisted on addressing the judge as Citizen President – he shouted 'Long live revolution! Long live anarchism! Death to the bourgeois judiciary! Long live dynamite! Bunch of idiots!'[1] Gallo was, in fact, very characteristic of one type of young terrorist, on the borderline of insanity, half delinquent, half fanatic. He was an illegitimate child, abandoned by his mother. He was not unintelligent and had managed to get some sort of education. At the age of twenty he was imprisoned for forging money and in prison apparently discovered anarchist ideas, which he determined to put into practice on his release. Certainly at his trial, after his attack on the Bourse, when he was sentenced to twenty years' hard labour, he remained impenitent and regretted that he had not succeeded in killing anyone. He gave the jury an hour and a half lecture on anarchist theory and said specifically that he had intended to carry out 'an act of propaganda by the deed for anarchist doctrine'.[2]

The most famous of these attacks on the institutions of the bourgeois state was that on the Chamber of Deputies in Paris in 1893. Auguste Vaillant – again a man who had been abandoned by his parents as a child – had worked at a number of jobs and had become a member of various small revolutionary groups. He spent a couple of years in the Argentine as restlessly and unsatisfactorily as in France. On his return to France he seems, however, to have made an effort to support himself, his daughter and the girl with whom he was now living; but, according to his

own account, it was the difficulty of doing this that finally
spurred him to revolutionary action. He raised enough money
from an anarchist burglar to rent a room in which to make a
bomb, and determined to kill himself in a last gesture that would,
he said, be 'the cry of a whole class which demands its rights and
will soon join acts to words'.[1] He prepared a powerful bomb
which was designed to scatter a large number of projectiles, and
at four o'clock on the afternoon of 9th December 1893 hurled it
from one of the balconies of the Chamber of Deputies. There was
a loud explosion. As the smoke cleared and revealed a scene of
blood and broken glass, the President of the session, M. Dupuy,
made himself famous by announcing loudly: '*La séance continue.*'
Although no one had been killed, Vaillant was condemned to
death and, in spite of a moving appeal by his daughter, he was
executed, exclaiming at the last minute: '*Vive l'anarchie!* My
death will be avenged.'

The prophecy appeared to be a true one: on 24th June 1894,
Sadi Carnot, the President of the Republic, who had refused to
exercise his prerogative of mercy in favour of Vaillant, was
stabbed to death while on a visit to Lyon. The assassin was a
twenty-one-year-old Italian, Santo Jeronimo Caserio, who had
been expelled from Italy because of his anarchist ideas, which he
proceeded to carry to a logical conclusion when the opportunity
arose. He seems to have been inspired by a desire to carry out a
spectacular act of propaganda by the deed rather than by the
direct intention of avenging Vaillant. The murder of President
Sadi Carnot was the climax of a series of terrorist actions by the
French anarchists, which finally obliged the police to take serious
measures against everyone suspected of anarchist views. Houses
were searched, papers and periodicals were suspended, and
known anarchist agitators were liable to be visited by the police
several times a day. Moreover, the police attempted to accuse
the anarchist theorists and journalists of common crimes of theft
and assault. In one of the most famous trials of the decade, in
August 1894, thirty people were accused of forming a criminal
association. They included prominent anarchist journalists such
as Sebastien Faure and Jean Grave, the editor of *Le Révolté*,

which had succeeded Kropotkin's *La Révolte* as the main organ
of serious anarchist discussion, along with ordinary burglars.
Some of the accused, for example Emile Pouget, the editor of
the tough, slangy anarchist paper *Le Père Peinard*, and Paul
Reclus, the nephew of Elisée, fled abroad; the rest were acquitted,
since it was quite impossible to make the charge of conspiracy
stick. The trial included the appearance of Stéphane Mallarmé
in the witness box to give evidence for one of the accused, the
writer and critic Félix Fénéon. In fact, the *Procès des Trente* serves
to illustrate the peculiar mixture of politics and bohemian revolt,
ordinary crime and idealistic action, which is characteristic of
Parisian anarchism in the eighties and nineties.

It was indeed the true anarchist crimes, often apparently
pointless, which contributed most to the formation of the conventional picture of the anarchist, bomb in pocket and dagger in
hand. Some criminals claimed that they were anarchists who
were simply redressing the wrongs of society. When, for example,
Clément Duval was arrested in 1886 for burglary, he attacked
the policeman and is said to have defended his action with the
words: 'The policeman arrested me in the name of the law; I hit
him in the name of liberty.' At his trial (which made the reputation of his young defending counsel, Labori, who was later to be
Dreyfus's lawyer) he persisted in maintaining that his crimes were
committed simply in order to obtain a redistribution of wealth:
'When society refuses you the right to existence, you must take
it.' Finally, he was led out of the court, crying, 'Long live
anarchy! Long live the social revolution! Ah, if ever I am freed,
I will blow you all up!'[1] In fact, he did not carry out his threat;
although sentenced to death, he was pardoned by President
Grévy and in 1901 escaped from prison, ending his life in New
York, where he died in 1935, admired by the Italian anarchist
colony there.

Two other individual criminals in the Paris of the 1890s
became legendary and controversial figures in the anarchist
movement. On 11th July 1892 François-Claudius Ravachol was
executed after being convicted of a strange series of brutal
murders for petty theft and pointless large-scale bomb outrages.

Ravachol is a difficult figure to assess and remains as puzzling to us as he was to his contemporaries.[1] It was only after his execution that anarchists accepted him, and even then with some reserve, as one of themselves. The nature of his crimes, and an initial suspicion that he was a common crook turned police informer, meant that it was only after his death that he acquired a reputation as an anarchist martyr in whose honour ballads were written and who gave his name to a verb – *ravacholiser*: to blow up.

Ravachol was born in 1859 near Saint-Etienne; the name was his mother's, as he had been abandoned by his father as a child. He was good to his younger sister and brother, and indeed seems always to have been polite, amiable and apparently respectable, although, it is said, vain to the extent of putting a touch of rouge on his cheeks to relieve their sallowness. He worked at various jobs in the Saint-Etienne area and became an anarchist, having lost his belief in God after reading a novel by Eugène Sue. It was at this time that he committed a number of mean and violent crimes – the murder of an aged rag merchant, the murder of a very old hermit, whose savings he stole, the pillaging of the grave of a dead countess, the murder of two old maids who kept an ironmongery shop. Subsequently, Ravachol only admitted violating the tomb and murdering the hermit, and alleged that he had only done these acts in order to raise money for the anarchist cause. He was arrested, but succeeded in escaping and went to Paris under an assumed name. Here he began seriously planning some truly anarchist acts of 'propaganda by the deed'. He took lodgings in Saint-Denis, recruited a devoted young assistant, 'Simon called Biscuit', and began to acquire the tools and materials for making bombs. (Articles on chemistry in the home were a common feature in the anarchist periodicals of the day.) His aim, he claimed later, was to perform a spectacular act of vengeance against certain judges who had sentenced workers for their part in the May Day demonstrations in 1891. In fact, although he succeeded in doing considerable damage to the apartment blocks where the judges lived, in the Boulevard Saint-Germain and the rue de Clichy, in both cases the bomb was placed outside the wrong door, and the only result was to damage the buildings without killing any of the inhabitants. By this time the police had – on the information, it is thought, of Ravachol's landlord – linked up the author of the murders in the Saint-Etienne area with the perpetrator of the explosion in the Boulevard Saint-Germain, and when the building in the rue de Clichy was attacked they were actively looking for him.

Ravachol, after placing his bomb in the building in the rue de Clichy, went off to lunch at a small restaurant – the Restaurant Véry – where he tried vainly to convert the waiter to his anarchist ideas. However, he seemed to like the restaurant sufficiently to return there a day or two later, and by this time the waiter was able to connect his anarchist talk and his references to the recent explosion with the description of Ravachol which the police had now published. Ravachol was arrested in the restaurant. On the day after his trial opened the Restaurant Véry was destroyed by a bomb and its proprietor killed (giving, so the anarchists claimed, a new meaning to the word 'verification'), although the waiter had the good luck to escape and was rewarded for his part in Ravachol's arrest by a minor post in the police. The author of the explosion was never discovered, but it sufficed to surround Ravachol's trial with an atmosphere of vengeance and terror. The jury, for whatever reason, found him guilty of the bomb explosions, but with extenuating circumstances, and he was not condemned to death. This was left to the court at Montbrison, which tried him for his earlier murders. By this time Ravachol's impassive bearing, his frank admission of responsibility and the cry of *Vive l'anarchie!* with which he had received the Paris verdict had overcome the hesitations which many anarchists had earlier felt about him, and this impression was confirmed by his behaviour at his execution, when he went bravely and impenitently to his death, singing a ribald song against the proprietors he had attacked and the church whose ministrations he had just refused. And, after his death, the mounting series of explosions in Paris was celebrated in anarchist circles to the refrain:

Dansons la Ravachole!
Vive le son, vive le son,
Dansons la Ravachole,
Vive le son
De l'explosion![1]

Ravachol was at once proclaimed a martyr by the anarchists and their sympathizers, and the symbolist writer Paul Adam declared, 'In this time of cynicism and irony, a saint has been born to us.'[2] Although Ravachol's anarchist beliefs and connexions seem to have been genuine enough, his character remains obscure, and we are left wondering what desire to impose himself on society led him to so strange, if consistent, a course.

One other of the terrorists who were responsible for the epidemic of explosions in France between 1892 and 1894 – eleven major explosions in Paris, as well as the assassination of President Carnot in Lyon – provides an even more frightening, because more logical and intellectual, example of the anarchist temperament. This was Emile Henry, a younger man than Ravachol, and from a bourgeois and educated background. He was born in 1872 in Spain, the son of one of the men exiled for his part in the Commune; he returned to Paris when his father was amnestied, and was a brilliant pupil at school. However, after passing successfully into the Ecole Polytechnique, he became intellectually convinced of the truth of anarchist doctrine, gave up his studies and the prospect of an assured and successful career, and plunged into anarchist propaganda by the deed. He seems to have had some associates, though they were never discovered, and certainly some years later there were people in Paris who boasted they had been his friends, such as a young poet whom Oscar Wilde met in 1898.[3] Emile Henry's first terrorist attack – with a bomb made by himself – was on the Paris offices of the Société des Mines de Carmaux, a company which had recently suppressed a strike in its coalfields with considerable brutality. In the event the bomb was discovered by the police, who carried it back to their police station, where it exploded and killed five of them. Henry was not caught. A little more than a year later he committed a crime which shocked everyone, including a large number of anarchists themselves. On the evening of 12th February 1894 – one week after the execution of Vaillant for his attack on the Chamber of Deputies – Henry deposited a bomb in the Café Terminus near the Gare Saint-Lazare at a time when a large crowd of modest Parisian shopkeepers, clerks and even workers were quietly drinking and listening to the band. The bomb caused a great deal of damage; twenty people were wounded, one of whom subsequently died. Henry was arrested after a short chase.

Emile Henry's behaviour at his trial and before his execution showed him to be an intellectual to the end. His actions were inspired by a cold logic and a controlled, fanatical hatred of existing society. When reproached with killing innocent people, he simply replied: '*Il n'y a pas d'innocents*'.[1] When faced with the death penalty, he accepted it, saying: 'We inflict death; we will know how to endure it.' He refused to accept the help of a family doctor, who tried to give evidence that his mind was deranged as a result of illness in childhood. In prison he had long conversations with the governor, for whom he wrote a lucid essay setting forth anarchist philosophy. And in the dock he propounded what is in some ways the clearest and most uncompromising statement of the terrorist position: 'I was convinced that the existing organization was bad; I wanted to struggle against it so as to hasten its disappearance. I brought to the struggle a profound hatred, intensified every day by the revolting spectacle of society where all is base, all is cowardly, where everything is a barrier to the development of human passions, to the generous tendencies of the heart, to the free flight of thought. . . . I wanted to show the bourgeoisie that their pleasures would no longer be complete, that their insolent triumphs would be disturbed, that their golden calf would tremble violently on its pedestal, until the final shock would cast it down in mud and blood.' The bomb in the Café Terminus was a reply to all the injustices inflicted by bourgeois society. Anarchists have no respect for human life, because the bourgeois do not respect it. Anarchists, Henry said, 'do not spare bourgeois women and children, because the wives

and children of those they love are not spared either. Are not
those children innocent victims who, in the slums, die slowly of
anaemia because bread is scarce at home: or those women who
grow pale in your workshops and wear themselves out to earn
forty sous a day, and yet are lucky when poverty does not turn
them into prostitutes; those old people whom you have turned
into machines for production all their lives, and whom you cast
on to the garbage dump and the workhouse when their strength
is exhausted? At least have the courage of your crimes, gentlemen of the bourgeoisie, and agree that our reprisals are fully
legitimate!' Finally, Emile Henry explicitly linked his acts with
the international anarchist movement: 'You have hung men in
Chicago, cut off their heads in Germany, strangled them in
Jerez, shot them in Barcelona, guillotined them in Montbrison
and Paris, but what you will never destroy is anarchism. Its roots
are too deep: it is born at the heart of a corrupt society which is
falling to pieces; it is a violent reaction against the established
order. It represents egalitarian and libertarian aspirations which
are battering down existing authority; it is everywhere, which
makes it impossible to capture. It will end by killing you.'[1]

3

The anarchist movement in the 1880s and '90s was genuinely
international, and the various acts of propaganda by the deed,
whether of individual protest against society as a whole or
directed against monarchs and political leaders, symbolized a
deep sense of uneasiness and of revolt against industrial society.
Conditions in many industries both in Europe and America produced a feeling of real class warfare. Outbreaks of violence took
place that were more spontaneous and direct than the calculated
acts of the assassins or the bomb throwers. The miners of Mont-
ceau-les-Mines who murdered an unpopular overseer, the demonstrators at Fourmies in northern France who were shot down on
May Day 1891, the strikers in the Rio Tinto mines in Spain or
the peasants in Sicily or Andalusia whose risings were suppressed
by the army, all provided martyrs whom the anarchists claimed

as their own. Wherever the situation seemed desperate, the landlords or employers particularly harsh and grasping and the conditions of work intolerable, anarchist ideas found some sympathy
and easily served as a spur to action. The studied protests of the
individual terrorists seemed to be the symbols of mass discontent
and latent revolutionary passion.

Such situations were not only to be found in Europe. Anarchists from Europe brought anarchist ideas to the United States
and, for a short time at least, influenced the development of the
labour movement there. The most famous apostle of anarchism
in the U.S.A. was a German, Johann Most, who arrived there in
1882. Most was born at Augsburg in Bavaria, the illegitimate son
of an impoverished clerk and a governess.[1] He was brought up
by a stepmother whom he hated, and at the age of thirteen he
had an operation on his face which left him badly disfigured –
though later he was partly able to cover it with a thick beard. He
was apprenticed as a bookbinder and in the 1860s was in Switzerland, where he joined the International. After ten years or so of
socialist agitation in Germany and Austria, during which he was
briefly a member of the German Reichstag, he left for London in
1878, after a period of imprisonment for speaking and writing
against the Kaiser and the clergy. During the next few years he
broke with the German socialists and abandoned all belief in the
possibility of effective political action. He was expelled from the
German social democratic party, who over the next twenty
years were assiduously expelling anyone tainted with anarchist
heresy. Most was influenced by Bakunin's ideas, especially
through some of Bakunin's Belgian followers and also by Auguste
Blanqui, the veteran French revolutionary, for whom the act of
revolution was almost an end in itself. In London, Most founded
a paper, *Freiheit*, and used this to preach the doctrine of direct
action. In 1881 he was sent to prison for sixteen months because
of an article approving the murder of the Tsar Alexander II. His
paper was by now suspected of fomenting assassinations of all
kinds, and when Lord Frederick Cavendish was murdered in
Dublin by Irish nationalists who had nothing to do with the
anarchist movement and of whose aims Most would have

thoroughly disapproved, *Freiheit* was again raided and two of its printers arrested. When Most himself came out of prison he decided that further activity in London was impossible, and in December 1882 he sailed for America.

In Germany itself Most had had little influence, and the anarchists there were limited to those individuals who had been in direct contact with the followers of Bakunin and Guillaume in the Jura. However, even the disciplined atmosphere of Germany was not totally unaffected by the epidemic of terrorism. In addition to the attacks on the Kaiser in 1878, which were anarchist in method even if the two assailants had had little or no contact with anarchist groups and ideas, there were one or two attempts at propaganda by the deed. Thus a young man called August Reinsdorf planned to blow up the National Memorial at Rudesheim on the Rhine on the occasion of its opening in the presence of the Kaiser and the German princes. Unfortunately for Reinsdorf, he hurt his foot shortly before the ceremony, and had to entrust the operation to two of his associates, who forgot to buy a waterproof fuse for the bomb. As it poured with rain the night before the attempt, the bomb, not surprisingly, failed to go off. However, a few weeks later there was an explosion in the main police station at Frankfurt, and the Police President, Rumpf – who may indeed have arranged the explosion himself – succeeded, in his subsequent investigations, in discovering, through the indiscretion of Reinsdorf's friends, the story of the abortive plot to blow up the Kaiser and princes. In December 1884 Reinsdorf was arrested and he was executed early in 1885, going to his death with the ritual formula: 'Down with barbarism! Up with anarchy!'[1]

It looked as though Reinsdorf had already had his revenge, for shortly before he was executed Police President Rumpf was murdered. A young anarchist who had recently arrived from Switzerland was accused and charged with the murder, though the evidence against him was slight and he swore he was innocent. When the state prosecutor asked for the death penalty, the young man shouted, in true anarchist style: 'You will not ask for another death sentence.' In this case, there was no need for another act of anarchist vengeance, as the prosecutor shortly afterwards went mad. However, these were isolated acts, and anarchist ideas in Germany soon virtually vanished, except among a few bohemian intellectuals such as the Bavarian writer, Gustav Landauer, and a few dissident social democrats who were expelled from the socialist party for advocating direct revolutionary action.

In America, on the other hand, Most found more fruitful ground for his agitation than he had in Germany or England. When he arrived there had recently been strikes all over the country, and the movement in favour of an eight-hour working day was well under way. Many of the recent immigrants, especially the Russians and Italians, had brought their anarchist ideas with them and kept up contacts with anarchists at home. (It was a group of Italian anarchists in Paterson, New Jersey, who planned and executed the assassination of King Umberto I in 1900.) In the tough world of expanding American capitalism an industrial dispute could easily turn into a real war between workers and employers, as when, for example, strikers at the Carnegie Corporation's steel mills at Homestead, Pennsylvania, engaged in a pitched battle with the Pinkerton men hired by the employers to break the strike. Most himself started up *Freiheit* as a German-language anarchist paper, and there were soon Italian and Spanish anarchist journals to propagate the ideas and methods of the anarchist social revolution, as well as anarchist periodicals in French, Czech and Yiddish. Indeed, during these years the anarchist movement in the U.S.A. was almost entirely a foreign one; and it was in German, Russian, Italian or Yiddish that the famous agitators made their speeches. The violence of this propaganda and the explicit incitement contained in pamphlets like Most's own *Science of Revolutionary Warfare* ('a manual of instruction in the use and preparation of Nitroglycerine, Dynamite, Gun-cotton, Fulminating Mercury, Bombs, Fuses, Poisons, etc.')[1] all contributed to the anarchists' being held responsible for any violent disturbances. Anarchist demonstrations, complete with the black flag which was by now the official anarchist emblem, might well be suspected of leading to something worse, when anarchist papers were publishing exhortations like the following: 'Dynamite! Of all the good stuff, that is the stuff. Stuff several pounds of this sublime stuff into an inch pipe . . . plug up both ends, insert a cap with a fuse attached, place this in the vicinity of a lot of rich loafers who live by the sweat of other peoples' brows, and light the fuse. A most cheerful and gratifying result will follow. . . . A pound of this good stuff beats a bushel of ballots hollow – and don't you forget it!'[1]

It was in this atmosphere that one of the most famous incidents in the history of American anarchism occurred. The situation in 1886 in Chicago was tense: the city was a centre of agitation in favour of the eight-hour day; there was an active group of anarchists, mostly of German origin; and there had been repeated clashes between strikers and blacklegs at the McCormick harvester works. It was in Chicago that May Day was first celebrated as a day of working-class demonstrations and, although 1st May 1886 had passed off quietly, two days later the police fired shots during a clash at the McCormick works. As a result, the local German anarchist paper, the *Arbeiterzeitung*, published a leading article by the editor, August Spies, headed, 'Revenge! Working men! To Arms!' At the same time plans were made for a protest meeting at the Haymarket, a large open space in the city, at which, so the handbill announced, 'Good speakers will be present to denounce the latest atrocious act of the police, the shooting of our fellow workmen yesterday afternoon'.[2]

The meeting passed off peacefully enough, and towards the end a heavy storm drove many of the crowd away. At this point the police ordered the closing of the meeting, in the middle of a speech by Samuel Fielden, one of the leaders of the demonstration. Fielden objected and said that the meeting was a perfectly orderly one. The police lieutenant insisted, and at that moment a bomb was thrown into the crowd. A policeman was killed and several others wounded, and the police opened fire: in the confusion which followed more policemen and demonstrators were killed or wounded. The responsibility for the original bomb has never been wholly cleared up; as so often in episodes of this kind, there have been suggestions that it was an act of provocation by the police themselves.

The city was soon in a panic as violent as any produced by later 'red scares' in the United States. As a contemporary journalist put it: 'Good men forgot reason and clamoured for revenge.'[1] The police decided to arrest nine prominent anarchist agitators and journalists. Of these two could not be found; one of them, Schnaubelt, who may indeed possibly have thrown the bomb, disappeared; another, Albert Parsons, later surrendered so as to share the fate of his comrades. Eight men appeared in the dock charged with murdering the policeman, and after a trial which accurately reflected the popular mood of alarm and vengefulness rather than impartial justice, four were sentenced to death and the remainder to long terms of imprisonment. One of them, Lingg, was, in fact, a true terrorist who had manufactured bombs, but there was no evidence that he had any connexion with the Haymarket bomb. The evidence against the rest was even more slender. They challenged the court's competence and used a second trial as an opportunity to make defiant and unrepentantly anarchist speeches. Parsons spoke for eight hours and Fielden for three, while Schwab called for 'a state of society in which all human beings do right for the simple reason that it is right and hate wrong because it is wrong'.[2] Lingg expressed contempt for 'your "order", your laws, your force-propped authority'.[3]

In spite of appeals to the higher courts and petitions for mercy – including one signed by eminent writers, among them Bernard Shaw and Oscar Wilde – four of the accused were executed, testifying to their anarchist beliefs and deliberately claiming martyrdom: one of them especially, August Spies, became famous for his dramatic words from the scaffold: 'There will come a time when our silence in the grave will be more powerful than the voices you strangle today.'[4] As a result of these events, John Most was arrested, after addressing a meeting of sympathy in New York. For the rest of his life he was in and out of prison, struggling to keep his paper *Freiheit* going and becoming involved in controversies with other anarchists, both American and foreign. Some of these were extremely bitter; and on one occasion the

tempestuous and intrepid Emma Goldman tried to horsewhip
him at a meeting. Until his death in 1906, Most remained an
unremitting and dedicated propagandist, whose subversive message seemed wholly at odds with his industrious 'petit-bourgeois'
nature, at once affectionate and crabbed, generous and suspicious.

The Chicago trial fired the imagination of many young revolutionaries and reformers. The young Russian Jewess, Emma
Goldman, who had already experienced the harshness of American working-class life, threw herself passionately into anarchist
agitation and embarked on what was to be, both personally and
politically, a long and turbulent career.[1] Her friend, another
Russian, Alexander Berkman, was so moved by the Carnegie
Corporation's lock-out at their works at Homestead, Pennsylvania, that he resolved to assassinate Henry Clay Frick, the
Chairman of the Board. Accordingly, he, Emma Goldman and
a young anarchist painter, who all lived as a *ménage à trois* running an ice-cream parlour in Worcester, Massachusetts, planned
the murder; and, leaving Emma to raise funds in New York by
any possible means, including an unsuccessful attempt at prosti-
tution, Berkman set off on his mission. He succeeded in being
shown into Frick's office, but failed to do more than wound him.
He was arrested and sentenced to twenty-two years' imprisonment. Emma Goldman worked hard to arouse support for a
campaign in favour of a remission of his sentence, but Berkman
was not released till 1906.

In the meantime, in 1901 President William McKinley was
assassinated at Buffalo by a young man of Polish origin called
Czolgosz. Czolgosz was probably not a member of any regular
anarchist organization and seems to have acted on his own,
prompted only by his inner sense of persecution and injustice.
However, he had been to a lecture by Emma Goldman, and she at
once started a vigorous speaking tour on his behalf, although she
did not know him and declared that she did not approve of murdering the President. Czolgosz was executed, and Emma Goldman
was arrested, as was Most, in spite of the fact that he had long
declared himself against individual terrorism, and although his
lack of sympathy with Berkman nine years earlier contributed to

his breach with Emma Goldman, once a devoted disciple who had previously been, according to her own account, on the point of becoming his mistress.

The assassination of President McKinley convinced the authorities that there was a real anarchist peril. Theodore Roosevelt, the new President, denounced it in his message to Congress in December 1901 and Congress passed a law excluding from the U.S.A. any person 'who disbelieves in or is opposed to all organized governments'. The fear of anarchism remained alive into the 1920s, as the trial of Sacco and Vanzetti showed; but, although active anarchist groups continued to flourish among foreign immigrants, and although a number of intellectuals fell under the spell of anarchist doctrines or of Emma Goldman's personality, in fact individual acts of terrorism were largely abandoned, and it was in direct industrial action that the anarchist spirit remained an important influence in the United States for a few years longer.

In general, however, the experience of two decades of 'propaganda by the deed' forced all anarchists in Europe and America to think again about their methods and aims. In spite of the temporary reaction after the Commune, and in spite of the recurrent crises of the capitalist economy, by the end of the nineteenth century the legal and constitutional machinery for obtaining social reform and economic improvement was more efficient than it had been at any time since the industrial revolution. In the more advanced countries, therefore, it seemed more sensible to join a political party or a trade union and to agitate legally for piecemeal reforms rather than to make the apocalyptic gestures of the anarchists. Indeed, it was only in countries where, as in Spain, the possibility of open working-class political activity scarcely existed that the direct violence of the anarchists still had a wide appeal.

Moreover, propaganda by the deed could easily become better propaganda against than for anarchist ideas. As Octave Mirbeau, one of the French writers of the nineties who was highly sympathetic to anarchism, wrote at the time of Emile Henry's trial: 'A mortal enemy of anarchism could not have done better than Emile Henry when he hurled his inexplicable bomb in the midst of peaceful anonymous people who had come into a café to drink a beer before going to bed. . . . Emile Henry says, affirms, claims that he is an anarchist. It is possible. But anarchism has a broad back, like paper it endures anything. Today it is a fashion for criminals to claim a connexion with it when they have perpetrated a good crime. . . . Each party has its criminals and its lunatics because each party has its human beings.'[1] Not all of the anarchist intellectuals were as uncompromising in condemning terrorism, but all of them were conscious of the dilemma it posed. John Most saw all criminal acts as the inevitable result of existing society. 'I recognize a "wild" anarchist in every criminal, whether he is otherwise sympathetic to me or not, because a man of this kind, even when he acts on his own for personal advantage, is simply a product of his age.'[2] Elisée Reclus, the eminent geographer and a man of real scientific ability, who brought to his anarchist beliefs the conscientious scruples of his Huguenot background, suspended judgement: 'If an isolated individual filled with rage takes his revenge on a society which brought him up badly, fed him badly, advised him badly, what can I say? It is the result of terrible forces, the consequences of deep passions, the eruption of justice in its primitive phases. To take sides against the unfortunate man, and so justify, however indirectly the system of humiliation and oppression that weighs on him and millions of his fellow men – never!'[3] It was an attitude that annoyed Jean Grave, the editor of *La Révolte*, whose belief in himself as the repository of true anarchist ideals and doctrine won him the nickname of 'the Pope of the rue Mouffetard'. 'As far as his tolerance and goodness are concerned,' he wrote of Reclus, 'I must admit that they have more than once got on my nerves and have often brought us into conflict with each other over propaganda questions. . . . Have idiots or knaves the right to destroy the ideas we defend? . . . We often quarrelled, especially over theft. "Thieves," he once wrote to me, "we are all thieves and I myself among the chief thieves, as I work for a publisher to try and earn ten or twenty times the wages of an honest man. Everything is robbery." '[4]

Still, terrorism had made its effect; and as a technique for drawing attention to a cause it is still familiar. The Paris papers of the early 1960s with their accounts of the bombs planted by the terrorists of the O.A.S. bear a striking resemblance to those of the 1890s. Even if terrorism made enemies for the anarchists, it aroused profound and intense fears in respectable breasts. The very fact that all the terrorist acts, whatever their motive or aim, were committed by individuals or by very small groups tended to make detection and police precautions very difficult. The French police, according to M. Maitron's researches which have illuminated the French anarchist movement at the end of the century so vividly, reckoned that there were in France about 1,000 active anarchist militants and 4,500 sympathizers who regularly read anarchist papers, but that there were also 100,000 people who were vaguely anarchist in sympathy and up to a point prepared passively to support their aims. In the absence, however, of any regular organization, it was hard to control the movement, especially as the terrorist acts were often not the work of known militants, and the perpetrators were therefore all the harder to catch. In the circumstances, the well-known leaders of anarchist thought – Kropotkin, Malatesta, Elisée Reclus or John Most, for instance – were inevitably regarded as responsible, even though nothing could be proved against them. Never has the gap between theory and practice seemed wider than that between mild, scholarly and thoughtful men like Kropotkin, living quietly in Harrow or Bromley or Brighton, lecturing to the Royal Geographical Society and entertaining William Morris and G. F. Watts,* and those who, like Ravachol or Emile Henry, defied society with acts of blind and brutal terrorism.

It was during the years when 'propaganda by the deed' was making anarchism notorious as a creed of revolutionary action that the thinkers of the movement were trying, not wholly successfully, to turn it into a respectable political philosophy. The trouble was that those who were excited by the sensational

---

* Even Stepniak, a professed technician of revolution, specializing in manuals on guerrilla warfare and home-made explosives, used to entertain girls from Lady Margaret Hall, Oxford, to tea.

violence of the assassins and bombers were likely to find Kropotkin's views somewhat tame, while those who were attracted by the high-minded optimism of anarchist theory were the people who were most apt to be shocked and outraged by the indiscriminate cruelty involved in propaganda by the deed, or, in fact, any other form of violent revolutionary action. It is typical of the gulf between anarchist theory and terrorist practice that when the enterprising editor of the tenth edition of the *Encyclopaedia Britannica* invited Kropotkin to write the article on anarchism, it was the editor who felt obliged to append a footnote saying: 'It is important to remember that the term "Anarchist" is inevitably rather loosely used in public, in connexion with the authors of a certain class of murderous outrage', and added a résumé of 'the chief modern so-called "Anarchist" incidents', since Kropotkin had wholly omitted to mention them. By the beginning of the twentieth century, however, serious attempts were being made to resolve the problems which had confronted the anarchist movement in the 1890s: how to combine a confident belief in rational cooperation and enlightened progress with faith in the purifying value of the revolutionary act, and how to convert an essentially undisciplined individualistic creed into an effective basis for practical action.

CHAPTER VI
Saints and Rebels

' "I'm one of many thousands of young men of my class . . .
in whose brains certain ideas are fermenting. There's nothing
original about me at all. I'm very young and very ignorant; it's
only a few months since I began to talk of the possibility of a
social revolution with men who have considered the whole
ground more than I could possibly do. I'm a mere particle,"
Hyacinth wound up, "in the grey immensity of the people.
All I pretend to is my good faith and a great desire that justice
should be done." '   *Henry James:* The Princess Casamassima

'I am fifty years old and I have always lived in freedom; let
me end my life free; when I am dead let this be said of me:
"He belonged to no school, to no church, to no institution, to
no academy, least of all to any régime except the régime of
liberty." '   *Gustave Courbet, on rejecting the Legion of Honour*

I

All over Europe in the 1890s new ideas and new movements were
challenging the political, moral and artistic conventions of the
previous generation. The more industrial society seemed to be
expanding, the more people began to be aware of its inequities.
The richer the rich became, the solider and more ostentatious the
outward signs of their wealth, the greater the gap appeared to
be between them and the working classes, and the more dis-
satisfied intellectuals and artists became with the social values of
capitalist society. As the morality and conventions of society
seemed to many to stifle individual expression and to force men
into hypocrisy, so the idea of a total revolt against the established order acquired a personal as well as a social and political
connotation. Thus, the end of the nineteenth century and the
coming of the twentieth seemed to symbolize the possibility of a
new social and moral order for the future.

While anarchism had a natural appeal to the workers in countries where they were denied the possibility of peaceful change and reform, to the intellectuals in the great capitals of western Europe it seemed to offer a political theory which could combine a vision of a just society with the assertion of individual freedom; and those artists and writers who believed in a bohemian rejection of bourgeois conventions found in anarchism – and especially in *le propagande par le fait* – a compelling example of total revolt. Eager for social change and for violent sensations, many young intellectuals, for a time at least, were prepared to follow Kropotkin or Nietzsche indiscriminately, or to move from anarchism to various forms of violent nationalism. (Later, as their passionate desire for action waned with age and their sense of what was practicable grew, many of them turned to the more humdrum paths of orthodox social democracy.) As Léon Blum put it: 'The whole literary generation of which I was a part was impregnated with anarchist thought.'[1]

Of the figures who inspired the anarchists, both those who wanted political and social revolution and those who wanted to assert the sanctity of the individual against the anonymity of industrial society and the hypocrisy and constraint of bourgeois 'Victorian' morality, Peter Kropotkin was perhaps the most influential. When he finally settled in England in 1886 he was forty-four years old, but his time in prison had left him in delicate health and his days as an active leader of revolutionary movements were over. In fact, although before leaving Russia he had advocated the use of armed bands to stir up revolution among the peasants, and although he had shared the hopes of many anarchists in the seventies and eighties that revolution was near, he soon reverted to the belief which he had derived from N. V. Tchaikovsky, that it was by means of the printed word that the cause of the revolution could best be served and that a clandestine pamphlet was worth more than the terrorist's bomb or the assassin's dagger.

By 1886 he had suffered for his beliefs. He had spent two years in the fortress of Peter and Paul in St Petersburg and three as a political prisoner in France, and these sentences, as well as his dramatic escape from Russia, had made him a legendary figure in revolutionary circles. During these years, too, he had read and reflected further on the nature of social change. His personal experience of prison life had made him a passionate advocate of penal reform; indeed, for the rest of his life there were few warm-hearted liberal movements with which he did not sympathize, and no meeting or letter of protest against injustice was complete without his presence or signature. In England, where he lived in extremely modest circumstances – his estates in Russia had been confiscated – he became a respected and much-loved figure, whose simplicity and sincerity impressed even those who dis-agreed with his opinions, and he ended by being considered as a sort of anarchist saint, whose integrity and goodness could be set against the violence and terror with which the anarchist move-ment was popularly associated. As the great Danish critic, Georg Brandes, wrote: 'Seldom have there been revolutionists so humane and mild. . . . He has never been an avenger but always a martyr. He does not impose sacrifices upon others; he makes them himself.'[1]

In England, Kropotkin became a friend of all sorts of radicals. He respected and liked William Morris, but could not agree with his rejection of machines and technical progress, since, for Kro-potkin, as for Godwin, it was mechanization that would eventu-ally liberate men from innumerable tedious and degrading tasks. 'William Morris's hatred of machines', he wrote, 'proved that the conception of the machine's power and gracefulness was missing from his poetical genius.'[2] He was a friend of trade-union leaders like Ben Tillett and Tom Mann, and had been enormously im-pressed by the solidarity and mutual loyalty of the London dockers in the great strike of 1889. At the same time, his geo-graphical writings made him respectable in academic circles – at one moment there was even a rumour that he was going to be given a chair at Cambridge. He attended dinners of the Royal Geographical Society and firmly refused to rise and drink the health of the queen. To the end of his life he was consistent in his refusal to acknowledge the state or to accept anything from it. When he eventually returned to Russia in 1917 he refused an

invitation to join the provisional government and, again, after
the bolsheviks had taken power, he would not accept Lunachar-
sky's offer of a government subsidy towards the cost of reprinting
his works. The one point in his career when, it seemed to many
of his friends and disciples, he was inconsistent, was during the
First World War, when he warmly supported the war against
Germany. He shared Bakunin's dislike of the Germans and his
populist faith in the innate virtues of the Russian people, and
believed, as Bakunin had in 1870, that a German victory would
mean a strengthening of the regimented, disciplined state which
he continued to hate. His attitude led him to break with old
associates such as Malatesta, who continued to insist that a man
'ought never to fight except for the social revolution',[1] and it also
brought expressions of contempt from rival revolutionaries, so
that Stalin, for example, wrote, 'the old fool must have completely
lost his mind'.[2]

In fact, Kropotkin, for all his dislike of terrorism – 'On his lips
the word "Nechaevism" was always a strong rebuke', one of his
disciples reported[3] – believed that in certain situations violence
was justified, and that it might well be the only means of revolution. When the news of the 1905 revolution in Russia reached
him he went so far as to go and practise with a rifle in a shooting
gallery in case he had a chance of returning to Russia to fight.
This was one of the points which separated him from Tolstoy,
for whose views he otherwise had much sympathy and for whose
genius he had great admiration. The difference between the
anarchist and the Tolstoyan position was well expressed by an
anonymous writer who provided an introduction to Tolstoy's
pamphlet on *War and Compulsory Military Service* when this was
published in 1896 by the anarchist *Bibliothèque des Temps Nouveaux*, with which Kropotkin, Jean Grave and Elisée Reclus were
all associated. Tolstoy is, the writer asserts, an anarchist: 'He
affirms as we do that every government functions in a patho-
logical fashion and by its very nature corrupts all it touches; he
denies in advance that any law, any regulation, any will from

above can have any power for good; he abhors the military
system as absolutely contrary to all freedom and justice; but he
repudiates all resistance to evil. He calls himself a Christian
anarchist. . . . For our part the words ['turn the other cheek']
attributed to the prophet of Nazareth seem to us an abomina-
tion. . . . Every man worthy of the name must resist to the limit
of his strength, not for himself but for all the other human beings
whom he represents, and whom he would degrade by his
cowardice and ennoble by his courage. The old Roman saying
remains for ever the expression of the truth: "Against the
enemy, revendication is eternal." Revendication, not vengeance,
for we know the determining influence of circumstances, and we
feel hatred for nobody.'[1]

Kropotkin himself, in a letter to an English friend a few years
earlier, had expressed a similar attitude towards revenge: 'We
may say that revenge is no aim in itself. Surely, it is not. But it is
human and all revolts have borne and for a long time will bear
the character. In fact, *we* have not suffered from the persecutions
as they, the workers, suffered; we who, in our houses, seclude
ourselves from the cry and sight of human sufferings, *we are no
judges* of those who live in the midst of all this hell of suffering.
. . . Personally, I hate these explosions, but I cannot stand as a
judge to condemn those who are driven to despair. . . . One
single thing – that revenge must not be erected into a *theory*.
That no one has the right to incite others to it, but that if he
keenly feels all that hell and does a desperate act, let him be
judged by those who are his peers, his equals in bearing those
pariah's sufferings.'[2]

Kropotkin's dilemma was that he had seen from his own
experience in Russia that there were often circumstances in
which a violent upheaval offered the only possibility of change,
while, at the same time, his own temperament and beliefs made
him dislike the prospect. His fear was always that the revolution
might be forced into the methods of the state which it was aiming
to destroy. 'Terrorism', he wrote in his history of *The Great
French Revolution*, 'is always a method of government.'[3] And he
was constantly repeating that a 'revolutionary government' was

a contradiction in terms, since the whole point of a revolution was to abolish government. However, he refused to accept, as Tolstoy did and as Gandhi was to do, that non-violence could be made into a principle of action, since there were, in his view, sometimes situations so desperate that violence was the lesser evil; and it is for this reason that Kropotkin's support for the allied cause during the First World War is not quite as surprising or as inconsistent as it first seems.

Kropotkin and Tolstoy never met, but Tolstoy saw exactly what Kropotkin's position was. 'His arguments in favour of violence', he wrote, 'do not seem to me to be the expression of his opinions, but only of his fidelity to the banner under which he has served so honestly all his life.'[1] In return, Kropotkin saw the point of Tolstoy's final departure from his home and of his rejection of all worldly values. 'I am not astonished to learn', he wrote at the end of Tolstoy's life, 'that Tolstoy has decided to retire to a peasant's house where he might continue his teachings without having to rely upon anyone else's labour for supplying himself or his family with the luxuries of life. It is the necessary outcome of the terrible inner drama he had been living through the last thirty years – the drama, by the way, of thousands upon thousands of intellectuals in our present society. It is the accomplishment of what he was longing for for a long time.'[2]

Kropotkin differed from Tolstoy because he refused to accept non-violence as a principle. He also differed from him in rejecting Christianity, even in Tolstoy's highly unorthodox form. He thought of himself first and foremost as a scientist, and his social philosophy and his ethical system were, he believed, soundly based on empirical observations. From the time of his early expeditions in Siberia he had become convinced that men worked better together and achieved more when they were co-operating freely and equally: the men who accompanied him on his explorations, for example, responded much more readily once they realized that Kropotkin was not relying on his position and privileges as a noble and an officer to secure their obedience. The primitive tribes he observed seemed to have customs and instincts which regulated their social life without the need of government or laws. For Kropotkin, primitive society, so far from providing an example of Hobbesian conflict and of the war of all against all, showed rather that cooperation and 'mutual aid' were the natural state of man if left uncorrupted by government and by laws which result from the 'desire of the ruling class to give permanence to customs imposed by themselves for their own advantage', whereas all that is necessary for harmonious living are 'those customs useful for society . . . which have no need of law to insure respect'.[1]

His own observations were, Kropotkin believed, reinforced by the theories of Darwin; and his most extensive theoretical work, *Mutual Aid*, was explicitly written to counter T. H. Huxley's interpretation of Darwin's evolutionary theory. Huxley thought that life was a continuous free fight and believed that it was as a result of this struggle for existence that species survived or evolved into new forms of life. Instead, according to Kropotkin, the law of nature was a law of cooperation, of mutual aid rather than of struggle. Within each species mutual support is the rule, and for each example of rivalry a counter-example of reciprocal assistance can be produced. 'Here you have the dominative swans; there the extremely sociable kittiwake-gulls among whom quarrels are rare and short; the prepossessing polar guillemots which continually caress each other. . . .'[2] Again and again in his writings Kropotkin comes back to Darwin's example of the blind pelican whom his comrades kept supplied with fish.

Kropotkin's optimistic and idealistic assumptions about the animal world were repeated in respect of primitive human societies. Man was originally sociable and innocent, and throughout history his instincts to cooperate have asserted themselves – in primitive communities, in the Greek city-states, in the medieval urban communes – only to be corrupted by the overelaboration of the machinery of society, by the blind covetousness of a few merchants, by the refusal of the citizens to exercise their rights and by their willingness therefore to delegate power to representative assemblies whose members are at best mediocrities and at worst tyrants. Kropotkin, for all his optimism and naïveté, realized that the ideal society could only be the result of eternal vigilance. Although man's natural instincts were on the whole good, the fundamental problem of ethics is to find a solution to the contradiction between those feelings 'which induce man to subdue other men in order to utilize them for his individual ends' and those which 'induce human beings to unite for attaining common ends by common effort: the first answering to that fundamental need of human nature – struggle, and the second representing another equally fundamental tendency – the desire for unity and mutual sympathy'.[1]

The latter instincts – those making for human solidarity and mutual aid and sympathy – must be encouraged in two ways, by means of a sound economic organization and by means of a fresh approach to systems of morality. By this means humanity could be helped towards the next step in evolution. 'The ideal of the anarchist . . . is a mere summing-up of what he considers to be the next phase of evolution. It is no longer a matter of faith; it is a matter for scientific discussion.'[2] On the moral plane what is needed is an ethical system which springs from man's own good instincts and which does not rely on any outside sanction to enforce it.

In his moral thinking Kropotkin was much influenced by a young French philosopher, M. Guyau, whose most important work, *Esquisse d'une morale sans obligation ni sanction*, was published in 1885, during Kropotkin's spell as political prisoner in the old convent of Clairvaux, where he himself was reflecting about the moral basis of society. Kropotkin called Guyau an 'anarchist without knowing it' and he repeatedly used the phrase 'morality without obligation or sanction' to describe his own ethical doctrines. Guyau was an interesting writer who coldly dissected previous moral philosophy and exposed its fallacies, showing that a belief which made morality dependent on an external metaphysical sanction was as erroneous as one based on the pleasure-calculus of the utilitarians; and, while he had considerable sympathy with the Kantian idea of an incontrovertible categorical imperative that imposes duty on us, he found this position, too, to be philosophically untenable. Man is thrown back on himself alone: the motives for his actions are within him, unconscious as well as conscious, and his conduct is necessarily the product of these. It was foolish to define duty except in terms of one's own capacities: '*Je puis donc je dois.*' It is pointless to expect man to behave other than as his nature dictates. 'Immorality is an interior mutilation.' Thought and action are one, and thought must lead to action: 'He who does not act as he thinks, thinks incompletely.'[1]

Guyau's neo-stoicism is a good deal bleaker than Kropotkin's morality based on the natural instinct for mutual aid. Guyau's picture of man is that of a mariner left at sea in a damaged vessel: 'No hand guides us, no eye sees for us; the rudder has long been broken, or rather there has never been one, we have to make it; it is a great task and it is our task.'[2] Nevertheless, Guyau stresses, as Kropotkin did, that man has generous instincts as well as selfish ones, and that sympathy and compassion are as natural to him as envy and hatred. 'Life is not just nutrition, it is also production and fecundity. To live is to spend as well as to acquire.'[3] For Kropotkin, Guyau reinforced the beliefs about the nature of man and of human progress which he believed were justified by his interpretation of the theory of evolution and his observation of primitive communities. What was necessary in order to put into practice a morality without obligation or sanctions was a new economic order of society which would promote only man's good instincts and give no opportunity for the expression of his bad ones. To achieve this goal a revolution was necessary and a total reorganization of society to produce a state of what Kropotkin called 'anarchist communism'. A revolution is necessary because 'everything hangs together in our society and it is impossible to reform anything without the whole structure collapsing. The moment you strike at private property in one of its forms – land or industry – you will be forced to strike at all the others. The very success of the revolution will impose this.'[4] Previous revolutions had failed because only by the immediate expropriation of stocks and fields and factories could the food supply be maintained while the foundations of the new society were being laid: '*Du pain, il faut du pain à la Révolution!*' This would not only avoid the economic difficulties, Kropotkin

optimistically hoped, which had led to the Terror in 1792 and
to the reaction against the Second Republic in 1848; it would
also be the first step towards the new order. 'To make prosperity a
reality, this immense capital – cities, houses, tilled fields, factories,
means of communication, education, must stop being considered
as private property which the monopolist can dispose of as he
likes. This rich productive equipment, so painfully obtained, con-
structed, developed, invented by our ancestors must become
common property so that the collective spirit can draw from it
the greatest advantages for everyone. We must have EXPRO-
PRIATION. Prosperity for all as an end, expropriation as a
means.'[1]

Once the act of expropriation had taken place the way would
be open for anarchist communism. Kropotkin was insistent that
this should be based on the principle of 'from each according to
his ability, to each according to his needs', and stated repeatedly
that it was not possible to allocate the fruits of labour according
to the actual work a man did. There was much argument in
anarchist circles on this point and on the whole question of
ownership. Proudhon had envisaged a society where each
member would have a small amount of domestic property, and
the various types of cooperative movement which he inspired
thought of the means of production as being owned in common
by the members, with each of them owning a share of the products or their proceeds. For Kropotkin, however, this was at
best a transitional stage. Eventually there would be no ownership at all and everything would simply be freely available to
him who needed it. Optimistically, he was always seeing in contemporary society developments which seemed to show that the
world was moving in the direction he wanted, and he was enthusiastic about the growth of free public services: 'The librarian
of the British Museum does not ask the reader what have been
his previous services to society, but simply gives him the books he
requires.'[2] He was impressed by the way in which, in the liberal
society of late Victorian England, the state appeared to be ab-
dicating, and voluntary associations taking over. Again and again
he pointed to the British Life-Boat Association as an example of

the way in which society might be organized on the basis of
free cooperation for humane causes by men who made their help
freely available to those in need. He summed up his beliefs as
follows: 'Common possession of the necessaries of production
implies the common enjoyment of the fruits of the common production; and we consider that an equitable organization of
society can only arise when every wage-system is abandoned and
when everybody, contributing to the common well-being to the
full extent of his capacities, shall enjoy from the common stock
of society to the fullest possible extent of his needs.'[1]

It is an ideal that the anarchists have shared with the communists. Mr Khrushchev, for instance, told the 22nd party congress of the communist party of the Soviet Union that in the
decade 1971–80 'the material and technical basis of communism
will be created, and there will be an abundance of material and
cultural benefits for the whole population; Soviet society will come
close to a stage where it can introduce the principle of distribution according to needs'.[2] Kropotkin and his anarchist disciples
thought, however, that these ends could be achieved, not by
centralized state direction, but by mutual cooperation and free
association. Just as he had been impressed by the work of voluntary societies in England, so he saw with optimistic approval
examples of voluntary cooperation on an international scale in
the running of vast enterprises without government intervention.
Indeed, in his enthusiasm for the International Postal Union and
especially for the Compagnie Internationale des Wagon-Lits, he
comes close to a Saint-Simonian faith in the beneficent possibilities of large-scale business concerns. He believed that in the
intermediate stage of the revolution, before the ideal society was
finally established, mutual aid and good sense could solve all
problems. If there were temporary shortages, then rationing
would have to be introduced; and, if this is necessary, 'the last
rations would be reserved for those who need them most; an-
nounce that and you will see whether you will not obtain un-
animous agreement'.[3] He did not believe that such shortages
need last long. He – and still more his wife – was an enthusiastic
gardener, and shared with Fourier a belief in the pleasures and

virtues of gardening; and, indeed, in the difficult years at the end of his life, when he had returned to Russia after the Revolution, it was largely the products of Princess Kropotkin's vegetable garden that kept them alive. He believed that intensive modern methods of market-gardening, as he had observed them in the Channel Islands and elsewhere, could produce enough to feed large urban populations. The Department of Seine-et-Oise alone could, he thought, supply the whole of Paris if properly cultivated. The manufactured goods which the farmer would receive in return for his produce – money having, of course, been abolished – would soon be produced in abundance by improved mechanical processes. Kropotkin had great faith in the possibilities of machines, not only to increase production, but also to perform the tasks which, even in an ideal society, nobody would want to perform. 'If there is still work which is really disagreeable in itself, it is only because our scientific men have never cared to consider the means of rendering it less so,'[1] he wrote, and he was excited because a Mrs Cochrane in Illinois had invented a washing machine.

However, although machines might reduce tedious and unpleasant work, some manual labour would be desirable. Like Proudhon, Kropotkin believed that work had a virtue of its own and he thought that everyone should do some manual work, not only in order to contribute his share towards producing the communal necessities of life but also for its own sake. This was particularly necessary for the writer and artist: authors must first learn to be printers, and painters must experience the scenes they paint. 'He must have seen the sunset as he comes home from work. He must have been a peasant with other peasants to keep its splendour before his eyes.'[2] After a man had done the few hours' work that was needed, he would be free to follow his own pursuits and to produce for himself anything he wanted above what was available in the common fund. At no point would his labour be regulated; nothing would be required of him beyond what he was prepared to give. 'The anarchists conceive of society', Kropotkin wrote in a passage that sums up his main beliefs, 'in which all the mutual relations of its members are regulated, not by laws, not by authorities whether self-imposed or elected, but by mutual agreements between the members of that society and by a sum of social customs and habits – not petrified by law, routine or superstition, but continuously developing and continually readjusted in accordance with the ever-growing requirements of a free life stimulated by the progress of science, invention and the steady growth of higher ideals. No ruling authorities, then. No government of man by man; no crystallization and immobility, but a continual evolution such as we see in nature.'[1]

Kropotkin's appeal lay partly in the goodness and patent sincerity of his own nature, but partly, too, in his optimistic ability to reconcile apparently contradictory desires and values. The revolution need not mean the end of old values; for in the traditional associations and relationships of primitive societies lay the pattern for the new age. A society based on small units need not turn its back on the technical progress of the machine age: 'Have the factory and the workshops at the gates of your fields and gardens.'[2] The village communities would have up-to-date machinery in their communal factories. Moreover, unlike Marx, whose doctrine that all history was the history of class struggles implied that the revolution and the new order would emerge from a bloody clash, Kropotkin suggested that there were already signs in the development of existing society that the process of evolution was at work and that the beneficent processes of nature rather than the relentless forces of the historical dialectic would bring the new order into being.

Because he seemed to offer the best of so many worlds, Kropotkin's disciples and followers were extremely varied. Thus his *Paroles d'un Révolté* (a collection of articles from his paper) and his *Great French Revolution* were translated into Italian by the young socialist schoolmaster Benito Mussolini, who found the first book 'overflowing with a great love of oppressed humanity and infinite kindness'.[3] Gandhi and his followers responded to Kropotkin's populist message and his idea of natural village communities spontaneously springing up. Oscar Wilde was impressed by his personality and message: 'Two of the most perfect lives I have come across in my own experience', he wrote while in prison himself, 'are the lives of Verlaine and of Prince Kropotkin: both of them men who have passed years in prison: the first, the one Christian poet since Dante; the other, a man with a soul of that beautiful white Christ which seems coming out of Russia.'[1] And, in his *Soul of Man under Socialism*, Wilde produced a pamphlet which linked his own aestheticism and religiosity with ideas borrowed from Kropotkin. Few of Kropotkin's successors added much to his doctrine, but, in each generation since, a few gentle and dedicated men and women have found inspiration in his simple childlike optimism and in the hope he offered that man might not be as bad as he seemed and that scientific and technical progress need not necessarily involve a moral retrogression.

The other famous anarchist writers and theorists of the nineties – Malatesta, Jean Grave, Charles Malato, Elisée Reclus, John Most – in fact, added little to Kropotkin's main message, though helping to popularize his ideals. There were, however, naturally differences of interpretation. Malato quarrelled with Grave because the former believed that the anarchist movement needed leaders and some minimal organization. There were constant arguments about the exact nature of the economic organization of the future anarchist world. Was society to be communist, and everything available to all on the principle of 'from each according to his ability, to each according to his need', or was it to be 'collectivist', with the members owning their fields and factories in common on a cooperative basis and preserving some private property? How far could the anarchist movement include the extreme individualists who rejected not only all authority but sometimes all cooperation? In general, however, although passionately conducted and although personal differences often accentuated theoretical divergences of opinion, most of these discussions were rather unrealistic. The essence of anarchism, after all, was freedom of choice and the absence of central direction. There were some anarchist writers who saw that these discussions were at the moment unreal and irrelevant, and one of the most intelligent of the Italian anarchists, Saverio Merlino, summed up the possibilities open for the future as follows: 'Pacts of association can differ much from each other. In one association the workers will pledge themselves to give a certain number of hours of work, in another to carry out a given task in a definite time. The workers in one association will prefer to put the products of their labour in common; others to take a part proportionate to their work.'[1] And, after all, in the meantime the revolution against existing society had still to be made.

2

Among the French working class, already accustomed to hearing Proudhon's doctrines, and in many parts of Italy and Spain where Bakunin and his disciples had been the first to preach revolution, the ideas of Kropotkin, Malatesta and the other anarchist thinkers took root and played an important part in the development of working-class movements and organizations. At the same time, however, anarchism as a political philosophy was particularly attractive to a number of artists and writers who combined a genuine social conscience and sympathy for the poor, among whom out of economic necessity their lives were often spent, with a desire to free themselves from the conventions and hypocrisies of bourgeois life; and so, especially in France, a number of painters and writers became associated more or less closely with the anarchist movement. Not many of them painted or wrote in a style that was particularly anarchist; perhaps it was only the Dada movement a quarter of a century later that attempted to do for artistic conventions what Ravachol or Emile Henry were doing to the social structure.

Proudhon, it is true, had had strong views about the arts, and was in some ways the founder of the doctrine of social realism which has become the official communist aesthetic line in our own day. Art, he thought, must serve a moral and social purpose; it must bring home to people the realities of the life of the poor and move them to change the social system. Art he defined as 'an idealist representation of nature and ourselves with the aim of perfecting our species physically and morally'.[2] He was, as might be expected, opposed to the idea of the artist as an anti-social bohemian or as a devotee of the doctrine of art for art's sake. 'Art for art's sake', he wrote, 'is a debauch of the heart and dissolution of the spirit.'[1] In the society of the future the artist would be 'a citizen, a man like any other; he will follow the same rules, obey the same principles, observe the same conventions, speak the same language, exercise the same rights, fufil the same duties. . . .'[2]

One great painter, Gustave Courbet, was a close friend of Proudhon, as has been mentioned. Courbet inspired much of Proudhon's thinking about art, even though Proudhon's own appreciation of painting was strictly limited. Indeed, Courbet claimed to have written part of Proudhon's *Du Principe de l'Art* himself, though this is probably just an example of the vanity that was so important a trait in Courbet's character. Courbet was, of course, an artist and not a thinker – '*plus artiste que philosophe*', as Proudhon said. Nevertheless, he was a rebel by temperament and, on occasion, an active political as well as artistic revolutionary. He first met Proudhon in the turbulent days of 1848 and soon became interested in his ideas. Some, at least, of his paintings began to have a social message of the kind of which Proudhon approved. When he painted *The Stone Breakers* in 1849, Courbet wrote: 'As I was driving in our carriage on the way to the chateau of Saint-Denis near Maisières, to paint a landscape, I stopped to watch two men breaking stones on the road, the most complete personifications of poverty. An idea for a picture came to me at once. . . . On one side is an old man of seventy, bent over his task, sledge-hammer poised in the air, his skin tanned by the sun, his head shaded by a straw hat; his trousers of coarse material are all patched; inside the cracked sabots torn socks which had once been blue show his bare heels. On the other side is a young man with a dusty head and swarthy complexion; his back and arms show through the holes in his filthy tattered shirt; one leather brace holds up the remnants of his trousers, and his leather boots, covered with mud, gape dismally in several places. The old man is kneeling, the young one stands behind him holding a basket of crushed rock. Alas!

in labour such as this, one's life begins that way, it ends the same way.'[1] Proudhon later made this message explicit in a way that Courbet perhaps did not consciously intend: '*The Stone Breakers* is a satire on our industrial civilization, which constantly invents wonderful machines . . . to . . . perform all kinds of labour . . . and yet is unable to liberate man from the most backbreaking toil.'[2] For Courbet himself, however, the political message of his realism was incidental: 'I stirred up,' he said, 'not deliberately, but simply by painting what I saw, what *they* [the reactionaries] called the social question.'[3]

However, from time to time Courbet painted what he called a 'subversive' picture, of which the most famous is the anti-clerical *Return from the Conference* – a group of drunken priests on their way back from a meeting – which so shocked Catholic opinion that a devout son of the church bought the picture and destroyed it. Courbet's revolutionary temperament made him an active participant in the Commune of 1871. He was himself a member of the Commune and in charge of artistic policy. Thus he was involved in the plans for demolishing the Vendôme Column – a monument, it seemed to him, to Bonapartist despotism and militarism – and as a result he not only served six months in prison but also spent his last years in exile in Switzerland, defending himself against a lawsuit by which he was personally to be held responsible for the cost of re-erecting the column.

Courbet's dissolute bohemianism was far removed from Proudhon's ideal of the artist who would be just like any other citizen. (Indeed, the social nonconformity of artists has been a constant trial to reformers attempting to fit them into a political system.) James Guillaume, who never lost a certain school-masterishness, remembered Courbet at an anarchist congress in the Jura in 1872: 'This good-natured, childish colossus sat down with two or three friends he had brought with him, at a table which was soon covered with bottles; he sang all evening without being asked, in a rough, peasant voice, monotonous country songs from the Franche-Comté, which ended up by boring us.'[4] (Guillaume was not the only one to be distressed by Courbet's tuneless singing, for this had also irritated Berlioz when he was sitting for his portrait.) When Courbet died in 1877 one of the anarchist papers did not claim more for him than to say: 'The greatest merit of Courbet . . . is in our view that he has not created a closed school in the name of realism. Courbet's pupils do not copy him slavishly and do not imitate him; they develop him.'[1]

However much Courbet enjoyed his association with Proudhon and the link between his art and Proudhon's philosophy, it was in art itself that he was truly revolutionary. While art must, he thought, be related to the world in which the painter lived – 'in my opinion, art and talent for an artist can be only means for the application of his personal abilities to the ideas and objects of the age he lives in'[2] – it was in destroying past artistic styles that Courbet's own revolution was made. As he himself wrote of one of his most famous paintings: '*Burial at Ornans** was in reality the burial of romanticism. . . . Through my affirmation of the negation of the ideal and all that springs from the ideal, I have arrived at the emancipation of the individual and finally at democracy. Realism is essentially a democratic art.'[3]

It is true that Courbet's totally unsentimental peasants, his sombre, powerful, unromantic and unidealized landscapes did provide a vision of the world which was in keeping with anarchist philosophy; and the painters of the next generation who were closest to anarchism – Camille Pissarro, Seurat, Signac – were to attempt something similar. Of these painters Camille Pissarro was the most consistently and actively a member of the anarchist movement. He was exiled after the Commune and in 1894 he had to take refuge in Belgium to avoid the persecution of the anarchists in France after the murder of President Carnot.[4] Some of his lithographs, such as *Les Porteuses de bois* and *Les Sans-Gîte*, were executed for anarchist periodicals, and he designed a cover for a pamphlet by Kropotkin. He was a friend of the anarchist editor and publicist, Jean Grave, and had read a considerable amount of political theory, including Marx as well as Kropotkin. His attitude towards the latter was best expressed in a letter he

* In the Louvre.

wrote in 1892: 'I have just read Kropotkin's book (*La Conquête du Pain*). I must confess that, if it is utopian, it is in any case a very beautiful dream. And, as we have often had the example of utopias which have become realities, nothing prevents us from believing that this may well be possible one day, unless mankind founders and returns to complete barbarism.'[1]

When in 1894, the Paris police seized the subscription list of *La Révolte*, Jean Grave's paper which had previously been edited by Kropotkin, the names it contained were impressive and included Alphonse Daudet, Anatole France, Stéphane Mallarmé and Lecomte de Lisle, as well as those artists and writers more actively and practically involved with the anarchist movement, such as Signac, Maximilien Luce, Camille Pissarro and Octave Mirbeau. Few of the artists, however, who knew Jean Grave personally or subscribed to *La Révolte* bothered to work out their anarchist beliefs very far. For them, anarchism was simply the natural creed for artists who regarded themselves aesthetically as in the *avant-garde* and therefore as irrevocably opposed to bourgeois society, which treated them with ridicule and refused to buy their work, and which, at the same time, refused very many of their fellow citizens a decent way of life. 'Everything new', the critic Felix Fénéon wrote in an article about Pissarro, 'to be accepted requires that many old fools must die. We are longing for this to happen as soon as possible.'[2] Most artists and writers were too occupied with their own aesthetic discoveries and experiments to worry about anarchist ideas in any detail. Mallarmé, although he replied, when asked for his views on terrorism, that he 'could not discuss the acts of these saints', was nevertheless more interested in the development of his own esoteric, symbolist poetic world. Seurat, too, the most self-consciously theoretical of the post-impressionist painters, although he seems to have had anarchist sympathies, and although pictures like *La Baignade à Asnières*,* with its working-class bathers and background of factory chimneys, show aspects of urban industrial life, was primarily concerned with his scientific theories of colour which, he claimed, provided a new basis for painting, rather than

---

* In the National Gallery, London.

with anarchist theories which would provide a new basis for society, or at least a new range of subject-matter for painters.

Even Signac, who was more politically involved – and, unlike Seurat, who died in 1891 at the age of thirty-two, not only lived through the anarchist decade of the nineties but also survived long enough to end up as an active supporter of the communist party – had a clear conception of the frontier between ideology and art. 'The anarchist painter', he said in a lecture in 1902, 'is not one who will show anarchist paintings, but one who without regard for lucre, without desire for reward, will struggle with all his individuality, with a personal effort, against bourgeois and official conventions. . . . The subject is nothing, or at least is only one part of the work of art, not more important than the other elements, colour, drawing, composition . . . when the eye is educated, the people will see something other than the subject in pictures. When the society we dream of exists, the worker, freed from the exploiters who brutalize him, will have time to think and to learn. He will appreciate the different qualities of the work of art.'[1] Signac himself occasionally executed allegorical paintings or works with direct propagandist implications, but his art was never dominated by them. In spite of his anarchist sympathies, he and the others among the disciples of Seurat who shared these beliefs – Luce or Théo van Rysselberghe – did not produce anarchist art; still less did the most philosophical and reflective artist to be associated with them, Camille Pissarro.

It was the anarchist critics and journalists who persuaded many artists and writers that their instinctive revolt against bourgeois society and their sympathy with the sufferings of the poor should drive them to active support of the anarchist movement. Felix Fénéon, for example – the critic who first recognized Seurat's genius and originality and who coined the term 'post-impressionism' – was a convinced anarchist, in spite of his dandified appearance and his post as a minor civil servant in the War Ministry. He was associated with a number of advanced literary and artistic periodicals, and, after his dismissal from the War Ministry, he became assistant editor of the most important and influential of all of the artistic reviews of the 1890s, the *Revue*

Blanche. He was a friend of the symbolist poets Mallarmé and Jules Laforgue, as well as of Verlaine and the post-impressionist painters. He made no secret of his anarchist beliefs and when, after the murder of President Carnot, thirty men were accused of criminal conspiracy, he was one of them. He seems to have enjoyed the occasion: when the judge asked him where the detonators which were found in his office came from, he replied: 'My father picked them up in the street.' 'How do you explain detonators being found in the street?' the judge asked. 'The police magistrate asked me why I had not thrown them out of the window,' Fénéon answered. 'You see, one may find detonators in the street.'[1] It is hard to tell how far Fénéon's conspiratorial anarchism went, and how far it was an affectation; but it cost him a spell in prison and lost him his job in the ministry. Another Parisian anarchist writer, Laurent Tailhade, who coined a famous phrase about terrorism – '*Qu'importe les vagues humanités, pourvu que le geste soit beau*' – was less fortunate and became the victim of his own beliefs, for he lost an eye when a bomb exploded in the restaurant where he was eating.

In general, however, for the artists and writers, anarchism represented a general attitude to life rather than a specific theory about society, except for those who, like Pissarro, Signac and Octave Mirbeau, were linked with Jean Grave and *La Révolte*, or who, like Steinlen, sometimes wrote or drew for one or other of the anarchist papers or periodicals. While some of them, such as Camille Pissarro, were attracted by the generosity of Kropotkin's ideas and the vision of a world where men would live in free association with each other, others were excited by the assertion that there should be no limits to an individual's freedom other than those imposed by his own nature; their emotions were deeply stirred by the violent gestures of the anarchists. Alongside the social anarchism of Kropotkin or Malatesta there grew up a wild, bohemian, individualist anarchism which was often an embarrassment to the more constructive and philosophical anarchists. Maurice Barrès, for example, one of the most brilliant of a brilliant generation, in the novels of his youth grouped under the title of *Le Culte du Moi* and, more specifically, in *L'Ennemi des*

Lois (1892), makes his heroes look at ethical systems, philosophies
and ways of life in search of a means of total self-expression without regard to convention or the needs of others. In *L'Ennemi des
Lois*, the protagonists – after studying Saint-Simon, Fourier and
Marx – are converted by a scene in a vivisection laboratory into
anarchists, and retire to the country to lead a life of selfish
altruism: 'For them, other selves exist to the same extent as their
own, so that the conditions of the happiness of others are blended
with the conditions of their own happiness. They do not break
the flowers which they love to smell; if they suffered it would
diminish their pleasure; their refined sensuality suppresses all
immorality.'[1] Although the search for self-development and self-
expression was one way of expounding a 'morality without
obligation or sanctions', it was a very different one from that of
Kropotkin and his disciples. As Jean Grave pointed out when
writing of *L'Ennemi des Lois*: 'The anarchism presented in this
book is only an anarchism appropriate to millionaires. To free
oneself from the laws it is necessary to have an income of 100,000
francs or to marry a wife who has it. . . . Nevertheless this is an
interesting book to read in that it proclaims the individual freed
from society and the sole judge of his happiness.'[2]

Into the intellectual world of Paris, already familiar with the
notions of a morality without obligation or sanctions and eager
to assert the freedom of the individual from the restraints of
society, came the doctrines of Nietzsche. His works began to
appear in French translation in the late nineties and, however
much people may have differed about the meaning of their
message, at least he shouted defiance at bourgeois conventions and
encouraged the development of each personality to its limits,
regardless of the violence this might involve. Nietzsche was too
inconsistent a writer to supply anyone with a coherent pattern of
life, but his 'reversal of all values', the claim that 'God is dead'
and the command *Du sollst werden, der du bist** all encouraged
anyone who wanted to break with contemporary values, moral
aesthetic or political. As Emma Goldman put it: 'Nietzsche was
not a social theorist, but a poet and innovator. His aristocracy

* You must become who you are.

was neither of birth nor of purse; it was of the spirit. In that respect Nietzsche was an anarchist, and all true anarchists were aristocrats.'[1] A few intellectuals, around the turn of the century, already aware of Nietzsche's ideas in some form or other, discovered another German writer who seemed to some people to provide a philosophical basis for a doctrine of individualist anarchism. This was Max Stirner.

Stirner was the pen name of an obscure German philosopher, a retired teacher in an academy for young ladies who moved on the fringe of Hegelian circles. His main work *Der Einzige und sein Eigentum* (usually translated into English as *The Ego and Its Own*) was published in 1845 and aroused little outside interest, although Bakunin knew about his ideas. However, his work was rediscovered in the German-speaking world in the 1890s. It was known to the Danish critic Brandes and also to Ibsen, and extracts from a French translation appeared in the *Revue Blanche* in 1900. Stirner, in tortuous, obscure, repetitive, splenetic prose declared war on society and on all past philosophy. His immediate target was the Hegelian belief in spirit as the moving factor in human development, and especially the religious Hegelianism of Feuerbach, but more generally he attacked both Christian moral teaching and that of Kant. 'The divine is God's affair; the human the affair of "humanity". My business is neither the divine nor the human, it is not what is True, Good, Right, Free, etc., but only what is *mine*, and it is not something general but is individual (*einzig*) as I am individual. For me nothing is higher than myself.'[2] This is his essential message, repeated in one form or another on every page, and it is summed up in his conclusion: 'I am owner of my own strength when I am aware of myself as an individual. In the individual even the owner (*Eigner*) returns to his creative nothingness out of which he was born. Every higher being over me, whether God or man, weakens the feeling of my own individuality, and only pales before the sun of my consciousness. If I place my trust in myself, the unique individual (*den Einzigen*), then it is based on its own passing mortal creator which itself vanishes, and I can say I have based my trust on nothing. (*Ich habe meine Sache auf Nichts gestellt.*)'[3] It is a doctrine that comes very near to some forms of later existentialism.

Stirner was not a very important thinker nor a very interesting one, though capable of the occasional striking phrase, such as: 'A Prussian officer once said, "Every Prussian carries a policeman in his breast." ' However the extreme nature of his views seemed to many young intellectuals the most complete expression of all their anti-conventional values. Benito Mussolini, who in his left-wing socialist days had considerable sympathy for anarchism, wrote in 1912: 'Let the way be opened for the elemental forces of the individual, for no other human reality exists except the individual. We shall support all that exalts, amplifies the individual, that gives him greater freedom, greater well-being, greater latitude of life; we shall fight all that depresses, mortifies the individual. Why cannot Stirner become fashionable again?'[1]

Individual anarchism was of little political importance and was often, in its extreme solipsism and violent self-expression, an embarrassment to the anarchists who believed in a social revolution rather than simply a rejection of conventional moral values. Nevertheless, it was a factor in the psychological make-up of many revolutionaries. Through the writings of Nietzsche and Stirner, it could produce a self-made superman like Mussolini; it could contribute to the defiant assault on the past by the Futurists. It could also produce the early twentieth-century version of the 'beat' of the 1950s – figures like the bearded, ragged, passionate man who called himself Libertad and founded in Paris a weekly called *L'Anarchie* and a series of *causeries populaires* to propagate his ideas of total individual freedom. It could haunt the imagination of writers, so that echoes of the ideas of individual anarchism can already be heard in Ibsen's *Peer Gynt*, as well as in later works such as Gide's *Immoralist* and in the *'acte gratuit'* of Lafcadio in his *Les Caves du Vatican*. It could drive men off to live in free communities – most of which only lasted a short time, and which were condemned by many anarchist thinkers, such as Elisée Reclus, who wrote: 'We must not shut ourselves up at any price; we must remain in the vast world to receive all its impressions, to take part in all its vicissitudes and to receive all its instruction.'[2]

There was a young Russian émigré who took the name of Victor Serge and who was later to become a successful writer and a member of the Left Opposition in the Soviet Union, though he was imprisoned there in the 1930s and later escaped from Russia. While he was moving in anarchist circles in Paris and Brussels in the early years of the century he visited an anarchist colony founded by Fortuné Henry, the brother of Emile Henry, the famous terrorist. Serge's account of the divergent tendencies among the people he met there shows how many beliefs were embraced by the label 'anarchist': 'Tramps, a little Swiss plasterer of prodigious intelligence, a Russian officer who was a Tolstoyan anarchist with a noble blond head, who had escaped after the failure of an insurrection and who a year later was to die of hunger in the Forest of Fontainebleau . . . then a formidable chemist who came from Odessa via Buenos Aires, all helped to answer the great problems. The individualist printer: "There's only yourself in the world; try not to be either a *salaud* or a *nouille*." The Tolstoyan: "Let us be new men, salvation is within us." The Swiss plasterer . . . "All right, but don't let's forget to use our fists in the factories." The chemist, after listening a long time said with his Russo-Spanish accent: "All that's humbug: in the social war we need good laboratories." '[1]

The whole point of anarchism in the 1890s was that it was not a coherent political or philosophical movement. A creed which could include Kropotkin and the extreme individualist disciples of Stirner, a criminal like Ravachol or a great artist like Camille Pissarro, bohemian intellectuals and tough working-class labour bosses – such a creed owed its attraction to the very fact that it embraced so many disparate individuals and temperaments. However, if it was to become a serious and effective social force in the twentieth century, new methods of action and fresh ideas were going to be needed. In the first quarter of the twentieth century the anarchists were to see yet another revolution going wrong, and to attempt new tactics and even accept a degree of organization in the hope of still achieving their own social revolution.

CHAPTER VII
The Revolution that Failed

'They have shown how the revolution is *not* to be made.'

Kropotkin

The atmosphere of academic, even though passionate, discussion about the future society, the growing strength of the political working-class parties in Germany, France and Italy, as well as the revulsion caused by the frequent acts of terrorism, all tended to make the anarchist intellectuals increasingly unrevolutionary, and their groups mostly became – like the devoted anarchist groups in London or New York today – centres for unorthodox speculation about society rather than cells preparing revolutionary action. As Lenin put it contemptuously in 1918: 'The majority of anarchists think and write about the future without understanding the present. That is what divides us communists from them.'[1]

Malatesta later remembered Kropotkin saying to him: 'My dear Errico, I am afraid we are alone, you and I, in believing that the revolution is near.'[2] In fact, even Kropotkin sometimes doubted it, but Malatesta never lost his revolutionary enthusiasm and temperament. 'It seems to me today', he wrote in 1906, 'that the anarchists have let themselves fall into the opposite fault to the violent excesses. We now need rather to react against a certain tendency to compromise and a quiet life which is displayed in our circle. It is more necessary now to revive the languishing revolutionary ardour, the spirit of sacrifice, the love of risk.'[3]

Malatesta had led the life of an exile after leaving Italy in the autumn of 1878. He went briefly to visit some Italian friends in Egypt, but the Italian authorities made representations to have him deported and he made his way to the great anarchist centre, Geneva, where he became a friend of Kropotkin and of Elisée

Reclus. But he was not left in peace and was expelled from the canton of Geneva after a few months. He went to Rumania for a short spell, and then to Paris, where he was able for a while to pursue his trade as a mechanic till the police again made life difficult for him. In 1881 he reached London, which was to be his main base for nearly forty years. However, whenever an opportunity occurred to return to Italy he took it; he was back in Florence and in trouble with the police in 1885. Then he went to South America and spent four years in the Argentine, where he spread anarchist ideas among the Italian immigrants and left an anarchist stamp on the organized working-class movement which was to last well into the twentieth century. But it was the revolution in Europe, and especially in Italy, that was his main concern, and at the end of 1889 he returned to London, waiting for a chance to go back to Italy again. The chance seemed to have come early in 1897, at a time when bad harvests and rising prices had led to peasant revolts, and when, as a result of the demand for strong action against strikers and rioters, constitutional government seemed to be in danger. Actually, Malatesta was not able to play any part in the industrial and political struggles in Italy in 1898 and 1899, since he was arrested early in 1898. He had gone to the port of Ancona, where there was an active anarchist group among the dockers and several anarchist publications,[1] and he had thrown himself into the cause of the anti-political revolution, opposing those anarchists such as Saverio Merlino who felt that in an emergency anarchists should participate in elections to support the liberal and social-democratic cause. It was a suggestion to which Malatesta's firm reply, made after he was in prison, was: 'I beg you not to make use of my name in the electoral struggle fought by the socialists and republicans. I protest not only that it would be without my agreement, but also with my express disapproval.'[2] Malatesta was arrested after riots in Ancona and charged with 'criminal association' – a charge, with its implication that anarchists were no better than common criminals, which brought a cry of rage from the international anarchist community. In the event, Malatesta and his friends were convicted of belonging to a 'seditious association'; Malatesta was sentenced to imprisonment and sent to the island of Lampe-dusa. However, in May 1899, he succeeded in escaping in a boat during a storm and returned to London via Malta and Gib-raltar.

After a visit to the United States and to the strong Italian and Spanish anarchist groups in New Jersey, he talked of visiting Cuba, but does not, in fact, seem to have done so. By the follow-ing year he was back in London, still waiting – like Mazzini half a century earlier – for the chance to take his place in the Italian revolution. During these last years of his stay in London, Mala-testa was watched closely by the British police, particularly after the assassination of King Umberto in 1900 by an Italian member of an anarchist group from Paterson, New Jersey – an act of pure anarchist propaganda by the deed, carried out by a man thirty years old, happily married, and moved only by a cold and fanati-cal fury. Because of the continuous suspicions of the London police, Malatesta was involved in one of the sensational criminal episodes of Edwardian England, the Houndsditch murders and the 'Siege of Sidney Street'.

On 16 December 1910 the police were called to a jeweller's shop in Houndsditch in the East End of London. A gang of thieves had attempted to break in by means of a tunnel from an empty house next door. When the police arrived three policemen were shot and the robbers escaped, although one of them had been wounded. The wounded man was taken to the house of a girl who had been regularly attending the meetings of the anar-chist groups in the East End, and there he died. The girl was arrested, but produced no information: she seems to have known very little about the criminals, whom she knew simply as Peter the Painter and Fritz. Then, among the equipment left in the empty house, a cylinder of oxygen and a blow lamp were found; near them was a card with Malatesta's name and address. What had happened, apparently, was that a Latvian who went under the name of Muromtsev had, some months earlier, asked the anarchists in the East End for assistance in finding a job. They had sent him to Malatesta, who himself was earning his living as a mechanic; and Malatesta had given him a card of introduction to his suppliers to enable Muronzeff to obtain the equipment for his trade, which turned out to be burglary rather than engineering. Malatesta was at once arrested and, although his innocence was very soon established, the attention of the popular papers had already been drawn to the sensational story of dangerous foreign criminal anarchists in London. The Houndsditch affair had an even more dramatic sequel. The murderers barricaded themselves in a house in Sidney Street in Stepney, and it was only after troops had been called out and the Home Secretary, Winston Churchill, had personally supervised their disposition, that the two remaining members of the gang were killed.

Although the whole affair might have led to a general anarchist scare – as the Chicago bomb and the assassination of President McKinley had done in the United States – it probably only served to emphasize the innocence of the anarchists in London. An attempt to deport Malatesta a year or so later failed, and the other anarchists in England remained unmolested. Rudolf Rocker,* a German anarchist who (although a Gentile himself) devoted years to social work among the Jews in the sweatshops of the East End tailors, recalled the descent of the journalists on his club after the Sidney Street affair, and reported the somewhat disappointed reaction of one of them, Philip Gibbs, who wrote in the *Graphic*: 'So I sat, a solitary Englishman, among all these foreign anarchists, for more than an hour, during which nothing happened except friendly greetings, handclasps, voluble conversation in subdued voices and a foreign tongue. . . . Nothing happened to me. I could laugh now at my fears. These alien anarchists were as tame as rabbits. I am convinced that they had not a revolver among them. Yet remembering the words I heard, I am sure that this intellectual anarchy, this philosophy of revolution, is more dangerous than pistols or nitro-glycerine. For out of that anarchist club in the East End come ideas.'[1] At least one foreign revolutionary, however, was enthusiastic about the exploits of Peter the Painter and his anarchist significance.

---

* Rocker was a characteristic anarchist in that he preferred to be turned back by the U.S. immigration authority rather than go through a ceremony of marriage with the woman with whom he lived devotedly and faithfully throughout a long life.

Peter and his companions were, Benito Mussolini wrote, 'anarchists . . . in the classical sense of the word. Haters of work, they had the courage to proclaim it once and for all, because physical work brutalizes and degrades man, haters of property which seals the difference between one individual and another, haters of life, but above all, haters, negators, destroyers of society.'[1]

Malatesta made another effort to get away into a truly revolutionary atmosphere in Italy – an atmosphere to which Mussolini was contributing as a left-wing socialist editor and agitator who was not without sympathy for anarchist methods. In 1913 Malatesta returned again to Ancona and took an active part in the anti-clerical and anti-parliamentary campaign which the anarchists were organizing. Then, in the famous 'Red Week' of June 1914, there broke out in central Italy a series of demonstrations which turned into an effective general strike. The anarchists tried to make this movement into a genuinely insurrectional one in accordance with their own beliefs. Malatesta recalled that, after the police had killed two young men in Ancona, 'The tramway strike paralysed the traffic, all the shops were shut and the general strike became a reality without the need of discussing or proclaiming it. On the next and subsequent days Ancona was in a state of political insurrection. The armouries were sacked, grain was requisitioned, a sort of organization was established to procure the necessities of life. The city was full of soldiers, there were warships in the harbour, the authorities sent out strong patrols, but they did not order repression, probably because they were not sure of being able to count on the obedience of the soldiers and sailors. Indeed, the soldiers and sailors fraternized with the people: the women, the incomparable women of Ancona, embraced the soldiers, gave them wine and cigarettes and exhorted them to mix with the people. . . .'[2] Although the movement spread, and others besides the anarchists – socialists and even liberal republicans – seemed ready for revolt, the General Confederation of Labour, which controlled most of the trade unions, called off the strike and the movement quickly collapsed. It was a sign of how little control the anarchists really had over the labour movement, in Italy at least, and how far the realities of the twentieth century were from the insurrectionary dreams of Malatesta's youth.

Malatesta returned sadly to London. He quarrelled with Kropotkin over Kropotkin's support for the war; and he remained a voice of the anarchist conscience constantly declaring that – to quote the title of one of his English articles of 1914 – 'The anarchists have forgotten their principles.' After the war, at the end of 1919, he finally returned to Italy and plunged with as much enthusiasm as ever into the social, political and industrial unrest of the years that ended with Mussolini's march on Rome. Malatesta, for all the revolutionary prestige he still enjoyed and in spite of his reputation for incorruptible honesty and warm humanity, was unable to influence events much. He refused to countenance political and parliamentary activity; at the same time he had grave doubts about using the trade unions as a means of making the revolution, for he believed that the unions demanded a degree of organization and, above all, the existence of permanent officials, which was something his anarchist principles would not allow him to accept. After some difficulty with the government and also with the French – who refused him permission to cross France because he had been expelled for political offences forty years earlier – Malatesta returned to Italy in triumph. (It is said that the seamen of Genoa stopped work and that all the ships' whistles sounded in his honour.) But his old age was spent in obscurity and disappointment, though his courage and spirit never failed.

Malatesta was imprisoned by the Italian government in 1921; he and his companions went on hunger strike as a protest against the delay in bringing them to trial. He was finally released some two months before the fascists came to power. In fact, they did not interfere with the old man – Malatesta was now nearly seventy – and he lived quietly in Rome, earning his living with his hands as he had always done, so that members of the Roman bourgeoisie were sometimes startled to learn that the small, gentle, elderly electrician who worked for them was, in fact, the terrible Malatesta. He died in 1932. His hopes that the anarchists in Italy would be strong enough to serve as a leaven in the revolutionary

movement and to turn it to truly anarchist ends had been disappointed. The Italian state was, at the end of his life, a stronger
and more formidable adversary than it had ever been.

What was equally disturbing, however, was that the Russian
Revolution had – like 1789, or 1848, or 1871 – left the anarchists
disappointed and disillusioned. Yet another revolution had taken
place and yet again it was the wrong revolution, so that the true
social revolution was still to be made. Malatesta had never had
any illusions about what had happened in Russia; and his
epitaph on Lenin sums up his attitude: 'Lenin is dead. We can
feel for him that kind of enforced admiration which strong men,
even when deluded, even when wicked, can extract from the
crowd, men who succeed in leaving as they pass a deep mark on
history: Alexander, Julius Caesar, Loyola, Cromwell, Robespierre, Napoleon. But, even with the best intentions, he was a
tyrant who strangled the Russian revolution – and we who could
not admire him while alive, cannot mourn him now he is dead.
Lenin is dead. Long live Liberty!'[1]

If Malatesta felt disillusioned by what had happened in
Russia, the disappointment was even more bitter for others of
his generation, and especially, of course, for Peter Kropotkin,
who all his life had believed in and worked for the revolution in
Russia. When it finally came, in February 1917, he was all too
ready to interpret the facts to fit his theories: 'What they reproached us with as a fantastic utopia has been accomplished
without a single casualty. The free organizations which sprang
up during the war to care for the wounded, for supplies for the
distribution of provisions, the unloading of trains, and so many
other ends, have replaced on 2nd March the whole ancient litter
of functionaries, police, etc. They have opened the prison gates,
declared the ancient government non-existent, and what is best,
have one after another disarmed and expelled all the police, high
and low.'[2] When he returned, after over forty years of exile, to
face the realities of Russia in the summer of 1917 he was bound
to be disappointed. His own position was a curious one, for his
support of the war had alienated from him nearly all the revolutionaries on the left, and his opposition to government as such

made it hard for him to collaborate very far with the moderate members of the provisional government. His personal position was a strong one and he had been given a warm welcome; but, quite apart from his political beliefs, his failing health prevented him from playing a very active role. After the October Revolution he devoted himself more and more to writing and for the most part lived quietly in the country, receiving a few Russian anarchists and friends from abroad – Emma Goldman and Alexander Berkman, or the British socialist Margaret Bondfield. After the bolshevik revolution he was able to forget his differences with the Russian anarchists on the issue of the war, but, although in touch with some of them, he was unable to take any practical part in the movement or to prevent its liquidation by the communists.

Kropotkin himself was left unmolested: but he did not hesitate to attack Lenin – with whom he had at least one interview – in the most bitter terms. When the bolsheviks took hostages from Wrangel's anti-revolutionary army, Kropotkin wrote to Lenin: 'I cannot believe that there is no single man about you to tell you that such decisions recall the darkest Middle Ages, the periods of the Crusades. Vladimir Ilyich, your concrete actions are completely unworthy of the ideas you pretend to hold. . . . What future lies in store for communism when one of its most important defenders tramples in this way on every honest feeling?'[1] While he made the best of the situation when talking to foreign visitors and never gave up his innate optimism, his last months (he died in February 1921) were full of doubts and anxieties, and in one of the last documents he wrote he expressed the helplessness of a whole generation of revolutionaries:

'The revolution will advance in its own way, in the direction of the least resistance, without paying the slightest attention to our efforts. At the present moment the Russian revolution is in the following position. It is perpetrating horrors. It is ruining the whole country. In its mad fury it is annihilating human lives. That is why it is a revolution and not a peaceful progress, because it is destroying without regarding what it destroys and whither it goes.

'And we are powerless for the present to direct it into another channel, until such time as it will have played itself out. It must wear itself out. . . . Therefore the only thing we can do is to use our energy to lessen the fury and force of the oncoming reaction. But in what can our efforts consist?

'To modify the passions – on one side or the other? Who is likely to listen to us? Even if there exist those who can do anything in this role, the time of their début is not yet come; neither the one nor the other side is yet disposed to listen to them. I see one thing: we must gather together people who will be capable of undertaking constructive work in each and every party after the revolution has worn itself out.'[1]

The actual experience of the Russian anarchists in the revolution justified Kropotkin's pessimism and, indeed, showed that an anarchist revolution in Europe was even more remote than it had ever been. The situation in Russia had, at first, seemed to provide an excellent opportunity for putting Bakunin's teachings into practice with more hope of success than there had ever been in, for instance, Italy at the time of the ill-fated risings in Bologna and the south in the 1870s. There was, in 1917, a virtual breakdown of the authority of the state; workers' and peasants' soviets had formed and these might be expected to form the basis of anarchist communes; all over the country there was a great deal of spontaneous, as yet undirected, revolutionary activity and a profound desire for social change. There were a number of anarchist groups in Russia, although they had been obliged to operate secretly, and, in any case, were only a small minority compared with the other left-wing parties – the social revolutionaries and the two branches of the social democrats, menshevik and bolshevik. The anarchists, too, were divided among themselves: some were anarcho-syndicalists and placed their hope of revolution in the action of the workers' unions which would take over the factories. Others were communist anarchists and disciples of Kropotkin, who saw social revolution coming about through the formation of local communes which would then join in a federation. Again, there were a certain number of individualist anarchists, distrustful of any except the freest and most spontaneous forms of association; others were followers of Tolstoy who were opposed to violence and who, it was said, refused as a matter of principle to kill the lice which they plucked from their beards.

During the summer of 1917 these various and diverse small groups tried to intensify their propaganda and their influence. The Federation of Anarchist Groups in Moscow produced a daily paper; in Petrograd the Union for Anarcho-Syndicalist Propaganda, run by a group of anarchists headed by Voline, who had recently returned from exile in New York, published weekly their *Golos Truda* (The Voice of Labour); in the Ukraine a Confederation of Anarchist Organizations took the name of *Nabat* (Tocsin) from their newspaper. What all anarchists could agree on was the necessity of throwing themselves into the revolution and, as Bakunin had taught, trying by their revolutionary example to steer it along anarchist lines. As *Golos Truda* wrote in the critical days preceding the bolshevik seizure of power: 'If the action of the masses should commence, then, as anarchists, we will participate in it with the greatest possible energy. For we cannot put ourselves out of touch with the revolutionary masses, even if they are not following our course and our appeals, and even if we foresee the defeat of the movement. We never forget that it is impossible to foresee either the direction or the result of a movement by the masses. Consequently, we consider it our duty to participate in such a movement, seeking to communicate *our* meaning, *our* ideas, *our* truth to it.'[1]

Determined as the anarchists were not to corrupt the revolution by using means which would, in their view, merely reestablish the equivalent of the old order, they opposed even the slogan 'All Power to the Soviets!' because they objected to the concept of power. And it was this disregard of the fact of power that made them unable to achieve very much, and made it possible, within three years, for the bolsheviks to destroy the anarchist movement in Russia completely. If, as occasionally happened, the anarchists were sufficiently influential in a factory to persuade the workers to take it over and run it on anarchist lines, then quickly the local bolshevik leaders would force it to close. If a prominent anarchist wanted to give a lecture or hold a meeting, he would find that the bolsheviks in control of the local soviet would see that there was no hall available. 'Liberty,' Lenin remarked to Alexander Berkman, 'is a luxury not to be permitted at the present stage of development.'[1]

There were circumstances, however, when Lenin was temporarily too weak to control the anarchists or when he was prepared to tolerate them temporarily if they were effectively fighting a common enemy. Thus, in the Ukraine, an anarchist-led guerrilla army was able to carry on an effective existence for over two years. This was almost entirely the work of Nestor Makhno, a tough young revolutionary who emerged from prison in 1917, after nine years' imprisonment on a charge of murdering a police officer.[2] Makhno was born in 1889 into a family of the poorest peasantry. He found work in a local foundry and, after the 1905 revolution, took up anarchism. While in prison, he had been much influenced by a self-taught anarchist theorist, Arshinov. When he was released he went back to his native town in the southern Ukraine and, by the force of his personality, succeeded in building up an anarchist movement which seemed to the peasants to give them just what they wanted – an immediate seizure of the land, which they carried out in September 1917. After the October Revolution the local soviet watched the growth of Makhno's influence uneasily, but did nothing to stop him – even when he successfully negotiated, on the best anarchist principles, a direct exchange of grain produced by his peasants for textiles produced by anarchist workers in a Moscow factory. In his own area Makhno was carrying out the basic anarchist strategy of working for the revolution with others, especially the left social revolutionaries, fighting on the same side in the face of the threat from the white armies, while at the same time spreading anarchist ideas, methods and influences.

The Treaty of Brest-Litovsk in March 1918, by which the bolshevik government made peace with Germany (much to the indignation of the social revolutionaries and anarchists, who had hopes of combining a protracted guerrilla war with a social revolution), gave the Germans and Austrians control of the

Ukraine. The advance of their troops drove the various guerrilla bands out of the area, and for the time being put a stop to Makhno's activity. He himself set out on a tour of Russia, and was disappointed to find that, with the establishment of bolshevik power, the anarchist groups had been largely dissolved and many anarchists had been arrested or had disappeared. He visited Kropotkin, and the old prophet gave the young rebel a word of advice: 'One must remember, dear comrade, that there is no sentimentality about our struggle, but selflessness and strength of heart on our way towards our goal will conquer all.'[1] Makhno also managed to see Lenin and to talk with him about conditions in the Ukraine; and he was both impressed and bewildered. Lenin made no concessions to Makhno's anarchist beliefs, but he seems to have been struck by his toughness and energy, and he probably felt that it was better to send so vigorous a young revolutionary back home to fight the Germans than keep him waiting in Moscow. Accordingly, with the help of the bolshevik authorities, Makhno succeeded in returning to the Ukraine and there set about organizing an effective guerrilla force – the Insurgent Army of the Ukraine – to harass both the German and Austrian occupation army and the puppet Ukrainian government which they had established. Makhno's supporters were not all anarchists, and he was constantly having to intervene to curb the expression of anti-Semitic feelings among the peasants, to whom the Jew was a traditional scapegoat and the Jewish money-lender or pedlar a symbol of the economic order they were aiming to destroy. Makhno claimed, as opposed to the bolsheviks, that his army remained 'unchangeably true to the Revolution of the Peasants and Workers, but not to instruments of violence like your Commissars and Chekas'.[2] He made it clear that his army was dedicated to the anarchist cause, and they carried the anarchist black flag throughout.

Makhno had at once to face the problems confronting anarchists in practice, and found, just as the Spanish anarchists were to do when engaged in a civil war nineteen years later, that compromises had to be made. One of the main subjects of discussion was whether the army should be recruited voluntarily or whether the soldiers should be conscripted from the areas which it controlled. Makhno decided for conscription – partly because the peasants were less afraid of reprisals from the other side if they could say they had been forced to serve. Makhno's following was mainly in the countryside – he remained himself a peasant in outlook and manners – and the problems of organization in the towns proved more difficult. When, for example, the railway workers of Alexandrovsk complained that they had had no pay, they were given the almost Godwinian advice to come to an equitable understanding with the railway users. And, at a congress of peasants, workers and insurgents in October 1919, a peasant voiced one of the perpetual problems of anarchist social organization: 'If there is a bridge between two of our villages and the bridge gets broken, who is to repair it? If neither village wishes to do the work, then we shall not have a bridge and we will not be able to go to town.'[1]

Still, the anarchist bakers of Alexandrovsk produced a scheme for providing bread for the population; and, in the areas controlled by Makhno, certain anarchist principles were established. Plans were made for anarchist education modelled on Ferrer's experiments in Spain;* freedom of the press was established, though not freedom of political organization, since this was contrary to anarchist belief. The basis of anarchist justice was also laid down: 'On the question of the need to organize a judicial administrative apparatus we suggest as a basic principle that any rigid court and police machinery and any definite codification of laws constitute infringements of the population's rights of self-defence. . . . True justice cannot be administratively organized, but must come as a living, free creative act of the community. . . . Law and order must be upheld by the living force of the local community and must not be left to police specialists.'[2] As in the Spanish Civil War, it was a principle that could very easily be used to justify summary execution and arbitrary terror.

Within the limits imposed by conditions of guerrilla warfare, Makhno seems indeed to have done his best to run the areas he controlled on anarchist lines. The seizure of land in September

* For Ferrer's career and ideas see Chapter IX below.

1917 had been followed by the establishment of agricultural communes; and, in a remote rural area cut off by war from the outside world, and where economic organization was in any case primitive, some sort of anarchist system of production and exchange worked to the satisfaction of the peasants. At the same time, Makhno, although retaining the military command in his own hands, adopted the idea that supreme authority rested with the new periodical congresses of workers, peasants and insurgents.

In the main, however, his task was necessarily a military one. During the summer of 1918 he harried the German and Austrian forces in a series of raids and, when they were obliged to withdraw because of the armistice in the west, Makhno used the opportunity to seize their stores and ammunition. During the next months his relations with the bolsheviks remained comparatively friendly. He was fanatically determined to wage ferocious war against all enemies of the revolution, whether they were Germans or white generals, and he was perfectly willing to do this in alliance with the bolsheviks. However, the appeal of Makhnovite anarchism to the peasant soldiers in the Red Army was enough to arouse bolshevik hostility; and when Makhno invited soldiers in the bolshevik forces to attend his anarchist congresses, this was something the bolshevik leaders could not forgive. In the spring of 1919 they decided that Makhno was no longer an ally, though at this point, when they themselves were being pressed on all sides, there was little they could do to deal with an army which by now numbered some 15,000. In the meantime Makhno conducted his campaign with considerable efficiency, but also with considerable brutality. His personal habits – he was drinking heavily and his affairs with women were notorious – and the inevitable compromises in which anarchist principles were sacrificed, worried some of his anarchist supporters from the *Nabat* group: 'While possessing many valuable revolutionary qualities,' they were to say of Makhno in 1920, 'he belongs unfortunately to that class of person who cannot always subordinate their personal caprices to the good of the movement.'[1] And the anarchist intellectual who, under the name of Voline, wrote the most complete account of the fate of the anarchists in the Russian Revolution said severely of him: 'He had no theoretical or historical political knowledge; he was thus unable to make the necessary generalizations and deductions.'[1]

Nevertheless, Makhno's achievement in organizing an army and conducting a campaign was, till then, unique in the history of anarchism and was only to be equalled by some of the successes of the Spanish anarchists in 1936–7. The liquidation of Makhno's forces by the bolsheviks was therefore a blow to anarchists everywhere. By the autumn of 1920 the Red Army had sufficiently established its power in the south of Russia to dispense with Makhno's aid; and in November 1920 an order was issued that all insurgent units were to be absorbed into the Red Army. Makhno resisted throughout that winter, but by August 1921 his support among the terrorized peasants had dwindled and he was forced to flee into exile. He died in Paris in 1935 in poverty, obscurity and bitterness.

Although, in the confusion of the civil war, Makhno was able to maintain his independence till the summer of 1920, other anarchist groups were less successful. The anarchists made one or two attempts at direct action against the bolsheviks, as when they placed a bomb in the headquarters of the Moscow communist party in September 1919, but such actions merely provided the bolsheviks with a useful label to be attached to anyone who challenged their right to rule. In April 1918 the Red Army and secret police raided the anarchist centres in Moscow and arrested several hundred people, using as an excuse the complaint by Raymond Robins, the American Red Cross representative, that anarchists had seized his car. This was accompanied by the allegation that the arrested anarchists were common criminals, and a denunciation of 'the criminal activity of the armed detachments of counter-revolutionary burglars and robbers which had taken refuge under the black flag of anarchy'. It was a charge with which anarchists everywhere were already familiar, and indeed, as we have seen, there were always people connected with the movement whose acts of social protest looked very like

the acts of ordinary crooks. Throughout the next two years the
bolsheviks tried to maintain the fiction that it was only criminals
who were in jail and that, as Lenin reassured the American
anarchist Emma Goldman, 'Anarchists of ideas are not in our
prisons.'[1]

Emma Goldman and Alexander Berkman arrived in Russia at
the end of 1919, after being deported from the United States.
Both of them were famous in the international anarchist movement, and they were at first welcomed warmly in the country
from which their families had originally emigrated. Emma Goldman, now fifty years old, had lost none of her fire, courage and
oratorical enthusiasm. For more than thirty years she had been
advocating anarchism and practising free love, and had lectured
all over the United States on subjects ranging from Ibsen to
birth control, as well as running an anarchist periodical, *Mother
Earth*. She had been repeatedly in trouble with the authorities –
for her defence of Berkman's attack on Frick and her campaign
in favour of McKinley's assassin, Czolgosz, as well as for her
outspoken advocacy of contraception and frank discussion of
topics such as homosexuality. She was several times imprisoned,
and indeed had only just been released from a sentence resulting
from her agitation during the war against conscription when the
order for her deportation was made. She was a woman of total
sincerity, warm-hearted and cultivated, who, like Kropotkin,
had won the friendship and respect of many people who were
not anarchists but who were impressed by her unfailing courage
in support of freedom in all its forms. (Her autobiography,
Living My Life, though often prolix, gives an unforgettable picture
of the anarchist world and deserves a place alongside Kropotkin's
Memoirs of a Revolutionist as one of the classical accounts of the
anarchist life.)

Berkman, her close friend and associate (although by now their
association had become a purely professional one), lacked Emma's
warmth and broad humanity, but his passion for the anarchist
cause and for truth and justice was equally strong. After his
attempt on the life of Frick he served a prison sentence of four-
teen years, but on his release he soon resumed his life as an

agitator, regardless of public hostility and police oppression. In 1916 a bomb had exploded at a parade in San Francisco; and when Berkman and Emma Goldman heard of it she exclaimed: 'I hope they aren't going to hold the anarchists responsible for it.' 'How could they?' their secretary asked. 'They always have,' Berkman replied.[1] Indeed, two labour union leaders, Thomas Mooney and Warren K. Billings, were arrested and the police tried, though unsuccessfully, to implicate Berkman. Mooney and Billings were sentenced to death by a California court; their sentences were eventually remitted, after suggestions that their trial had been framed, and after an agitation led by Berkman, which had received support of an unusual kind when the bolshevik government in Russia threatened to arrest the American diplomatic representative in Russia if Mooney and Billings were not pardoned. Although the police had failed to involve Berkman in the Mooney and Billings affair, they were soon able, in the atmosphere of wartime America, to charge him with his agitation against conscription. In spite of his own able defence at the trial, at which both he and Emma Goldman sat in the dock, he was imprisoned and released only to be deported. While waiting to leave he heard the news of the death of Frick, whom he had tried to murder a quarter of a century before. 'Deported by God,' was Berkman's comment.

Emma Goldman and Alexander Berkman arrived in Russia as honoured guests and, although they had already had doubts about some of the activities of the bolsheviks, they were as anxious to be impressed by the revolution as Kropotkin had been. However, they were increasingly worried and disappointed, and soon began to be an object of suspicion to the secret police. Berkman himself sensed a change in his personal situation after he had refused to translate Lenin's *State and Revolution* because he disagreed with it. They were shocked at the imprisonment of so many Russian anarchists, at the liquidation of Makhno's insurgent army and at the refusal of the government to release anarchist prisoners to attend Kropotkin's funeral in 1921 – the last occasion when the black flag of the anarchists was carried through the streets of Moscow.

Two weeks after Kropotkin's funeral the sailors at the naval base of Kronstadt revolted against the bolshevik government. Although there had been anarchist influences among the sailors at Kronstadt in 1917, the rising in 1921 was, it now seems,[1] not directly anarchist in inspiration but rather an attempt by disillusioned revolutionaries to restore what they regarded as the purity of the original Soviet idea against the dictatorship of the bolsheviks. However, the programme which the sailors issued contained as one of its items, 'Freedom of speech and press to workers and peasants, to anarchists and left socialist parties'; and to label the whole thing as an anarchist plot was an easy way of discrediting it. Coming so soon after Kropotkin's death and Lenin's refusal to release the anarchist prisoners, the brutal suppression of the Kronstadt revolt was a bitter blow to the foreign anarchists in Russia, even if its aims had not, in fact, been those of the anarchists. It is true that in the summer of 1921, after the anarchists in prison had gone on hunger strike, some of them were released in order to impress the delegates to the International Conference of Red Trade Unions, but this was the last concession. With the dissolution of Makhno's army, the increasing rigour of the government towards all opposition and the arrest and persecution of the anarchists, anarchism in Russia was at an end. Trotsky's boast, 'At last the Soviet government, with an iron broom, has rid Russia of anarchism',[2] seemed justified.

By the end of 1921, Emma Goldman and Alexander Berkman decided to leave. 'Grey are the passing days,' Berkman noted in his diary. 'One by one the embers of hope have died out. Terror and despotism have crushed the life born in October. The slogans of the revolution are forsworn, its ideals stifled in the blood of the people. The breath of yesterday is dooming millions to death; the shadow of today hangs like a black pall over the country. Dictatorship is trampling the masses underfoot. The revolution is dead; its spirit cries in the wilderness. . . . I have decided to leave Russia.'[3] Exiled from Russia, exiled from America, Berkman and Emma Goldman went to Germany and France, after the usual difficulties which anarchists experienced in obtaining visas and residence permits. Worse still, when they published their books criticizing the bolsheviks, they found themselves estranged from many of their friends and associates on the left, for whom the Russian Revolution was still beyond criticism. It took courage to admit that yet another revolution had failed and that the anarchist society was farther away than ever.

Alexander Berkman continued to write and to work for the anarchist and syndicalist movement, but his years in prison had left him in delicate health and he died in Nice in 1936. Emma Goldman, after living for a time in England, went to France. On the outbreak of the Spanish Civil War she inevitably plunged into the struggle. After the liquidation of the Spanish anarchists and the defeat of the republic, she continued to be an active propagandist against the new Spanish régime and, while on a speaking tour in Canada, she collapsed and died in 1940.

The experiences of the anarchists in the Russian Revolution had shown that the theoretical differences between Marx and Bakunin meant in practice bitter strife and bloodshed. Communists and anarchists were henceforth irrevocably on different sides. At the same time, it was the anarchists who had failed to take the lead in a great revolution, just because their principles made organization so difficult. The Marxists, by their success in Russia, now appeared to be a far more effective revolutionary force than the anarchists; and it was thus even harder for the anarchists to win and retain the support which would enable them to put into practice their own ideas of what the revolution should be. Already before the First World War the anarchists had made occasional attempts to organize themselves into a regular disciplined movement, but each time their divisions and their uncompromising and often impressive insistence on the right to differ made these attempts ineffective. They were more at home providing a noisy and disruptive element in the early congresses of the Second International (until they were excluded by the socialist majority after 1896) than in holding congresses of their own.[1] Nevertheless, congresses, national and international were held; theory and tactics were repeatedly discussed. And in France, Spain and the United States many of the younger

5. Michael Bakunin

6. Errico Malatesta

generation of anarchist-minded working-class leaders had tried
to introduce new ideas and practices into the anarchist movement, even though the result of these new trends was often to
divide the movement still further. Some at least of the anarchists
realized that it was on the organized force of the trade-union
movement that a revolution might be based; and it was in the
trade unions that the battle between communists and anarchists
was to be finally fought out.

CHAPTER VIII

Anarchists and Syndicalists

'Les historiens verront un jour, dans cette entrée des anarchistes dans les syndicats, l'un des plus grands évènements qui se soient produits de notre temps.'

Georges Sorel

'Are you poor, forlorn and hungry?
Are there lots of things you lack?
Is your life made up of misery?
Then dump the bosses off your back.
Are your clothes all patched and tattered?
Are you living in a shack?
Would you have your troubles scattered?
Then dump the bosses off your back.

Are you almost split asunder?
Loaded like a long-eared jack?
Boob – why don't you buck like thunder?
And dump the bosses off your back.
All the agonies you suffer
You can end with one good whack.
Stiffen up, you orn'ry duffer
And dump the bosses off your back.'

From the IWW Song Book

I

Even before the communist party in Russia had shown that a successful revolution was possible, and before Lenin's achievements had given new encouragement to Marxists as against anarchists, there had been many anarchists who were worried by the futility of individual terrorism and the sterility of academic discussions. Anarchism was, after all, a working-class movement. It was from among the workers that it had recruited many of its most devoted militants; it was in the daily recognition of the realities of the class struggle – at least in certain industries and countries – that its strength lay. The doubts about individual acts of propaganda by the deed and about the action of small conspiratorial groups, which men like Kropotkin and Elisée Reclus had often expressed, were reinforced by the increased pressure from the police and government after each act of terrorism. If anarchism were going to be more than an individual protest, it was going to have to find a new basis in the masses, and new means of action in an increasingly industrialized society. As Kropotkin put it: 'If the development of the revolutionary spirit gains enormously from heroic individual acts, it is none the less true . . . that it is not by these heroic acts that revolutions are made. . . . Revolution is above all a popular movement.'[1] For anarchism to become a revolutionary popular movement in the face of the rival attraction of the growing political parties which the socialists were building, it needed to show its effectiveness as an organization capable of producing revolutionary social and economic change. As one anarchist paper put it at the time of the assassination of King Umberto I of Italy in 1900: 'It is not the political head that we should be striking. It is the economic head, Property, that we must aim at.'[2]

These ideas were, in a sense, a return to the classical anarchism of Proudhon and Bakunin. They had never vanished from the anarchist movement, but, at least in the popular mind, they had tended to be overshadowed by the spectacular gestures of the individual terrorists and the resulting counter-measures which showed how seriously the police all over Europe took the anarchists. Proudhon had outlined a programme by which the workers in their workshops would themselves take over the means of production without the need of political institutions; Bakunin, although largely concerned with the possibility of revolution among the backward peasantry of Russia or Italy, had also thought of the workshop or factory as a possible nucleus of social revolt. The only method of emancipation, he had written in 1869, is that of 'solidarity in the struggle of the workers against the bosses. It is the organization and federation of "caisses de résistance".'[3] The anarchists of the Jura, concerned as they were with a day-to-day struggle to protect their interests, had responded readily to these ideas and they accepted the principle of direct action by the workers in pursuit of their own social and economic ends. As James Guillaume put it: 'Instead of having recourse to the state, which only possesses such strength as the workers give it, the workers will settle their business direct with the bourgeoisie, will pose their own conditions and force them to accept them.'[1]

The method by which this battle was to be fought was the strike, and already in 1874 one of the leaders of the Jura anarchists, Adhémar Schwitzguébel, put forward the idea of the general strike as the simplest and surest way of winning control of the means of production: 'The idea of a general strike by the workers which would put an end to the miseries they suffer is beginning to be seriously discussed. . . . It would certainly be a revolutionary act capable of bringing about the liquidation of the existing social order and a reorganization in accordance with the socialist aspirations of the workers.'[2] However, the watchmakers of the Jura were not numerous or powerful enough to create a large, effective organization, even though, in the difficult years after the Commune, it was among them that the ideas of Bakunin were most vigorously and effectively kept alive.

It was in France that the new forms of industrial organization and tactics were developed; and they provided the anarchists with new possibilities of action – and also with new possibilities of disagreement. Whereas, in Germany and Britain, the new trade-union movements which developed in the 1880s were movements aiming at piecemeal improvement in the wages and conditions of employment of the industrial workers, and soon established very close relations with the growing socialist political parties, in France, from the time when trade-union activity was first permitted in 1884 after the repression following the Commune, the unions rapidly became committed to a doctrine of direct industrial action independent of any political parties. In the 1880s, it is true, Jules Guesde, the man most responsible for introducing Marxist ideas into French politics, tried to develop trade unions in close association with the socialist party he had founded. However, the alliance did not last long, and at a congress of unions at Bordeaux in 1888 there was already a majority in favour of direct action by means of the general strike and against any political action. Finally, in 1894, the followers of Guesde walked out of a congress of syndicalists at Nantes. For some fifty years the French trade unions and socialist party were to act independently of each other.

Meanwhile, it was on the basis of Proudhon's teaching that the new working-class organizations in France were being developed. These took two forms. In the first, the workers in individual factories, and in some cases in individual industries, formed unions ('syndicats'). Secondly, from 1887 on, 'Bourses du Travail' were formed alongside these syndicates. These were organized on a local basis, and workers in all trades belonged to them. The purpose of the Bourses du Travail was primarily to find jobs for workers, but they very quickly assumed functions beyond this and became centres for education and for the discussion of all the problems affecting the life of the working class. The movement spread rapidly and in 1892 the Bourses du Travail, already functioning in many parts of France, were linked into a national federation.

In 1895, Fernand Pelloutier was appointed the secretary-general of the Fédération des Bourses du Travail, at the age of twenty-eight, and it was he who made the movement into a powerful force and inspired it with a particular kind of anarchist idealism which not only influenced French working-class thought and action but also provided a pattern for other countries, notably Spain. Pelloutier came from a family of officials and professional men, originally Protestant, but converted to Catholicism in the early nineteenth century. He was sent to a Catholic school, but, although he was very intelligent, he failed to matriculate, and was, like so many of his generation, in trouble with the masters for writing an anti-clerical novel. His family lived in Brittany, and the young Pelloutier soon became the associate of a young lawyer in Saint-Nazaire, Aristide Briand, who was at the beginning of a long political career and, at this stage, a representative of the extreme left and much involved in the

defence of anarchists and syndicalists in trouble with the authorities. Pelloutier's political activity in support of Briand soon got
his father, a Post Office official, into difficulties and he was
moved by the ministry to Meaux, and then, at the end of 1893,
to Paris. Here Fernand continued his career as a spokesman and
organizer of the working class, and within two years he was
appointed secretary-general of the recently founded *Fédération des
Bourses du Travail*. Here for seven years, in spite of ill health (he
suffered from a painful and disfiguring tubercular affection of the
face), he threw himself single-mindedly into the task of making
the *Bourses* real centres for working-class education and a nucleus
which would serve as a pattern for a future reorganization of
society on the basis of workers' control of industry.

Although the numbers belonging to the *Bourses du Travail* were
never very large, the ideas disseminated by them have never
wholly disappeared from the French working-class movement.
For Pelloutier the main task was, above all, the education of the
workers and their preparation for their role in the new society.
First of all, they had to be taught the rational basis for their
instinctive revolt against their present situation: '*Ce qui manque à
l'ouvrier, c'est la science de son malheur.*'[1] The *Bourses du Travail* were
accordingly to be 'centres of study where the proletariat could
reflect on their condition, unravel the elements of the economic
problem so as to make themselves capable of the liberation to
which they have the right'.[2] Pelloutier and his followers believed
that any trade-union movement must be truly revolutionary and
aim at the total transformation of society, and that, at the same
time, it must not fall into the errors of the society it intended to
replace. 'Must even the transitory state to which we have to
submit necessarily and fatally be the collectivist jail?' he asked.
'Can't it consist in a free organization limited exclusively by the
needs of production and consumption, all political institutions
having disappeared?' The workers' union was both a means of
revolution and a model for the future. Thus the syndicalist movement 'declared war on everything which constitutes, supports
and fortifies social organization'. Officers must be temporary;
members must be free to leave. 'What is a syndicate?' Pelloutier

wrote. 'An association you are free to enter or leave, without a president, having as its only officials a secretary and treasurer who are instantly dismissible.'[1]

This was carrying Proudhon's ideas to their natural conclusion; and the anarchists were quick to see the possibilities of the new movement for the spread of their ideas. Already in 1892 the Paris police had seized a circular from the anarchist exiles in London instructing anarchists to use the syndicates as a method of action. The tactics were the same as those envisaged by Bakunin twenty-five years earlier (and to be put into effective practice by the *Federación Anarquista Ibérica* in Spain twenty-five years later). 'It is very useful', the circular ran, 'to take an active part in strikes as in all other working-class agitations, but always to refuse to play the star role. We must profit by every opportunity to make anarchist propaganda and to warn the workers against the authoritarian socialists who will be the oppressors of tomorrow.'[2] Pelloutier's ideas seemed to link this aim with a new and positive role for the anarchists in the working-class movement, and many anarchists joined the new syndicalist movement enthusiastically. Emile Pouget, for example, who edited *Le Père Peinard* and whose racy, popular journalistic polemics had made him a successful anarchist propagandist among the working class who wanted something more down to earth than the intellectual anarchism of a Jean Grave or a Kropotkin, became the editor of the main syndicalist weekly in 1900.

Pelloutier's main practical aim after he became secretary of the Federation was to amalgamate the revolutionary and educational activities of the *Bourses du Travail* with the action being carried on by the trade unions organized on a factory or industrial basis. The *Fédération des Syndicats et des groupes coopératifs* had been in existence since 1886; but in 1895 it split into two on the issue of whether to support political action by a political party. The majority adopted the view that Pouget had expressed a few years earlier when he wrote: 'The aim of the syndicates is to make war on the bosses and not to bother with politics.'[3] Once the supporters of Jules Guesde, who wanted a close association with the political socialist movement, had been defeated, the way was open for the syndicates to join with the *Bourses du Travail*. Nevertheless, the process was a slow one. The syndicates formed their own confederation (the *Confédération Générale du Travail* – CGT) in 1895, but it was a comparatively weak and ineffective organization, and the almost total failure of a railway strike in 1898 marked how great the distance was between the hopes of effective and dramatic strike action and the actual capacities of the working class. Pelloutier was anxious that his comparatively strong and well-run Federation should not weaken itself by becoming submerged in a less efficient and less militant body; and, in fact, the unification of the syndicates and the *Bourses du Travail* did not take place in his lifetime.

Pelloutier died in 1901 aged only thirty-four. His tuberculosis had grown steadily worse and he had ruined his health still further by working not only as secretary-general of the *Fédération des Bourses du Travail* but also as editor of a review which was intended to provide the workers with serious articles and facts about the economic situation, and which Pelloutier and his brother produced almost unaided, even doing the actual printing themselves. Pelloutier's dedication, his mixture of practical gifts with moral enthusiasm, his devotion to the ideal of education and self-improvement among the workers, together with his early death, made him a legendary figure among his followers; and it was they who finally succeeded in uniting the *Bourses du Travail* with the CGT in 1902. Under the new charter, the CGT was composed both of syndicates and of *Bourses du Travail*; each section was autonomous, but each syndicate had to belong to a local bourse or an equivalent local organization. Thus the CGT was now based both on the federation of unions, and thus on the various industries, and on the federation of the *Bourses du Travail* and so on a system of regional and local decentralization. The spirit of Proudhon seemed to have triumphed.

However, although the syndicalist movement had now achieved a unity which in 1902 the French socialist parties still lacked, and although they were committed to direct economic action and to opposition to all forms of political activity, they were, in fact, still very weak numerically. At the beginning of the twentieth century the industrial workers were in a minority in France. It is estimated that in 1906 39 per cent of the wage-earners in France were engaged in commerce and industry; and of these not more than 11 per cent belonged to any sort of trade union, and only 4 per cent to the CGT.[1] The membership fluctuated considerably according to economic conditions and between one industry and another. Thus any effective industrial action was bound to be limited in its results, unless it could succeed in paralysing a key industry or service, such as the railways. Under these circumstances there was necessarily much disagreement about what the unions could achieve. Were they to be, as their anarchist members wished, militant organizations preparing the way by their example for the revolution and the new society? Or were they to be content with achieving what practical gains they could in limited sectors of industry? The discussion that divided the socialist political parties in these years, about whether reform or revolution was the first aim, was paralleled in the trade-union movement. The anarchists who saw in the unions a means of making the revolution were quite clear what they were trying to do. One of them, Paul Delesalle, who was one of the assistant secretaries of the CGT for several years, wrote that their role was to 'demonstrate the foolishness of partial reforms and develop the revolutionary spirit among the union members'.[2]

It was just because the syndicalist movement was weak that the idea of direct revolutionary action seemed attractive. If short-term gains were as hard to win as final victory, there was no reason why the latter should not be an immediate aim. Just as many German social democrats thought that the logic of history would bring them victory without their having to do very much about it, so many French syndicalists believed that somehow the capitalist order would fall at a single blow. The more serious militant syndicalists were constantly reproving this heresy. 'If you only had to blow on the old society to overthrow it,' Emile Pouget wrote on May Day 1904, 'it would really be too easy. If we deceive ourselves about the size of the effort required, we are

preparing for cruel disillusion. . . . The social revolution will not
be accomplished without the necessity of a formidable effort.'[1]
Nevertheless, no one disputed the possibility of imminent revolution provided the will to it was there.

In 1906 the CGT formally accepted the views of militants like
Pouget and recognized that it was a revolutionary organization
which aimed at the seizure of economic power by means of direct
action culminating in a general strike. Paul Delesalle described
the plan of campaign as follows:

'(1) A general strike by individual unions, which we can com-
     pare to manoeuvres of garrisons.
(2) Cessation of work everywhere on a given day, which we
     can compare to general manoeuvres (*"grandes manoeuvres"*).
(3) A general and complete stoppage which places the pro-
     letariat in a state of open war with capitalist society.
(4) General strike – revolution.'[2]

The problem which confronted the CGT was how to combine
a state of war against capitalist society with the pursuit of immediate and limited gains for the workers. The months before
the Amiens congress had been filled with industrial unrest; the
campaign for the eight-hour day was in full swing and there had
been extensive strikes in support of it, especially among the
miners, who were the largest of the unions belonging to the CGT.
The government had been sufficiently alarmed by the threat of
demonstrations on May Day 1906 to order the arrest of the
federal secretary and the treasurer of the CGT, and it was in this
atmosphere of militancy that the CGT congress assembled later
in the year. The congress reaffirmed the divorce between the
syndicates and the socialist parties and laid down that, although
members of the CGT were entirely free outside the unions to
adopt the form of struggle which corresponded to their political
or philosophical views, they were not to introduce these views in
the unions; and the unions themselves should not 'concern themselves with parties or sects, which are free outside and apart from
the unions to work for social transformation as they think fit'.
What linked the members of the unions was a consciousness of

the need to struggle for the abolition of the wage system and a 'recognition of the class struggle, which, on an economic foundation, puts the workers in revolt against every form of exploitation, material and moral, that is operated by the capitalist class against the working class'. At the same time, the Charter of Amiens tried to reconcile this with the need for day-to-day action in the following terms: 'In respect of everyday demands, syndicalism pursues the coordination of the workers' efforts, the increase of the workers' welfare through the achievement of immediate improvements, such as the shortening of the hours of labour, the raising of wages, etc. This, however, is only one aspect of its work: it is preparing the way for the entire emancipation that can be realized only by the expropriation of the capitalist class. It commends the general strike as a means to this end and holds that the trade union, which is at present a resistance group, will be in the future the group responsible for production and distribution, the foundation of the social organization.'[1]

It is obvious how much this programme owed to anarchist ideas, from Proudhon to Kropotkin and Pelloutier, but for some anarchists the assertion that the syndicates had a 'double task of day-to-day activity and of the future' went too far in its implicit acceptance of existing society. There was, indeed, a formal public debate on these questions at an international congress, summoned by the Dutch and Belgian anarchists at Amsterdam in 1907. Many representatives of the young revolutionary syndicalists from France attended, together with many of the most respected international anarchist figures – Emma Goldman, the Dutchmen Cornelissen and Nieuwenhuis, Rudolph Rocker, and Malatesta – 'perhaps', as one of the French anarchists put it, 'the last representative of the old insurrectional anarchism'.[2] The usual eccentrics were also present to make the proceedings more difficult; one of them objected on principle to any votes being taken, because this infringed the liberty of the minority, while another extreme individualist proclaimed that his motto was '*Moi, moi, moi . . . et les autres ensuite*'. However, there was a serious discussion of the whole question of trade-union action which, according to reports from the various countries represented, was everywhere dividing the anarchist movement. For the young French syndicalists, Amédée Dunois and Pierre Monatte, the trade-union movement provided a means of bringing anarchism back to a direct contact with the workers. As Dunois put it: 'By involving ourselves more actively in the working-class movement, we have crossed the gap which separates the pure idea . . . from the living reality. We are less and less interested in the former abstractions and more and more in the practical movement in action', and he went on to echo Pelloutier and say: 'The workers' trade union is not simply an organization of struggle, it is the living germ of future society, and future society will be what we have made of the trade union.'[1] Pierre Monatte, a twenty-six-year-old blacksmith's son from the Auvergne, made the connexion between anarchism and the new syndicalism even more explicit. 'Syndicalism', he said, 'has recalled anarchism to the awareness of its working-class origins; on the other hand, the anarchists have contributed not a little towards putting the working-class movement on to the path of revolution and to popularizing the idea of direct action.'[2] And for him, too, syndicalism was a moral as well as a social force: 'Syndicalism does not waste time promising the workers a paradise on earth, it calls on them to conquer it and assures them that their action will never be wholly in vain. It is a school of the will, of energy and of fruitful thought. It opens to anarchism, which for too long has been turned in on itself, new perspectives and experiences.'[3]

The idea of linking the future of anarchism to the trade unions was not, however, accepted by many anarchists. Emma Goldman, for example, was afraid that it might swamp the individual in a mass movement: 'I will only accept anarchist organization on one condition: it is that it should be based on absolute respect for *all* individual initiatives and should not hamper their free play and development. The essential principle of anarchism is individual autonomy.'[4] Malatesta, too, although he had always accepted some degree of organization and had, like Proudhon, thought that it was the autonomy of small social groups rather than of individuals that was important, was nevertheless worried that the new movement involved the risk of dividing the working class, since the interests of all workers were not necessarily the same, and that it might create a bureaucracy of just the type which the anarchists were working to abolish: 'The official is to the working-class movement a danger only comparable to that provided by the parliamentarian; both lead to corruption and from corruption to death is but a short step.' Above all, anarchism must not be limited to one particular class, even if it is the working class who most need revolution because they are the most oppressed. 'The anarchist revolution we want', he said, 'far exceeds the interest of one class; it has as its aim the complete liberation of humanity which is totally enslaved from three points of view – economically, politically and morally.'[1]

Malatesta not only attacked some of the basic conceptions of the syndicalists; he also attacked their tactical methods. Revolution was revolution and could not be disguised as anything else. The bourgeoisie and the state would not give way without a fight, and once fighting started it was an insurrection – and this was not the same as the general strike. 'The general strike', he said, 'is pure utopia. Either the worker, dying of hunger after three days on strike, will return to the factory hanging his head, and we shall score one more defeat. Or else he will try to gain possession of the fruits of production by open force. Who will he find facing him to stop him? Soldiers, policemen, perhaps the bourgeois themselves, and then the question will have to be resolved by bullets and bombs. It will be insurrection, and victory will go to the strongest.'[2] The compromise resolution with which the discussion ended did not resolve the dilemma; but, as far as effective action by the anarchist movement was concerned, it was Monatte rather than Malatesta who was right. The ideas of anarcho-syndicalism and of direct industrial action were to give the anarchist movement a new lease of life; in France, at least until 1914, and still more in Spain, anarchism in association with trade unionism was to show itself, for the only time in the history of the anarchist movement, an effective and formidable force in practical politics.

2

During the years of the growth of syndicalism in France, a retired civil engineer, Georges Sorel, had been thinking about its
implications and developing certain theories about the proletariat
and its role in modern society. He thought of himself as a successor to Proudhon; indeed, on the opening page of his *Materials
for a Theory of the Proletariat*, published in 1918 at the end of his
life and dedicated to the syndicalist bookseller Paul.Delesalle, he
called himself, with a slightly pathetic rhetorical touch, 'an old
man who like Proudhon obstinately remains a disinterested servant of the proletariat'. To his Marxist enemies he was always a
'reactionary, petty bourgeois Proudhonist'. He was like Proudhon
in the unsystematic nature of his thought and also in the divergent
views which he is said to have inspired. He himself was sceptical
about his own influence. 'I don't believe much in the influence of
a single man,' he said to a friend in 1922, just before his death. 'I
believe that when a mind puts forth an idea, it is because this idea
is in the air. . . . Is it necessary for a man of the first rank like
Lenin to have read my work to see clearly? Frankly, I don't
think so. . . . You see I am far from sharing the flattering opinion
of those who talk of my influence on Lenin and Mussolini.'[1]

It is typical of Sorel that although he devoted thirty years of
his life to attacking bourgeois society, he was a characteristic
member of it. He came from a middle-class family in Normandy
– his cousin was the great historian Albert Sorel – and he had a
perfectly respectable career as a government engineer. He retired when a little over forty, with a Legion of Honour and a
small inherited income. In 1889, when he was forty-five, he
published his first book. For the rest of his life he lived quietly
in a cottage at Boulogne-sur-Seine, taking the tram once a
week to Paris, where he spent the day listening to Bergson's
lectures and talking for hours with his young friends. He soon
became a familiar figure in the lives of the young intellectuals
who gathered in the offices of the advanced reviews. His circle
included Romain Rolland and Charles Péguy, and (among the
younger men, some of whom were to become his bitterest

critics) Daniel Halévy and Julien Benda. He lived among intellectuals – although hostility to intellectuals was a central feature of his teaching; and those anarcho-syndicalists he knew best were those who were, like Paul Delesalle, by nature interested in theory.

Sorel's admiration for the proletariat, for direct action and revolutionary violence, which brought him close to the militant anarchists and led to his being regarded as the theorist of anarcho-syndicalism, was only one part of an all-out attack on most of the political and social values of the late nineteenth century. Above all, according to him, it was the intellectuals and the rationalists who were ruining society and filling it with false values. Already in his first book, *The Trial of Socrates*, he states the case which he repeated for the rest of his life. The Athenians, he maintains, were right to condemn Socrates; Socrates did corrupt the youth and undermine the tacitly accepted values that held Athenian society together. It is easy to see why much of Sorel's teaching appealed to the right more than to the left and why he spent the later years of his life closer to the Action Française than to his former anarchist friends. As in Proudhon, there is often in his work a nostalgia for a vanished past where men were bound to each other by ties deeper than the mechanical devices invented by liberal constitutional theorists, by positivists and by all the people who believed that problems have solutions and who are therefore optimistic – or if they are pessimistic, it is only because their own pet schemes have gone wrong.

All Sorel's doctrine is based on the assumption that the intellectuals are misleading the masses, debauching them with false ideas and cheap sentimentality, making them believe that 'irrealizable things are possible in order the better to lead them by the nose'.[1] Intellectuals impose a pattern on the world that does not correspond to reality. 'It is impossible', Sorel says (and here we can see how attentive he must have been at Bergson's lectures), 'to reach a point where you can describe with precision and clarity; sometimes we must beware of attempting to make language too rigorous because it will be in contradiction to the fluid character of reality and thus language will deceive us. We

must proceed by feeling our way (*"par tâtonnements"*)'.[1] The
intellectuals have prostituted true science; they are only interested in results, not in the nature of the world. 'Science is for the
bourgeoisie a mill that produces solutions for all problems; science
is no longer considered as a perfected way of knowing but only
as a recipe for pursuing certain advantages.'[2]

The bourgeois intellectuals, according to Sorel, have broken up
the natural solidarity of society and disintegrated the old order
without replacing it by a new one in which men will be more than
atoms whose behaviour is studied and predicted by the social
scientist. If society is to be transformed, there must be a new
elite to transform it, since the traditional elites of the past have
long since forfeited their role. Sorel had studied Marx and had
been much influenced by him, even though he bitterly attacked
the Marxists in his *Decomposition of Marxism*; he shared Marx's
belief that the next revolution would be made by the proletariat;
and thus it was the proletariat which, in his view, was to be the
new force that would regenerate society. At the same time, he
realized that Fernand Pelloutier was attempting to turn the
Bourses du Travail into centres of education which would train
the working class and its leaders for just the role for which Sorel
had cast them. As Sorel himself wrote, the *Bourses* were to be 'a
matter of conscience rather than an instrument of government'.[3]
The militants of the new trade-union movement would provide
the proletariat with the leaders who would ensure their victory
in the coming revolution.

Sorel already had much in common with the anarchists when,
in the late nineties, he realized the potentialities of the syndicalist
movement and the power of Pelloutier's ideas. He was full of
contempt for governments and politics. 'All our political crises',
he wrote, 'consist in the replacement of intellectuals by other
intellectuals; they always therefore have as a result the maintenance of the state and sometimes its reinforcement by increasing
the number of people with a vested interest.'[4] It was the failure
of the Dreyfus crisis to bring about any real change in the structure of French society that finally disillusioned him with politics
and existing political figures. At this time he was getting to know

7. Two covers by Steinlen for pamphlets published by Les *Temps Nouveaux*

(b) Federica Montseny

8. (a) Emma Goldman

Pelloutier and his ideas, and it was to the syndicalist movement that he turned in the hope that this might regenerate society where the political leaders had failed. 'The liquidation of the Dreyfusian revolution', he wrote later, 'obliged me to recognize that proletarian socialism or syndicalism realizes its nature fully only if it is by its own will a labour movement directed against the demagogues.'[1]

The militant leaders of the proletariat now seemed to promise the possibility of a true revolution which would obliterate the corruption and false sentimentality of the liberal age and which would draw its strength from deep, primitive, instinctive forces in man's nature. It was the working class alone that had the moral integrity to make such a revolution; and the militants of the syndicalist movement were the elite of the new age. A violent destruction of the existing state by the revolutionary proletariat would be not just a political revolution but a moral revival: 'Not only can proletarian violence ensure the future revolution, but it also seems to be the only means at the disposal of the nations of Europe, numbed as they are by humanitarianism, to recover their energy.'[2] And elsewhere he expressly talks of revolutionary socialism as being the Nietzschean reversal of moral values – the *Umwertung aller Werte*.

These are the ideas Sorel elaborated in his most famous book, *Reflexions on Violence*, published in 1906. It is here that the passionate and romantic nature of his thought is most apparent. He is as conscious as Nietzsche was of the decadence and weaknesses of modern society and its reluctance to use violence even to defend itself. On the other hand, if the proletariat is prepared to use violence it will win an easy victory; and this sort of violence will somehow be morally pure. Sorel contrasts it with the force used by upholders of the existing state or advocated by those socialists who only want to gain possession of the state machine instead of destroying it altogether. Sorel sometimes writes as if, for all the purifying effect of violence, physical violence might not actually be needed and the proletariat's faith in its own power might be sufficient to cause the revolution.

In almost all his works, indeed, Sorel insists on the importance of faith in producing political and social change. The organizations that survive in history, the causes that triumph, are those inspired by an irrational belief in their own destiny and mission, and not those based on intellectual constructions and rational analysis. The most successful example – and Sorel comes back to it again and again – is the Roman Catholic church. The church has always shown astonishing powers of survival. 'I believe', Sorel said in one of his essays, 'that Christianity will not perish: the mystical faculty is something very real in man and experience shows that it does not decrease in intensity through the ages . . . it is not weakened by scientific development.'[1] Indeed, he thinks that it is only when the church begins to compromise with liberalism by trying to give its theology an appearance of rationalism that it is in danger of losing its power.

Sorel believed – and it is perhaps his most original contribution to political thought – in the power of the Myth in politics. These myths cannot be analysed; they are not utopian descriptions of a future state of affairs, but moral beliefs acting on present conduct. 'They are not descriptions of things,' Sorel says, 'but expressions of will.'[2] It does not matter if they are symbols of a state of affairs that will never be realized. 'Myths must be judged', he wrote, 'as a means of acting on the present; any discussion on the method of applying them practically to the course of history is meaningless. It is only the myth taken as a whole that is important.'[3] The success of the Catholic church is, for Sorel, one example of the effectiveness of the myth in action: the deep faith in the possibility of change that made the French Revolution is another; and so is Mazzini's almost religious faith in Italian unity.

The myth – the mystical belief in the ultimate triumph of one's cause, one's will to victory – is kept alive and propagated by an elite. In the periods when the Catholic church was in danger it was the monastic orders that kept the myth alive. In the twentieth-century workers' movement this task is performed by the militant syndicalists. And the myth which they must believe in is that the proletariat has in its possession a weapon that will infallibly enable it to overthrow the existing order. That weapon is the general strike. By the time that Sorel produced the *Reflexions on Violence* the idea of the general strike was already well established in many working-class organizations. Although the leaders of the German trade unions repeated at intervals 'General Strike is General Nonsense' (*'Generalstreik ist Generalunsinn'*), it had been used as an effective political weapon to obtain franchise reforms in Belgium, and the mass stoppages of work on May Day had, in many countries, provided an impressive demonstration of the potential strength of the working class. By 1906, the idea of the general strike had been accepted by the CGT in France and formally embodied in the Charter of Amiens. Sorel was not therefore launching a new strategy for the working classes in their struggle, but rather trying to fit what they were already doing into his own highly personal, subjective and romantic view of society and history. By temperament he was closer to those anarchists for whom the violent revolutionary overthrow of society had a purifying value of its own than to the conscientious trade-union organizers, and he said very little about what would happen after the revolution. He is like Proudhon in his awareness of the power of the irrational and also in his puritanism. 'The world will become more just only to the extent to which it becomes more chaste.'[1]

If the passionate nature of Sorel's hatred of the liberal world and his belief in the purifying effects of violence bring him close to a certain type of anarchist temperament, and if his recognition of what the trade unions might achieve and of the possibilities of the general strike fitted into a general theory of society which the syndicalist leaders had been trying to put into practice, it is nevertheless with the revolutionaries and reactionary theorists of the right that Sorel has been rightly linked in the works recently devoted to him.[2] Sorel's syndicalism was only a part of his unsystematic, voluminous, wide-ranging critique of society and of his attack on intellectuals, rationalists and bourgeois politicians; and it was only for a few years of his life that he was in active contact with the syndicalist leaders. In fact, his anti-intellectualism and his obsession with dynamic violence make him closer to Mussolini (who reviewed *Reflexions on Violence* when it first

appeared in Italy) than to Kropotkin or Pelloutier. He remains
a paradoxical figure whom it is hard to classify; an anti-intellectual who spent his time in the company of intellectuals and in
reading, writing and theorizing; a man of the left who ended up
nearer to the right; a technician who rejected the possibility of
exact science. An English writer, Wyndham Lewis, for whom
Sorel had a particular fascination, summed him up as follows:
'George Sorel is the key to all contemporary thought. Sorel is,
or was, a highly unstable and equivocal figure. He seems composed of a crowd of warring personalities, sometimes one being
in the ascendant, sometimes another, and which in any case he
has not been able, or not cared, to control. He is the arch ex-
ponent of extreme action and revolutionary violence *à l'outrance*;
but he expounds this sanguinary doctrine in manuals that often,
by the changing of a few words, would equally serve the forces of
traditional authority and provide them with a twin evangel of
demented and intolerant class war.'[1] Another of his friends and
disciples, Daniel Halévy, said of him in 1940: 'Those who listened
to him forty years ago owe it to him that they have not been
surprised at the changes in the world.'[2] Perhaps it is as an analyst
and commentator on the forces which led to the governments of
Mussolini and Hitler, Pétain and Franco, rather than as a
theorist of anarcho-syndicalism that he should be remembered.

3

At the beginning of the twentieth century not all the syndicalist
leaders in France were anarchists, and even fewer were friends of
Sorel, as Pelloutier or Delesalle or Pouget were. Some were still
hankering after a trade unionism which would concentrate on
collective bargaining for immediate gains; others, such as Victor
Griffuelhes, the secretary-general of the CGT from 1902 to 1909,
were tough labour bosses whose ideology, such as it was, had been
formed by the Blanquists who believed in direct action for its own
sake rather than by those who believed in social theories or
educational programmes. ('I read Alexandre Dumas,' Griffuelhes
is reported to have said when asked if he had been influenced by

Sorel.)[1] Nevertheless, in the years before 1914 the French trade-union movement made many attempts at revolutionary direct action and it became a model which militant syndicalists in other countries, especially Spain, were prepared to follow.

In one way, at least, the experience of the French syndicates seemed to show that Sorel was right. Although there were a number of effective strikes in individual industries, the general strike and the collapse of bourgeois society which was to follow from it remained a myth – a hope and inspiration for the future rather than a possibility for the present. Of the great strikes in this period – the postal strike of 1909, the rail strike of 1910, the miners' and metalworkers' strikes in 1913 – none had in themselves achieved either partial success in the shape of immediate reforms nor had they played the part of preparing a breach in capitalist society which the militant anarchists in the trade union assigned to them. The constant agitation, the violent revolutionary tone of these years, was not without effect, but it was not always the effect which the syndicalist leaders had hoped to obtain. Certainly in the first decade of the century the French trade-union movement had increased in strength; on one estimate the CGT had increased its membership six times over between 1902 and 1912 – even though the total figure was still only 600,000.[2] Their unremitting agitation had created an atmosphere of class struggle and had undoubtedly drawn attention, as never before, to the existence of the social question in France and of a militant, underprivileged proletariat. Yet the very fact that the government had taken notice of some of their grievances, and had introduced laws for the improvement in the conditions of work and for workers' pensions, weakened the appeal of a purely revolutionary syndicalism. Moreover, when it came to a showdown the government always seemed able to win. Under the former radical republican, Clemenceau, or under Aristide Briand, the former advocate of the general strike who had abandoned his syndicalism for a long and successful government career, the government had broken strikes, mobilized strikers and sown dissension among syndicalist leaders. At the same time, personal rivalries and differences of opinion had prevented the

CGT from presenting the appearance of a solid workers' front which it would have to do if the myth of the general strike were to be effective. Victor Griffuelhes was forced to resign from the office of general secretary in 1909. His authoritarian temperament and impatience of criticism laid him open to attack ('*Ceux qui n'ont pas confiance en moi, je les emmerde,*' he once said),[1] and he resigned when his financial integrity was wrongly called in question. After a brief interval Léon Jouhaux became general secretary, and for nearly fifty years he was the organizer and inspirer of the French trade-union movement.

Jouhaux and the other most influential syndicalist leaders of his generation, Alfred Merrheim and Pierre Monatte, had all started as anarchists; but their experience of working-class organization in a democratic state made them move a long way towards coming to terms with existing society and obliged them to temper their revolutionary ideals with a considerable amount of practical reformist action. Proudhon and Pelloutier were Jouhaux's masters; and throughout his long career he never wholly abandoned their teaching. Even after the dark experiences of the Second World War, he was still speaking their language: 'When will men come together again in a world regenerated by labour freed from all servitude to join in singing in unison hymns to production and happiness? On this first day of the new year [1944] I want to believe in the coming of these new lights, as I do not wish to doubt the reason of man.'[2]

The setbacks and crises of the years before 1914 convinced Jouhaux that the CGT needed more organization – even at the cost of more centralization – if it was to be effective. The total failure of the attempt at a general strike in 1912 disillusioned many syndicalists, but it was the experience of the First World War which forced them into thinking again about their whole position and basic beliefs and which made them abandon most of the anarchism in anarcho-syndicalism. In the years before the outbreak of the war the CGT had regularly debated the action to be taken to prevent war and regularly passed, by a considerable majority, a resolution calling for a general strike as the best means of stopping it. Amicable exchanges of visits with German and British trade unionists (although Jouhaux himself was shocked by the bourgeois appearance and habits of the English and German union leaders) served to obscure the differences in the nature of the movements in the three countries and the fact that, while the French were calling for a general strike against war, the German trade unionists were still repeating with equal regularity, 'General Strike is General Nonsense.'

August 1914 showed not only that the CGT was in no position to call a general strike against war, but also that nearly all its leading members did not want to. For some syndicalists it may have been fear of the consequences which made them obey the mobilization notices; for to fail to do so would make them deserters, and the penalty for desertion in wartime was death. But for most of them the sense of patriotism and a genuine fear of the Germans was enough to send them to the front, expectantly or resignedly according to their temperament; and it was only after two years that the militant and anti-militarist revolutionary spirit began to revive. In fact, the trade unions in France, as in the other belligerent countries, strengthened their own position immensely as a result of the war. Just as the governments were forced to realize that it is impossible to fight a war without the cooperation of organized labour, so the unions began to feel a certain sense of solidarity with the state. As Jouhaux himself put it in 1918: 'We must give up the policy of fist-shaking in order to adopt a policy of being present in the affairs of the nation. . . . We want to be everywhere where the workers' interests are being discussed.'[1] This is not to say that after 1914 the CGT wholly abandoned the anarchist ideas which had dominated it in the decade after 1899, but it did in practice give up the idea of an immediate revolution and it did, in theory and in practice, accept the existence of the state. The CGT remained resolutely anti-political; it refused continuously to associate itself permanently with any single political party. When calling for the nationalization of industry, Jouhaux was careful to point out that this must not mean state control but rather control by the workers. For a few years after the Russian Revolution some former anarchists in the CGT were attracted to communism as representing the most directly revolutionary force in the country; but most of those who joined the communists, such as Pierre Monatte, could not support the discipline or approve of the centralization which the Third International was determined to impose, and it was only in the 1930s, in very changed circumstances and with a new generation of trade unionists, that communist influence became a strong force in French trade unionism.

Jouhaux's own criticism of the Russian Revolution was not unlike that of Emma Goldman, or, indeed, that of Kropotkin. He was largely converted to an evolutionary view of social and economic change because he had been appalled by the economic chaos in Russia, and like Kropotkin, who had exclaimed many years before, '*Du pain, il faut du pain à la revolution*', Jouhaux saw that famine on the scale experienced in Russia made nonsense of the revolution. 'We are against the Third Communist International,' he said in 1920. 'We are against the Third International because it is a political grouping which concentrates in itself all political forces and wants to include most economic elements, but without being a specifically economic organization.'[1] The history of French syndicalism from 1920 onwards is the history of its struggle to remain a specifically economic organization in the face of increasing temptation to involve itself with political groupings whether communist or anti-communist; and to this extent its anarchist origins were never wholly forgotten.

The anarchists left their mark on French syndicalism, but they only influenced it seriously for ten or fifteen years; and after 1914 the history of the CGT had little to do with the history of the anarchists. In a sense, the French state proved too strong for them, since not only did it show before 1914 (and indeed repeatedly down to the present) that it could survive syndicalist attempts to paralyse it by means of direct action, but it also showed that it had considerable power of positive attraction. France as a state still, in spite of continuous anti-militarist propaganda, had the power of arousing patriotic support and enforcing obedience, while the political methods of obtaining social reform proved just as effective and attractive as the ideas of direct industrial action. Although the syndicalist movement never lost its revolutionary element nor its pacifist anti-militarist side (which made some of its members paradoxically enough come to terms with the authoritarian *Etat Français* of Vichy), it was, in fact, committed to reform rather than revolution, to negotiation with the state rather than to its abolition. Anarcho-syndicalist ideas on the French model had considerable influence elsewhere, but they did not survive in the face of governments which were prepared to permit trade-union activity and themselves to undertake social reform; nor were they strong enough to resist the appeals to solidarity in time of war. The one country where anarcho-syndicalism was to remain a serious force was Spain – where union activity was barely tolerated, where the government was both decrepit and reactionary, and where there had been no experience of a war to convince at least some of the working class that they shared certain interests with the bosses.

It was in France that the ideas and practice of anarcho-syndicalism were first developed; it was in Spain, where there was already a strong anarchist movement, that they were most effective. But elsewhere, in Latin America, for instance, where the labour movement was weak and the class struggle bitter, militant leaders were able to direct working-class organizations along syndicalist lines. In fact, however, anarchist ideas tended to flourish everywhere where there was a true class struggle between employers and labour and where the state either deliberately lent its authority to the employers or stood aloof from the battle. Thus for some fifteen years one section of the trade-union movement in the United States practised anarchist tactics and held largely anarchist beliefs, simultaneously with, though largely independent of, the development of anarcho-syndicalist ideas in France.

The innumerable immigrants from Italy, Spain and Russia or those Germans in the U.S.A. who had listened to the teachings of John Most had made anarchist ideas widely known in the United States, while the Haymarket affair, the ceaseless propaganda of Emma Goldman, Alexander Berkman and others, and the alarm caused by the assassination of President McKinley had kept the concept of an 'anarchist peril' before the public. John Most and some of his followers had, in the 1890s, turned against the practice of terrorism and had begun to see that there were possibilities of industrial action in the factories and mines which could be more effective: and it was these ideas, involving as they did the acceptance of a minimum of organization, which had separated Most from many of his anarchist colleagues. However, when certain American trade unions began to accept anarchist practice it was not the theorists who were responsible. American anarcho-syndicalism was rather a blind, instinctive reaction against bad labour conditions by ignorant labourers, largely immigrant, to whom the politicians seemed very remote, and to whom direct, often violent, action seemed a natural way of achieving their ends. In the mines and lumber camps of the West, or in the textile and other factories of the East and Middle West which relied on cheap immigrant labour, a few militant organizers could, at least for short periods, build up an effective industrial fighting force.

The history of trade unionism in America is as much a history of the rivalry between the unions as of the struggle between capital and labour. By the 1890s there was a powerful trade-union movement based on a craft organization and forming the American Federation of Labour. But to the vast mass of the unskilled, organized working class, the AF of L seemed to be just an organization for the preservation of the position of a minority of skilled workers, by means of a series of deals with the employers, to the disadvantage of the less skilled or more recently arrived workers. In the 1890s, along with attempts to form a socialist political party, various labour leaders began to see the potential political power of the unorganized workers. As one of these leaders, Daniel de Leon, put it: 'The organization of the future has to be built of the men who are now unorganized – that is, the overwhelming majority of the working class of the nation.'[1] It was this desire to organize the unorganized and to bring together all the men working in one industry into 'one big union' as well as to unite the unions into a really powerful force that led to the foundation in 1905 of the Industrial Workers of the World (IWW). The main support for this came from the Western Federation of Miners, whose chief, 'Big Bill' Haywood, was one of the most forceful exponents of the idea of direct industrial action to be found anywhere. The anarchists were few in number at the founding congress of the IWW, though they had a consistency and a sincerity that gave them a certain influence. Immediately, however, the organization became involved in a discussion which was to split it from the start and which went to the centre of the problems with which the anarchists were most concerned: how far should a working-class movement be involved with politics? How far should it be associated with a political party? Should the revolution be made by direct action by the workers, who would simply take over the means of production, or should it aim at conquering the state by political means?

De Leon, an intellectual Marxist, thought that the trade-union movement ought to be the industrial arm of a political movement, and, largely under his influence, the preamble to the constitution of the IWW contained a specific, if puzzling and contradictory, reference to political action: 'Between these two classes [workers and employers] a struggle must go on until all the toilers come together on the political as well as on the industrial field, and take hold of that which they produce by their labour, through an economic organization of the working class, without affiliation to any political party.'[1] This clearly went too far in the direction of accepting political action for many of the delegates, one of whom had declared: 'The ballot box is simply a capitalist concession. Dropping pieces of paper into a hole in a box never did achieve emancipation of the working class, and to my thinking never will.'[2] In fact, the lack of clarity in the debates at the foundation of the IWW was to lead to further trouble and division. Within a year Eugene Debs, one of the most famous leaders in the history of the American labour movement, had resigned from the IWW because he believed it was putting too little emphasis on political activity, and in 1908 Daniel de Leon, although he had originally maintained that 'the political expression of labour is but the shadow of economic organization',[1] broke away from Hayward and the Chicago leaders of the IWW, because he was committed to the ideas of political action by means of the Socialist Labour Party, of which he was also one of the leading members.

From 1908 to 1915 there was a confusing situation in which there were two groups both calling themselves the IWW – a group based on Chicago, led by Haywood and Vincent St John, who believed in direct action and who became increasingly anarchistic in feeling, and de Leon's group based on Detroit, which eventually took the name of the Workers' International Industrial Union. The anarchist element in the IWW had indeed already made itself felt in 1906, when they carried a resolution abolishing the office of president of the IWW and stating: 'Whereas the day is at hand when we must abolish anything that pertains to autocratic power and reactionary policy, the office of president of a class-conscious organization is not necessary. The rank and file must conduct the affairs of the organization directly through an executive based on a central committee.'[2] And, as a result of this decision the police had to be called in to help the organization to gain possession of the offices and files from the abolished president, who refused to give up his post.

During these years of bitter personal recrimination and faction rivalries mixed with genuine ideological differences the IWW achieved very little. Although it claimed 60,000 members in 1906, only 14,000 of these actually paid their dues and they were badly weakened by the various secessions, especially by that of the Western Federation of Miners, which abandoned Haywood in 1907. However, the militant section began to have a certain success just because of the violence and directness of their methods and the simplicity of their ideas, which appealed to overworked, underpaid and undereducated miners, lumberjacks and farmhands, so that in 1910 an observer could write of the farmhands at North Yamhill, Oregon, that they 'had been handing out the principles of revolutionary unionism in huge raw chunks'.[3] The IWW successfully led strikes in Pennsylvania in 1909; and in 1912 they had a great success with a strike at

Lawrence, Massachusetts, when for three months the IWW militants, although said to number only 300, kept 23,000 workers out. In the meantime, Haywood had been in Europe, where he met Pouget and other leading thinkers of French syndicalism, so that the techniques of direct action and sabotage practised at Lawrence were at once branded as un-American by the IWW's many enemies.

Still, for all its renunciation of politics and acceptance of direct action, the IWW failed to make itself truly anarchist. In 1912 attempts to enforce decentralization in the organization failed, so that Alexander Berkman commented sadly: 'The question of local autonomy, in itself such an axiomatic necessity of a truly revolutionary movement, has been so obscured in the debates of the convention that apparently sight was lost of the fact that no organization of independent and self-reliant workers is thinkable without complete local autonomy.'[1] Berkman and Emma Goldman found much to sympathize with in the militant IWW: they were the first to associate themselves with its claims for freedom of speech and agitation, and to campaign when its leaders were tried and imprisoned, but they were never wholly committed to it, and, indeed, the rivalries and feuds of the American trade-union movement were very far removed from the anarchist dreams of what a working-class organization should be like. However, Berkman and Emma Goldman were victims of the same circumstances as the IWW leaders when, after America's entry into the war in 1917, any 'subversive' organizations were made to suffer. They fought against conscription with the IWW leaders; they fought against the sentences imposed on Mooney and Billings at San Francisco in 1917. The same repression which put an end to their careers as agitators in the U.S.A. practically put an end to the IWW also, and sent Big Bill Hayward into the same disillusioning exile in Russia, where he died in 1925. By the end of the war anarcho-syndicalism in the U.S.A. had virtually disappeared and, although non-political industrial unionism was to continue, and although a streak of violence in the conduct of industrial disputes continued till the 1930s, it was no longer really anarchist in feeling.

The IWW experience had left a militant legend; it had

influenced some foreign trade unions for a brief period – notably in Mexico, where Mexican workers who had experienced IWW methods in the U.S.A. returned to join with the anarchists who, in the years of the Mexican Revolution, were learning anarcho-syndicalist practice from Spain.[1] But the growing prosperity of the United States, the end of immigration and the absorption of the foreign elements, as well as the slow mitigation of the rigours of uncontrolled capitalist expansion, all removed the basis of American anarcho-syndicalism. In the twenties and thirties anarchism was kept alive as a creed in the U.S.A. among the Italian or Spanish immigrants; and, indeed, they were to have a *cause célèbre* with the trial of Sacco and Vanzetti and the six-year legal battle between their condemnation in 1921 and their execution in 1927. Sacco and Vanzetti had been condemned for murder in the course of an armed robbery near Boston; and although the facts of the case are still a subject of controversy,* the knowledge that they were admittedly anarchists undoubtedly did much to create prejudice against them in the minds of the citizens of Massachusetts, while this in turn made them the rallying-point for liberals and men and women of the left of all shades of opinion. Yet the campaign in their favour soon seemed to be taken out of the hands of their original anarchist comrades; and it was the communists who became increasingly active in their defence – though occasionally embarrassed by an anti-Soviet remark from Vanzetti in his prison cell – while the anarchists who had formed the original defence committee became correspondingly uneasy and suspicious. This was perhaps the last time when old-fashioned anarchist bomb attacks – including ones against the houses of the judge and of one of the jurors – still gave the impression that anarchism was a potent force in the United States. By the mid-twentieth century anarchism in the U.S.A. has reverted to being a dream which intellectuals discuss or a symbol of revolt against the affluent society that still attracts idealistic students, but which has long since ceased to be an effective social force.

* The latest examination of the evidence by Mr Francis Russell, in his interesting *Tragedy at Dedham* (New York 1962, London 1963), suggests that Sacco may have been guilty (although perhaps his robbery was to raise funds for the anarchist cause), while Vanzetti was almost certainly innocent.

Before 1914 the ideas and practice of anarcho-syndicalism had been widespread. Beatrice Webb could write in 1912: 'Syndicalism has taken the place of the old-fashioned Marxism. The angry youth, with bad complexion, frowning brow and weedy figure is nowadays a syndicalist; the glib young workman whose tongue runs away with him today mouths the phrases of French syndicalism instead of those of German social democracy.'[1] Although these ideas did not survive either in the advanced capitalist countries or in the centralized Soviet state, they were still powerful in countries where the class struggle was violent and the state powerless or unwilling to intervene – in the Argentine, where the teachings of Malatesta had not been forgotten by the Italian immigrants; in Uruguay and Bolivia; in Mexico and Peru, where Spaniards and the occasional militant who had been to the U.S.A. and seen the IWW in action kept alive the tradition of direct action in a revolutionary situation.[2] But in one country alone did the anarcho-syndicalist ideas originating in France at the end of the nineteenth century take root so successfully that for a brief period in the summer of 1936 the anarchist revolution seemed about to be achieved. It is to Spain that we must look to see a serious anarchist movement effectively at work; and it was the defeat of that movement in 1937 which marked the end of anarchism as a serious political force, even if it still survives as an intellectual one.

CHAPTER IX

Anarchists in Action: Spain

'Paz a los Hombres, Guerra a las Instituciones.'

Spanish anarchist slogan

'The problem was not only one of Bread but one of Hatred.'

Salvador Cordón

'El Español vive mucho de afirmaciones y de negaciones categóricas.'

José Peirats

I

For nearly seventy years anarchism was a revolutionary force in Spain; and the movement achieved an influence there far greater than anywhere else in the world. It is in Spain, therefore, that the stresses and contradictions, the savagery and nobility, the apocalyptic vision and the rationalist conviction of the anarchists can be seen most clearly.

There is no simple explanation of the fact that anarchism became a mass movement in Spain to an extent that it never did elsewhere. A backward country; a weak government; a total gap between rich and poor; above all, a rural population living, in many areas, hopelessly near to starvation and moved by a smouldering hatred of landlords and priests – all these could be found elsewhere in Europe (in Sicily, for example). Perhaps it was, as some have believed, because the Spanish temperament responded to the extremism of anarchist doctrines, and because a population accustomed to centuries of religious fanaticism responded readily to a fanaticism of another kind. Perhaps, again, the individualism, the independent pride and self-respect, commonly held to be characteristic of the Spaniard, made him ready to accept a doctrine which, in a more extreme form than even the Protestant religion, places on each individual the responsibility for his own actions. Marxist historians have tried to account for the success of anarchism rather than Marxism in Spain by an analysis of the way in which the ties of the feudal order were broken in the nineteenth century, without being replaced by the relations resulting from modern industrial and financial organization, so that Spain was somehow out of step with the pattern of historical development elsewhere.[1] Others, again, have seen the Spanish anarchist movement as proving the truth of Bakunin's contention that only those with nothing to lose – the *Lumpenproletariat* or the landless labourer – are capable of becoming true revolutionaries.

It was perhaps for a number of such reasons that Fanelli's bringing of Bakunin's gospel* to Spain had such far-reaching results. Certainly, the moment of Fanelli's arrival was a propitious one for the spreading of any revolutionary doctrine. In 1868 the mounting discontent with the rule of Queen Isabella among large sections of the population of Spain had come to a head, and she had been forced to abdicate. The search for a successor – apart from producing a Hohenzollern candidature which provided the pretext for the Franco-Prussian War of 1870 – resulted in a brief period of weak constitutional monarchy, followed by a short-lived liberal republic, and finally, after a period of confusion and disorder, in a restoration of the Bourbons and a general reaction that made any revolutionary activity exceedingly difficult. However, during the period 1868–74, anything seemed possible in Spain. These years were marked by sporadic outbreaks of revolt in different parts of the country, started by both the extreme Carlist right and the federal republican left. It was in these conditions of near civil war that the early Spanish anarchists gained their first experience of action. Moreover, it was a period when many middle-class intellectuals were attracted by Proudhon's doctrines. Pi y Margall, the leader of the federalist party, and Prime Minister for a short period under the republic, had translated Proudhon, and his ideas of a federal society based on small self-contained and self-governing communes were sufficiently close to those of Bakunin's disciples for

* See Chapter IV above.

them to have much common ground. As one anarchist intellectual put it: 'Consciously or unconsciously, the doctrines of Proudhon make up the creed of the majority of people in Spain, so that, in one form or another, in every Spaniard you will find a federalist.'[1] Moreover, Pi y Margall had explicitly linked the idea of a federal state with the idea of social revolution, and had emphasized the fact that 'our revolution is not purely political; it is social'.[2] Thus, in the turbulence of the years 1868–74 new ideas of social organization were inextricably involved with ideas of federalism and separatism. Indeed, one of the reasons for the success of anarchism in Barcelona was that it provided a working-class equivalent for the Catalan nationalism and separatism of the middle classes.

At this time there was little true socialism in Spain. Clubs such as the *Fomento de las Artes* in Madrid or the *Ateneo Catalán de la Clase Obrera* in Barcelona provided small groups of men with the opportunity for discussing the ideas of Fourier and Proudhon and the possibilities of organizing society on a basis of mutual co-operation. These groups consisted of professional men, students and craftsmen, the latter mostly printers and cobblers. They were not yet revolutionary and one of Bakunin's early followers in Spain, Rafael Farga Pellicer, was obliged to report to Bakunin that socialism in Spain was not yet 'as developed as was to be wished'.[3] Nevertheless, it was these groups which provided Fanelli with his first audiences, and among them he recruited the twenty or so men who were the first members of the anarchist movement in Spain.

Fanelli's first converts were in Madrid; perhaps the most important was Anselmo Lorenzo, a young printer, who was a few years later to settle in Barcelona and become one of the leading anarchists there. After founding a group in Madrid, Fanelli went on to Barcelona. One of his new friends in Madrid, José Rubau Donadeu, in whose house Fanelli's first meetings had been held, put him in touch with a painter, José Luis Pellicer, and his nephew, Rafael Farga Pellicer. In Pellicer's studio Fanelli addressed a group of about twenty, and thus launched the movement in Barcelona. Farga Pellicer, the nephew, was an important figure in its development, for it was through him that links were established between the bourgeois intellectuals of his uncle's circle and the *Centro Federal de las Sociedades Obreras de Barcelona* which loosely grouped together the various existing working-class organizations of the city – a city in which an old-established textile industry had produced a more advanced and better-organized working-class movement than anywhere else in Spain. With these contacts the anarchists began to have the possibility of a genuinely proletarian following, though it was a long time before the revolutionaries were more than a minority in the Barcelona working-class movement.

Fanelli's immediate contacts called themselves the Spanish Section of the International and, like Bakunin himself, did not feel that the programme of the Bakuninist Social Democratic Alliance which Fanelli preached was in any way incompatible with the aims of the International. They were soon disillusioned and found themselves plunged into a struggle with the Marxists by which they were often bewildered and which left the Spanish working-class movement permanently and disastrously divided. During 1870 and 1871 they gradually became aware of the quarrel between Marx and Bakunin, and were compelled reluctantly to take sides. Two of the original group, Farga Pellicer and Sentiñon, went to the Basle congress in 1869 and met Bakunin himself; and they were present as impotent observers at the final *débâcle* of the International at The Hague in 1872. Anselmo Lorenzo went to the London congress in 1871 and was well received by Marx and Engels. He was, however, quickly disillusioned by the atmosphere of the congress. A man of uncompromising directness, honesty and simplicity, he had expected much from the congress of a movement which seemed to offer the Spaniards hope of real support. Although he was impressed by Marx's genuinely warm welcome, and still more by his erudition and scholarship, of the congress as a whole he later wrote: 'I have sad memories of the week spent at that conference. The effect produced on my mind was disastrous: I hoped to see great thinkers, heroic defenders of the working man, enthusiastic propagators of new ideas, precursors of that society transformed by the revolution, in which justice would be practised and happiness enjoyed, and instead, I found serious grudges and terrible enmities between those who should have been united in a single will to attain the same goal.'[1]

At the end of 1871, when the split in the International was widening, Marx's son-in-law, Paul Lafargue, arrived in Spain as the representative of the London General Council and tried to assume control of the section of the International there. He had little immediate success and, perhaps for this reason, succeeded in remaining on good personal terms with Anselmo Lorenzo and some of the other leading followers of Bakunin. It was nearly ten years before the Marxist socialist party assumed any importance and, under the leadership of Pablo Iglesias, a young printer who had been an early member of the International but who had followed Marx and Lafargue rather than Bakunin and his Spanish disciples, began to develop into a socialist trade-union movement and a socialist political party.

Actually, the progress made by the revolutionary movement in Spain, of whatever allegiance, was halted by the severe government action against the International, which was officially banned in January 1872. Nevertheless, until the fall of the republic in 1874 it continued to be active. Congresses were held to discuss the fundamental principles of revolutionary action and reflected the rivalries in the International. (It was at a congress at Córdoba in the New Year of 1873 that the Spanish section of the International declared itself formally for Bakunin rather than for Marx.) By the time the anarchist movement was driven underground after the restoration of the monarchy – and, of course, the very principle of decentralization and anonymity on which the movement was based made it particularly fitted for a clandestine existence – it had a number of successes to its credit and had already established its own legends. One of the principles most firmly maintained by the Spanish anarchists was that 'the emancipation of the workers must be the work of the workers themselves', and consequently they had taken the lead in a number of spontaneous strikes in Barcelona and elsewhere. One of these – a general strike in favour of the eight-hour day among

the paper workers at Alcoy, between Valencia and Alicante –
led to an insurrection in 1873 which made Alcoy a symbolic
name in the history of the anarchist movement. Delegates from
Alcoy had played a leading role at the congress at Córdoba, and
five of them were members of the Federal Council of the International in Spain. As a result, Alcoy had been chosen as the seat
of the Federal Council, so that a number of the chief figures in
the Spanish Section of the International were there to lead the
rising in person. The workers seized and burned the factories,
killed the mayor and marched round the town with the heads
of the policemen whom they had put to death. It was a frightening sign both of the potential power of the workers and of their
ruthlessness after years of oppression, and Alcoy became a name
with which to remind the workers of their militant traditions and
also to alarm the bourgeoisie with the threat of violence and
terror.[1]

However, the real achievement of the anarchist leaders during
the few years between Fanelli's arrival and the restoration of the
Bourbons was not just that they had begun to influence the
urban workers of an industrial centre like Barcelona, and to
practise the revolutionary strike some thirty years before the
development of anarcho-syndicalist doctrines in France. The
most remarkable fact about Spanish anarchism was its appeal
to the most depressed and desperate section of the whole population – the landless farm workers and the small peasants of the
south. It was this combination of the artisans and workers in the
most advanced industrial areas with the desperately poor rural
masses, whom Bakunin had seen as the best material for revolution, that gave the anarchist movement its broad basis of support
and its widespread appeal.

Throughout Spanish history there had been a series of spontaneous, disorganized and savagely repressed peasant revolts in
Castile, Aragón and Andalusia. In the nineteenth century the
lot of the peasants was perhaps harder than ever; the common
lands had been broken up and sold by governments anxious for
cash to balance their budgets; the landlords recognized fewer
and fewer obligations towards their peasants. As in the south of

Italy, absentee landlords began to regard their estates solely as a means of raising enough income to enable them to live in style and comfort elsewhere – or when they did live on or near their estates, as in the wine-growing area around Jerez, their scale of living only emphasized the gap between rich and poor. Several of Fanelli's first disciples in Barcelona were Andalusian in origin; and even before this there had been groups in the ports of the south – Málaga and Cádiz – who were familiar with the doctrines of Fourier and Cabet as well as of Proudhon.* It was in Cádiz that the first anarchist centre in the south was formed, and at first it was the artisans, schoolmasters and students in the towns who picked up the new ideas or learnt them from travelling apostles, such as Anselmo Lorenzo, who also spread the doctrines to Portugal. The first influential anarchists in Andalusia were men like Navarro Prieto, the son of a schoolmaster, who, having got himself to the university but having failed to pass his examinations, became a successful anarchist journalist; or Agustín Cervantes, a melancholy and hypochondriacal legal and classical scholar who lost his professorial chair because of his anti-clerical and radical views.

There was enough endemic unrest in the countryside for revolutionary material to be readily available. As in Sicily, bandits had always played a role in Andalusian life and many of them had become honoured legendary figures who had defied central authority and robbed from the rich to give to the poor. The new anarchist doctrines merely seemed to confirm what every peasant had long felt – that the landlord, the state and the church had combined to oppress him and deprive him of his natural rights. In 1844 the government had created a new police force, the *Guardia Civil*, to suppress banditry. In the confused and unruly years between 1868 and 1874 the Civil Guards were increasingly in evidence; and by the end of this period it was the anarchists against whom they mainly acted. 'From now on', in Gerald Brenan's words, 'every Civil Guard became a recruiting

---

* Even as *bien-pensant* a Spanish lady as the Empress Eugénie had read Fourier by the time she was eighteen years old. (See Theodore Zeldin, *Emile Ollivier and the Liberal Empire of Napoleon III* (Oxford 1963), p. 94.)

officer for anarchism.'¹ The state now seemed identified with the landlord, and the abolition of one must, it seemed, lead to the abolition of the other.

With the collapse of the republic and the end of the hopes of the liberal federalists and cantonalists, some federal republicans began to see in anarchism a way out of their disillusionment, just as some of the same sort of people in Italy turned to anarchism when disappointed with the ineffectiveness of Mazzini's republicanism. One of these, Fermin Salvochea, was to become a typical saint of the Andalusian anarchist movement. He came to anarchism in a way not unlike that by which Bakunin and Kropotkin had become social revolutionaries. He was the son of a prosperous merchant in Cádiz and was twenty-six years old at the time of Queen Isabella's abdication.² He had lived in England for a time and he was impressed by Bradlaugh's militant rationalism and had become an eager reader of Tom Paine. During the years after 1868 he was involved first in a republican rising in Cádiz and then in the federalist rising in Catalonia. In 1871, after being in and out of prison, he became the mayor (*alcalde*) of Cádiz, but again was soon involved in another federalist revolt and this time was sent to a penal colony in Africa. Here he read about and reflected on the nature of society and revolution and he became an intellectually convinced anarchist. He at once put his principles into practice: he refused a pardon which his family had used their influence to obtain for him, tearing it up in front of the prison governor and declaring that there were only two ways of obtaining freedom – by force or as part of a general amnesty for all political offenders. In 1886 he succeeded in escaping and returned to Cádiz, where he founded an anarchist periodical. During the next years he quickly became one of the most respected leaders of Andalusian anarchism, as much admired by the peasants and workers as he was detested by the members of the class from which he originated. On May Day 1890 and again in 1891 he organized great anarchist demonstrations all over Andalusia, with the result that he was soon arrested and imprisoned again.

While he was in prison, in January 1892, a band of 500

workers and farmhands marched into Jerez in an attempt to
liberate 157 anarchists who had been imprisoned there the year
before on charges of belonging to the mysterious *Mano Negra*, an
anarchist movement which, indeed, may never have existed outside the imagination of the police, who were always ready to
attribute isolated, unconnected acts of violence to a single master
organization. Although Salvochea was in jail in Cádiz at the
time, he was accused of organizing the raid and was condemned
to a further period of imprisonment, part of which was spent in
military confinement under conditions so bad that even Salvochea's spirit broke and he attempted suicide. When he was released in 1899 he was frail and ill, but till his death in 1907 he
remained an object of reverence to anarchists all over Spain. His
career is typical of the anarchist militants of his generation, men
who became the heroes and saints of the revolutionary movement
in Spain in the twentieth century. Moreover, the character of
men like Salvochea or Anselmo Lorenzo, austere, simple, dedicated apostles of the anarchist cause, was one which appealed to
a movement that had a strongly puritanical side. The really
serious anarchists, especially in Andalusia, neither smoked nor
drank, while their sexual morality was often extremely prudish.
Thus it was men like Salvochea, who remained celibate, or
Lorenzo, who lived faithfully and happily all his life with his
unwedded *compañera*, who were closer to the spirit of the movement than intellectual practitioners of free love like Francisco
Ferrer, although he became another of the famous martyrs of
the Spanish left.

During the 1870s the revolutionary movement in Spain worked
largely underground, and it is probably impossible to ascertain
its strength. In 1889 the return to power of the liberals made
open organization to a certain extent possible again; and this
gave the Marxist socialists the chance to develop a socialist
political party. However, throughout the 1880s it was the anarchists who had kept the idea of revolution alive. They were
associated – generally correctly – with many of the outbreaks of
violence and the strikes which took place in this period. The
doctrine of propaganda by the deed found a ready audience in

Spain, so that, in the 1890s, anarchist activity consisted both of support for any sort of strike or rising springing spontaneously from below and of individual acts of terrorism and symbolic vengeance such as the attack on General Martínez Campos or the murder of Cánovas del Castillo.* What made these acts particularly notable was the extreme severity with which they were punished. In September 1896 a law against anarchists was introduced and it was enforced with the utmost savagery. During the following ten years, to the accompaniment of protests from all the liberals of Europe, the anarchists suffered, often quite unjustly, a series of prison sentences and executions as frequent and severe as anything experienced until the totalitarian régimes of the twentieth century.

The most notorious of these trials and executions was that of Francisco Ferrer in 1909. Ferrer was the son of a prosperous peasant near Barcelona and was born in 1859.[1] Although his family were devout Catholics, one of his uncles was a free thinker, and his first employer, a grain merchant, was a radical atheist. Ferrer grew into a young man of violent anti-clerical views and revolutionary sympathies. The latter he was able to express practically by taking a job as the conductor of the train running across the French frontier between Barcelona and Cerbère, and using the opportunity to help political refugees cross over the border. Then, in 1886, he was involved in a republican rising and fled to Paris, where he stayed till 1901. For a time he ran a restaurant and then he became secretary to a Spanish republican politician, in exile like himself. At the same time he started to collect a few pupils, to whom he taught Spanish by new and experimental methods.

In his stay in Paris, Ferrer developed his ideas about society and, in particular, about education. Starting from his deep hatred of the Catholic church, and of its domination over such public education as there was in Spain, he dreamed of a Modern School where instruction would be based on rational principles and where children of all classes and both sexes could mix and only those whose families could afford it would pay. It was, in

* See p. 130 above.

effect, a return to the educational ideal of Rousseau's *Emile*, and an attempt to adapt some of the ideas of eighteenth- and nine-teenth-century educational reformers to the situation in Spain. What gave Ferrer's ideas their particular quality was the militant atheism which underlay them and the fact that public education in Spain was extremely backward, so that any proposals for reform seemed startling. The principle on which the schools were to be based was spontaneity: 'True education worthy of the name will obtain everything by spontaneity alone.'[1] It was through education of this type that the school should prepare 'a better humanity, more perfect, more just than present humanity'. 'I intend', Ferrer wrote in 1900, 'to form a school of emancipation, which will be concerned with banning from the mind whatever divides men, the false concepts of property, country and family, so as to attain the liberty and well-being which all desire and none completely realizes.'[2]

Ferrer denied that he was an anarchist; and he did not want to be directly involved with any revolutionary movement: '*Plutôt qu'un révolutionnaire, je suis un révolté*,' he said. He was con-sistent in his condemnation of anarchist acts of terrorism. Never-theless, in his insistence on individual responsibility and in his belief in the necessity of a rational, scientific education as a means of social reform, he was obviously near to the anarchists. Indeed, the Spanish Section of the International had already passed a resolution calling for an '*enseñanza integral*' as its congress at Saragossa in 1872, so that Ferrer's ideas seemed to fit in with theirs; and, when Ferrer returned to Spain to found his *Escuela Moderna*, Anselmo Lorenzo, who had first met him in Paris, became one of his closest collaborators.

Ferrer, in his exile in Paris during the stormy anarchist decade of the nineties, was determined to raise money to enable him to found a school on his own lines. In this he was lucky. He was separated from his wife, who indeed had tried to shoot him in a Paris street, and he met and fell in love with a girl called Léo-poldine Bonnard. Léopoldine became the companion to a rich elderly lady of extremely bigoted Catholic views. Nevertheless, Ferrer's eloquence and, presumably, his charm were such that she became converted by him and Léopoldine to their ideas, and when she died a few years later she left Ferrer all her money. When he returned to Barcelona in 1901 he thus had the means to realize his dream of founding the *Escuela Moderna* and a publishing house to produce the textbooks which a rational education demanded. He returned to Spain at a moment when, as a result of the defeat in the war with the United States in 1898 and the loss of almost all the remaining Spanish Empire, many intellectuals were discussing and criticizing the fundamental assumptions of Spanish life. Thus Ferrer's ideas aroused a considerable interest and were widely discussed. In fact, his school was extremely small; it had thirty-three pupils when it opened and never rose above fifty. But the challenge to accepted social and religious ideas which it represented soon made it notorious. Ferrer paraded his militant atheism by actions such as organizing a picnic for his pupils on Good Friday, while his private life increased the bad reputation which he had among the *bien-pensants*. He had separated, though in a friendly way, from Léopoldine Bonnard, by whom he had had a son, and had fallen in love with a beautiful girl called Soledad Villafranca, who had anarchist sympathies and was a teacher at his school. It was an association that was to contribute to Ferrer's tragedy.

On 31st May 1906 a bomb was thrown at the king and queen by a man named Mateo Morall, who had been a librarian at Ferrer's school and who had been an unsuccessful rival of Ferrer for the love of Soledad Villafranca. Ferrer was at once arrested and charged with complicity in the attempt to assassinate the king and queen. After a year's delay in prison, he was in fact, acquitted, but when he returned home he found that his school had been closed. After his release he visited Paris and London (where he called on Kropotkin), but returned to Spain to continue his publishing activities and to make propaganda for his educational methods.

In the summer of 1909 there was a growing political crisis in Spain. Revolution was in the air, especially in Barcelona. Alejandro Lerroux, the young leader of the left-wing radical republicans in Catalonia, had been conducting a campaign of violent

anti-clerical agitation, exhorting his followers to burn churches
and to sack convents, while the Catalan anarchists were perfectly
ready to add their quota of bombs and assassinations to the
general unrest. Then, in July, after a defeat of the Spanish army
in Morocco, the government decided to call up the reservists in
Catalonia for service in Africa. This was too much for a population which had already had enough of inefficient and oppressive
government, and for whom the disasters of the Cuban war were
still fresh in their minds. Barcelona rose in revolt and for a week
– the *Semana Trágica* – it looked as though a spontaneous social
revolution had broken out. As Anselmo Lorenzo wrote in a letter
on 21st July: 'It is amazing! The social revolution has started in
Barcelona, and it has been started by something so ill defined,
misunderstood and wrongly identified as that which is sometimes
called the vile rabble and sometimes His Majesty the People. No
one started it! No one led it! Neither liberals nor Catalan
separatists, nor republicans nor socialists nor anarchists. . . . A
week of intoxication, of holy rage, seeing that the fury of the
masses was justified by a hundred centuries of misery, oppression
and endurance.'[1]

One of the inevitable consequences of the anarchist doctrine
that anarchists must at once join and attempt to steer any spontaneous popular uprising was that they were always held responsible for such outbreaks, even though, in fact, it was nearly always
impossible to find out exactly how a particular revolt started.
After the *Semana Trágica*, however, it was not only the anarchists
who were to suffer in the repression that followed. Large numbers
of people were arrested and executed or deported; but the most
famous victim was Ferrer. During and immediately before the
riots he had been at his house in the country and visited Barcelona
only once to try and find out what was happening. He had been
on good terms with Lerroux, whose violent anti-clericalism he
found sympathetic, but he had never indulged in the inflamma-
tory mob oratory with which Lerroux had contributed to creating
the atmosphere that made the *Semana Trágica* possible. Yet, while
Lerroux survived to become a responsible bourgeois politician,
Ferrer was arrested and brought before a court martial. The fact

that he had been acquitted two years earlier doubtless contributed to the determination of the authorities to deal with him this time, and by now he had become a dangerous monster in the eyes of all supporters of the established order. The tribunal, although there was really no evidence against him, sentenced him to death; and he was executed on 13th October 1909. It is reported that his last words to the firing squad were: 'Aim well, my friends, you are not responsible. I am innocent. *Viva la Escuela Moderna!*'

The execution of Ferrer, like that of Sacco and Vanzetti in the United States some twenty years later, provoked an international outcry. In this case the Spanish government of the conservative Maura fell as a result of their mishandling of the events in Barcelona; and the new government opened a new phase in the Spanish crisis. Ferrer's fate is perhaps typical of the non-violent anarchist whose doctrines inevitably lead to his being identified with actions of which he disapproved. Ferrer himself had written: 'If I am called an anarchist for a sentence in which I spoke about "ideas of destruction in the mind", I will reply that in the collection of books and pamphlets published by the Modern School you can certainly find ideas of destruction, but please note that these are "ideas of destruction *in the mind*" – that is ideas of a rational and scientific nature, directed only against prejudice; is this anarchism? If so, I did not know it, but in this case I should be an anarchist in so far as anarchism would have adopted my ideas on education, on peace, and on love, and not because I would have adopted its methods.'[1] It is a dilemma which intellectual anarchists have only been able to escape in societies where violence was rare and not, as in Spain, an integral part of social and political life. It is the men with revolutionary ideas who are held responsible for revolutionary acts, in conditions when the only means of social change is violent action.

The *Semana Trágica*, however it started and however little it was in fact planned by the anarchists, firmly established them as the leaders of the revolutionary movement in Barcelona. With the revolutionary experience of 1909 added to their long list of heroic, bloody and hopeless risings, and with the new forms of action and organization which they were learning from the example of revolutionary syndicalism in France, the Spanish anarchists were by 1912 entering on a new phase of effective militancy.

2

The anarchist movement in Spain experienced in the most intense way the contradictory currents of ideas inherent in anarchist thought and practice everywhere; and each of the anarchist thinkers and leaders outside Spain had contributed to it. As we have seen, Proudhon's federalism had, by the 1860s, already become a doctrine shared by anarchists and many liberal republicans. The idea of the commune as the basis for the new social organization was taken for granted by the anarchists and, whenever they had the chance, the formation of a revolutionary commune was the first step they took. Bakunin's belief in the revolutionary potential of the suffering, ignorant masses, only awaiting the apostles of violent revolt to break out into effective action, seemed to find empirical confirmation in the enthusiasm with which the day labourers of Andalusia responded to the missionaries of 'the Idea', as the anarchist militants called it. Kropotkin's faith in human goodness and progress and his confidence in the possibilities of education seemed to be finding practical expression in the educational ideals of Ferrer and Anselmo Lorenzo. At the same time, these ideals and the fanatical devotion they inspired had their sinister side; nowhere more than in Spain was violent destruction an inherent part of the anarchist creed.

The 'tragic week' in Barcelona in 1909, with its spontaneous, disorganized acts of violence which the hastily improvised committees of the working-class movements, anarchist or socialist, were unable to control or direct, and the reprisals that followed, including the tragic execution of Ferrer, was both a culmination of the sporadic violence of the previous twenty-five years and the beginning of a new phase in the history of Spanish anarchism. In 1908 a new group in Barcelona, *Solidaridad Obrera*, tried to organize the workers on an anarchist basis; and, although its activities were suspended for a time as a result of the events of 1909, the idea of a libertarian, revolutionary syndicalist movement had taken root. In 1911 the *Confederación Nacional de Trabajo* (CNT) was founded in Barcelona. This was a body similar to the French CGT and to a large extent modelled on it. Although it was not until 1914 that it could operate legally, it began to be a formidable force in many centres – in Catalonia, Aragón, Andalusia, and later in Galicia, while the anarcho-syndicalists established contact with the anarchists of South America and provided the movement there with ideas and leaders. Although many of the ideas and tactics of the CNT were imported from France,[1] the revolutionary syndicalist movement in Spain was unique, both because anarchist ideas were more widely diffused than anywhere else and because of the alliance on which it was based between industrial and rural workers. In Barcelona and the other cities of Catalonia the federalist, anarchist tradition had been unbroken since the time of the First International; and it was now reinforced by an effective working-class organization. And, just as in the urban anarchist strongholds, there was an undercurrent of revolt that could turn a strike into a riot or a labour dispute into a street fight, so in the vast, arid, underdeveloped and overexploited south, a helpless and hopeless rural proletariat waited desperately for any sign that might suggest that an improvement in their condition was possible. Thus, as Díaz del Moral and Gerald Brenan have shown, there were in Andalusia periodical waves of excitement, agitation and expectation when new converts were made and when the revolution seemed imminent.

The ideas of anarchism in general and of the general strike in particular had been spread in the south by travelling propagandists, and still more by a large number of leaflets and pamphlets which were put out by the anarchist centres in the provincial towns and which, pored over in the dim light of the barracks where the day labourers lived herded together, or explained to the illiterates by those of their comrades who could read, stirred up hopes of an immediate regeneration of society. For landless day labourers or for the small peasants whose diminutive holdings did not produce enough for their families to live on, such regeneration was inevitably going to come about through the redistribution of land – *el reparto*. 'The Reparto', the historian of these movements has written, 'has constantly been the magic word in all the rural disturbances which, has electrified the masses.'[1] In 1903 there had been one of the recurrent waves of revolutionary agitation in Andalusia; in Córdoba the general strike was declared. But, as so often, the movement petered out in the face of resistance and still more in the face of the difficulty of maintaining enthusiasm and an effective organization among backward, scattered and remote communities. Moreover, the agitations of 1903 were followed in 1904 by a major famine – and, as Díaz del Moral has remarked, 'poverty and hunger are the worst enemies of proletarian agitation'.[2] For nearly fifteen years the anarchist movement in the south only just managed to survive, until another upsurge of hope and the revolutionary situation elsewhere in Spain and outside brought a new period of agitation.

During the dark periods of Andalusian anarchism – in the 1870s or in the period after the famine of 1904 – the 'idea' was largely kept alive by devoted propagandists and journalists, of whom José Sánchez Román was typical.[3] The son of a shoemaker, he had grown up in the 1870s and had learnt to read in the intervals of working in the fields and mending his comrades' shoes in the evenings. He was involved in the agitation attributed to the *Mano Negra* and was one of the moving spirits behind the famous attack on Jerez in 1892. Out of prison, he had read every anarchist pamphlet he could lay hands on; in prison he was able to learn at first hand from Fermin Salvochea and from a French anarchist who was a friend and disciple of Reclus. When he emerged in 1901 he became one of the most energetic, effective and widely read anarchist journalists in the south. However, the work of propagandists and journalists like Sánchez Román would not have been possible without the support of the anarchist workers who kept the doctrine alive in each village – the '*obrero consciente*', austerely devoted to the cause, who 'did not taste alcohol, did not smoke, did not gamble, never pronounced the word God, lived with his *compañera* without religious or legal ties or married before the municipal judge'.[1] It was these people who gave the movement its strength and continuity; and it was they who suffered, often heroically, in the repressions to which their activities gave rise. Sometimes they were attracted by even more uncompromising doctrines. At certain moments the most serious anarchists were vegetarians as well as teetotallers. These militants, while basing their belief on rational arguments, had the faith to live lives of such strict dedication that they can only be compared to the friars or missionaries of the Christian church.

In 1917–18, when reports of the distant revolution in Russia began to filter through to Spain, there was another intense proselytizing movement similar to that of 1903. Once again the pamphlets were circulated and those who could not read clustered round those who could to hear the doctrines of Kropotkin or of the French anarchist pamphleteers. The enthusiasm for the idea of Russia was so great that one leading anarchist, Salvador Cordón, changed his name to Khordoniev. Once again, too, the old dreams revived of an era when the landless labourers would become owners of a plot of land, when a system of irrigation might bring prosperity to the arid, stony fields, and the fertile plains no longer be in the hands of the rich. The CNT had increased its influence among the rural workers of Andalusia over the preceding years, so that local agricultural unions were able to organize effective strikes and to assert their short-term demands as well as dreaming of a future paradise.

In fact, between 1917 and 1923, all over Spain revolutionary strikes by the CNT were both producing a state of virtual civil war and also, inevitably, creating dilemmas for the anarchists about the way in which their movement was to be organized and about the relations of the anarchists and the CNT to other revolutionary opponents of the existing government. Spain had not been involved in the World War, and consequently the legacy of patriotic solidarity that was never totally forgotten by the trade-union movements in the belligerent countries did not affect the actions of the CNT. Moreover, during the war Spain had experienced a comparative boom; industry had flourished and for once there had been a labour shortage, so that the government and employers had been obliged to tolerate a certain amount of trade-union activity. The end of the war brought a slump; the cost of living rose; there was widespread unemployment, and the trade unions – both the socialist UGT and the anarcho-syndicalist CNT – were thrown back on the defensive. In a prolonged series of strikes they attempted to preserve their own legal existence and to gain a minimum wage and improved conditions of work, as well as asserting certain political aims.

For some five years, strikes, lockouts and violence of all kinds brought government in Spain almost to a stop and increased the economic distress which had originally inspired the strikes, while each act of violence by one side brought its reprisals from the other. Almost all parts of the country were affected, but it was in Barcelona that the struggle was bitterest. Barcelona was one of the great strongholds of the CNT, and it was in Catalonia that many of the most famous revolutionary syndicalist leaders were operating. Two of these, Angel Pestaña and Salvador Seguí, were revolutionary syndicalists in the French tradition, who believed in the necessity for organization and in short-term trade-union activity as well as in an ultimate revolutionary goal; and, as elsewhere, this was something which many true anarchists were not prepared to support. Certainly, the CNT leaders had some successes to their credit, notably the results of the notorious strike early in 1919 at the *Canadiense* works, a large hydro-electric concern in Barcelona. After a two-month strike which developed into a general strike in the whole of Catalonia, the government capitulated. It issued decrees instituting an eight-hour day and took other measures to meet some of the workers' grievances. However, these concessions were accompanied by a renewed attack on the revolutionary unions, and for the next four years there was open war between the CNT and the employers. One of the main means used against the revolutionary syndicalists was the foundation of independent unions – the *sindicatos libres* – which would, it was hoped, attract support away from the revolutionary syndicates. In the event, a kind of gang warfare developed between the two movements in Catalonia, with the employers hiring *pistoleros* to assassinate CNT leaders, and with the syndicalists replying in kind. In one of these attacks Salvador Seguí was murdered. He was a trade-union organizer of considerable gifts who had also turned himself into an intellectual revolutionary with ideas borrowed from Nietzsche as well as from his anarchist friends, but who had always used his influence against terrorism and in favour of organized trade-union activity.

For many years the CNT was seriously divided by the conflict of opinion between Seguí and Pestaña on the one hand and, on the other, those who wanted direct revolutionary action of a purely anarchist kind. This conflict naturally led to repeated arguments about anarchist first principles. During the years of open strife with government and employers, the issue was less acute, though a few militant anarchists, especially in Andalusia, refused to support the CNT. It was characteristic of this phase that the CNT congress of 1922 passed a resolution as confused and equivocal as the one with which the IWW in the United States had started its career. The CNT, the congress stated, 'being a completely revolutionary organism which frankly and expressly refuses parliamentary and collaborationist action with political parties, is at the same time wholly and absolutely political, since its mission is that of winning its right to review and to criticize all the evolutionary factors of national life, and to that end its duty is to exert decisive pressure, by means of joint action stemming from the capabilities and demonstrations of the CNT'.[1]

The anarchists also had many arguments about what was happening in Russia. The first enthusiasm for the revolution slowly ebbed as the true situation became known; but it was only reluctantly that the CNT gave up the idea of belonging to the Third International and it was only after bitter discussions that, in 1922, they finally withdrew from membership. Just as, sixty years earlier, the Spanish anarchists had gradually discovered that adherence to the First International and loyalty to Bakunin were not consistent with each other, so now they found that they were not long able to base their policy on the optimistic resolution passed enthusiastically at a national congress in 1919 which affirmed first that 'the CNT declares it is a firm defender of the principles of the First International maintained by Bakunin; and second, it declares that it adheres provisionally to the Communist International because of the revolutionary character which inspires it; meanwhile the CNT is organizing and summoning a universal workers' congress which will agree and settle the principles on which the true Workers' International will be based'.[1] The final break with the Third International in 1922 cost the anarcho-syndicalist movement some able and militant supporters, such as Andrés Nin and Joaquín Maurín, who, after a period as communists, led the dissident Partido Obrero Unificado Marxista (POUM) and further complicated the left-wing political scene in Catalonia, before becoming the victims of communist vengeance in 1937.

The years 1917–23 demonstrated both the power of the CNT and its limits. They could claim in 1919 over 700,000 members organized in industrial unions (*sindicatos de ramo*). They were able to maintain a continuous, violent and effective series of strikes and agitation in many parts of the country. They were extending their influence in areas such as Galicia, where they had been weak previously and far less numerous than their socialist rivals of the UGT. Yet, as so often, all this activity had failed to produce the final revolutionary situation which the syndicalist leaders expected and which their theories demanded, and even before the establishment of Primo de Rivera's dictatorship in 1923, the CNT had lost its initiative. The movement was weakened by its internal divisions about ends and means. The attempts made by the CNT and the UGT to collaborate never lasted very long and their rivalry grew more and more bitter. When Primo de Rivera established his dictatorship in 1923, the CNT's declaration of a general strike was not supported by the UGT, and within eight months the CNT was forced into becoming a clandestine organization once more. Anarchist periodicals were largely banned; anarchist and syndicalist offices were closed and over 200 leading militants were arrested. During the years of Primo de Rivera's dictatorship, as so often in the past, the Spanish anarchists were forced back on an examination of their tactics and obliged to reflect on their aims. They succeeded in keeping some of the federations of the CNT in being; but it was the anarchist militants who took the initiative in founding a new organization which would, they hoped, infuse new life into the movement and recall it to its true revolutionary aims, at a time when open syndicalist action was no longer possible. This new group was the *Federación Anarquista Iberica* (FAI), founded at a secret meeting in Valencia in July 1927. Within a few years the FAI became the driving force behind the Spanish anarchist movement. At first it had to operate in secrecy and obscurity, and was a true Bakuninist secret society of young, fanatical revolutionaries who were determined to restore the anarchist movement to a course of uncompromising opposition to the existing order, and to put an end to the flirtations with the republican politicians of which they suspected some of the CNT leaders. The FAI was, in fact, explicitly founded in imitation of Bakunin's own Social Democratic Alliance, and it was intended that it should perform the same role in the Spanish anarcho-syndicalist movement as the Alliance was meant to do in the International, that is to say, to provide a nucleus of dedicated and determined revolutionaries to inspire and control the whole movement.

During the period of Primo de Rivera's dictatorship, the possibilities of anarchist action were very limited. The CNT was able to retain its prestige as a true revolutionary organization, especially as the UGT and the socialist party were prepared to accept certain compromises with Primo de Rivera's régime. The price the CNT paid for preserving its revolutionary position was impotence and persecution. However, it was able to emerge from the period of dictatorship comparatively strong, and in 1931 could still claim over half a million members. The king's dismissal of Primo de Rivera in 1930 was followed by his own abdication in 1931. And, as in the years after 1868, suddenly everything seemed possible and a revolution not far away.

Inevitably, therefore, the anarchists had to take up the familiar debate about their relationship to the new republic and to the other revolutionary working-class parties, at a moment when a Constituent Assembly was preparing a new constitution. Inside the CNT the discussion had been going on for some time, with Angel Pestaña leading the wing which believed that something short of total revolution might be obtainable and desirable as a short-term goal, and Juan Peiró opposing any sort of association with politicians of whichever party. After the declaration of the republic in 1931, the CNT was no longer a clandestine organization and was reorganized once more as a national movement. In the face of violent denunciations of 'German bureaucracy' and 'centralism', the individual factory unions were reorganized into national industrial federations, and, in spite of protests from anarchists such as García Oliver that 'the Federations of Industry come from Germany and it looks as though they have come out of a barrel of beer', the new organization was accepted. The attitude of the CNT was necessarily ambivalent, both because of the differences of opinion about tactics between Pestaña and Peiró, and also because, as always, they were torn between a desire not to be left out of the new republican scene and a deep mistrust of the government's aims and motives. On the one hand, 'the Constituent Assembly is a product of a revolutionary act, an act which directly or indirectly had our support'. On the other hand, 'We hope for nothing from the Constituent Assembly, conceived in the womb of capitalist society and ready to defend its hegemony in its triple aspect, political, juridical and economic.'[1]

The republic, born in the midst of the world economic crisis, soon showed itself quite unable to deal with the worsening situation. Equally, the growing unemployment and distress created its own problems for the anarchists in the CNT. Pestaña and Peiró, although they had been divided previously about the question of contact with the politicians and support for the Constituent Assembly, were now united against the anarchists of the FAI, and in August 1931 they issued a manifesto with thirty signatures, setting out very clearly the differences as they saw them between revolutionary syndicalism and anarchism. After attacking the government's failure to deal with the economic situation, they attacked equally strongly the belief that a revolution could be

made then and there by a hastily improvised minority action:
'In the face of this oversimplified concept of the revolution –
classical and rather dangerous – which at present would deliver
us over to a republican fascism . . . we oppose another, true one,
the only practical and comprehensive one, which can lead us
unfailingly to the attainment of our final objective. . . . This
requires that the preparation should not only be preparation of
aggressive elements of combat, but that it should also have moral
elements, which today are the strongest, the most destructive and
the most difficult to defeat. . . . The revolution does not trust
exclusively in the audacity of more or less audacious minorities,
but rather it wants to be a movement developing out of the
people as a whole, of the working class marching towards its
final liberation, of the syndicates and of the Confederation which
will determine the act, the gesture and the precise moment of
the revolution. . . . We are revolutionaries, yes; but we do not
cultivate the myth of revolution.'[1]

Cultivation of the myth of revolution was, of course, just what
the FAI believed in, and by now their influence was strong
enough in the CNT to secure the expulsion of Pestaña, Peiró and
the other signatories of the manifesto of the thirty. All members of
the FAI had to be members of the CNT; and they were successful
in getting elected to the committees which decided CNT policy,
nationally and locally. As the CNT, on the best anarchist lines,
had no permanent officials and the minimum administrative
arrangements, the most militant and devoted people could win
considerable authority and prestige by their personalities alone,
and there was no bureaucratic hierarchy of conservative permanent officials to stop them adopting the most extreme courses.
Moreover, in the violent struggles of the post-war years and in
the period of clandestine illegal activity under Primo de Rivera's
dictatorship, the more brutal, tough and destructive members of
the movement tended to come to the fore. The younger generation were, some by temperament, some by intellectual conviction,
committed to uncompromising direct action more than ever
before. Typical of this generation of extremists was Buenaven-
tura Durruti, who was to become one of the great anarchist

heroes and martyrs of the Civil War. He was a railway worker
from León, born in 1896, and in the troubles of 1917 he organized
sabotage on the railways. He was exiled to France and, except
for a brief return to Spain when he was involved in an unsuccessful attempt on the life of Alfonso XIII and a successful one on the
life of the archbishop of Saragossa, he lived in France until 1931.
He was a man who stopped at nothing; he had robbed and
murdered in the anarchist cause, and the 'innocent expression'
which Gerald Brenan[1] noted is perhaps offset in his photographs
by a cruel mouth, and was certainly belied by his deeds. With his
friend Francisco Ascaso, he became a symbol of anarchist cruelty
and ruthlessness to his opponents.

During the years between the declaration of the republic in
1931 and the outbreak of the Civil War in 1936 there were a
number of occasions when the anarchists attempted to set up
insurrectional communes in various parts of Spain, in the hope
that their action would give the signal for general revolution.
The pattern of these actions was much the same everywhere and
recalls the comparable attempts made by the Italian anarchists
some fifty years before. The CNT took over the town; money
was declared abolished; the archives were burnt; the *Guardia
Civil* was disarmed and disbanded or murdered. In January 1932
such an attempt took place at two places in the upper Llobregat
valley in Catalonia. It was suppressed after five days of violent
fighting and, as a result, Durruti and Ascaso were deported to
an African penal settlement. It is worth quoting a letter which
Ascaso wrote as he left Spain, for it is typical of a certain eloquence and pathos that seem to have come naturally to even the
toughest and most ruthless anarchists: 'We are going away. . . .
To go away – according to the poet – is to die a little. Yet for us
who are not poets, departure has always been a symbol of life.
Constantly on the march, perpetually on the road like eternal
Jews without a country; outside a society in which we find no
environment in which to live; belonging to an exploited class,
without any place in the world, for us to travel is always a sign
of vitality.'[2]

During these years in which the anarchists were, so to speak, rehearsing for the great days in the summer of 1936, when final revolution seemed within reach, there were a number of such episodes. A revolutionary general strike was attempted in Seville in the summer of 1932, against an attempt by General Sanjurjo to seize power by a military coup. 'The only answer', the anarchists wrote, 'to such unworthy provocation is a revolutionary general strike, to start a civil war immediately, in the streets and in the fields. Let each house become a castle, let each roof become a fortress raised heroically against aggressive militarism and in favour of civil liberties.'[1] In this case the CNT's action was effective enough and Sanjurjo's rising was defeated by the strike in conjunction with the government's measures. Other anarchist attempts at revolution were less successful. In January 1933, for example, there were riots in Barcelona, and the south was ablaze with spontaneous risings; revolutionary communes were proclaimed in the Levante; and in Andalusia there were widespread peasant revolts. Of these, the most famous and the most brutally repressed was that at Casas Viejas.

Casas Viejas was a small village near Jerez, which had all the characteristics of a place where anarchism might well be expected to provide the only hope. It was desperately poor and riddled with malaria, in the middle of estates belonging to one of the largest and grandest landlords in Spain, the duke of Medina Sidonia. January was, as Mr E. J. Hobsbawm has pointed out,[2] the worst time of year for the landless labourer, when food was scanty and employment scarce. The village was already familiar with anarchist ideas and arguments; and there seems to have been a kind of anarchist dynasty in which young revolutionaries married into the families of old anarchist leaders. Thus, when reports began to arrive of risings elsewhere in Spain and rumours spread that the land was about to be distributed to the peasants (there were, in fact, some plans for land reform on neighbouring estates) the senior anarchist in the village, Curro Cruz, known as Seisdedos (Six Fingers), decided that the long-awaited moment was at hand and that the time for action had come. The mayor was told that a libertarian commune had been proclaimed; the four civil guards in the village were disarmed and shut up; the red and black flag of the Spanish anarchists was unfurled, and preparations made for the defence of the village and for the division of the land. So far, everything had taken place without violence; it was only with the arrival of government forces that fighting began, and it soon became apparent that the revolutionaries of Casas Viejas were isolated. Seisdedos seems to have done his best to prevent the population of the village as a whole from suffering, and he and his family and friends barricaded themselves in his house in the upper part of the village. After twelve hours of fierce fighting, ending with the burning of the house, some twenty-five anarchists were killed. The episode was typical of such anarchist risings in its courage, optimism and hopelessness; but at the same time the savagery of the government's response – it is alleged that they ordered that no prisoners were to be taken – showed both how precarious the leaders of the new republic felt its institutions to be and how right the anarchists were who expected no change in their relationship to the state under the new republican régime.

The result was that the FAI was able to increase its influence as against those CNT leaders who had hoped for some immediate gains from the republic. The split between the majority of the CNT and Peiró was only healed on the eve of the Civil War, while Pestaña broke away from the anarchist movement altogether and formed a political party of his own. The official line of the CNT over the next three years was to boycott the republic and to abstain from voting in elections: '*Frente a las urnas, la Revolución Social*' (Social Revolution rather than ballot boxes) was the slogan. In this atmosphere of social tension and unrest, and in the face of government impotence or hostility, there were naturally attempts by the movements of the left to draw together. In February 1934 – in spite of the hesitations of many of the more doctrinaire members of the FAI – the CNT and the socialist UGT succeeded in making some agreements for joint action on a local basis. Anarchist hostility to the socialists had been increased by the fact that the socialists had participated in the early governments of the republic. However, when, in November 1933, the left was overwhelmingly defeated in the elections and a right-wing government began to undo much of the legislation – inadequate though it had seemed at the time – by which the republicans had tried to limit the power of the church and the landlord and to protect the workers, then the socialists as well as the anarchists began to think in terms of revolution. In fact, the most important revolutionary outbreak in the *bienio negro* – the two dark years of repression that preceded the months of hope when the Popular Front came to power in 1936 – was the rising of the miners in the Asturias in October 1934, and this was the work of the socialists, although the CNT supported it. The local CNT leaders were supporters of the *treintistas* and thus local agreements were possible as they would not have been in Catalonia, where the CNT leadership was more extreme.

The Asturias rising, like so many other revolutionary outbreaks, failed because the government was able to isolate it. In Catalonia there had been a rising of separatists at the beginning of October, which the CNT had opposed; and in Madrid a socialist attempt at revolution had been crushed. In the Asturias the UGT and their CNT allies and a few communists were thus exposed to the full fury of the government forces. Moroccan troops and the foreign legion inflicted 10,000 casualties, killed and wounded, on the 70,000 workers involved. The events in Asturias added to the already existing tension and the allegations of atrocities on both sides contributed still further to the growing bitterness. The repression of the rising was followed by further persecution of the left. Throughout 1935, as in France at the same time, many of the rank and file of the working class began to press their leaders to forget their differences and to unite in a Popular Front to defend their basic liberties. As a result, the socialists, communists (still a comparatively insignificant party in Spain) and some of the republican groups agreed to fight the elections in February 1936 in alliance; and the result was a very considerable success for them. The CNT and the anarchists had, as previously, preached abstention from voting; but their exhortations often seemed half-hearted and certainly a large number of CNT voters must have swelled the majorities of the

Popular Front candidates, especially in the south, where the results of the elections were hardest to predict.

The anarchists had contributed much to the creation of an atmosphere of impending civil war.[1] Their ceaseless agitation and propaganda in favour of total revolution, the sporadic outbreaks and risings which had attempted to set up libertarian communes, and their consistent refusal to accept compromises, had increased the expectancy of revolution among the working class and the corresponding fear of revolution among the army and the right. During the spring of 1936 both sides were preparing for a clash. When the CNT met at Saragossa – one of the great anarchist strongholds – for their national congress representing some half a million workers, they were in a militant and revolutionary mood. What was typical of the anarchist movement, however, was that in addition to discussing practical measures of trade-union policy and voting in favour of an alliance with the UGT, as well as readmitting Peiró and some of the other syndicalists expelled a few years earlier, they spent a great deal of time discussing what would happen after the impending revolution; and here they were reiterating hopes that might have been expressed at any anarchist gathering during the previous fifty years: 'Once the violent aspect of the revolution is finished, the following are declared abolished: private property, the state, the principles of authority and, as a consequence, the classes which divide men into exploiters and exploited, oppressed and oppressors.' Then they went on to outline the way in which the communes would function, based on the free association of workers in their syndicates, producing and exchanging the necessities of life, and linked in 'regional and national federations for the realization of their general objectives', to form an Iberian Federation of Anarchist Communes. Decisions would be taken in the communes by elected committees to deal with agriculture, hygiene, culture, discipline and production, and statistics. 'All these functions will have no executive or bureaucratic character. Apart from those who discharge technical functions . . . the rest will perform their duties as producers, meeting in sessions at the end of the day to discuss the questions of detail which do not require the approval of the

communal assemblies.' Questions affecting more than one commune are dealt with by a regional federation – though very little
is said about this crucial problem, and the resolution is soon back
on easier ground affirming that 'the revolution will not operate
violently on the family', even though 'libertarian communism
proclaims free love'. Any difficulties this may produce would be
dealt with in a truly Godwinian way: 'For many illnesses a change
of water or air is recommended. For the illness of love, which is a
sickness that can become blind and obstinate, a change of commune will be recommended.'

Some of the measures proposed were, however, more practical:
a mass campaign against illiteracy was projected, similar to those
which have, since the Second World War, been put into practice
in Yugoslavia and Cuba, and schools would be based (as Ferrer
had preached) on the principles of helping men to form their own
opinions. There was to be no distinction between intellectuals
and manual workers. Certain distinctions, however, were to be
respected. It is thus explicitly stated that those communes which
are 'refractory to industrialization' or composed of naturists or
nudists may set up their own separate communities.

This long resolution[1] is a moving document, with its affirmation that man is not evil by nature, and its modest concluding
claim that it is not setting out definite rules for the revolutionary
proletariat, but rather 'the general lines of the initial plan which
the world of producers must complete, the point of departure for
Humanity towards its integral liberation'. In the bloodshed and
terror of the next months it is sometimes hard to remember that
it was these innocent and simple beliefs that inspired the Spanish
anarchists; yet their actions and their role in the Civil War will
not be understood if their point of departure is forgotten.

3

General Franco's revolt on 18th July 1936 not only started a
civil war; it also at once provoked a revolution. Indeed, Franco's
failure to secure control of all Spain by simultaneous military
action in the main centres was largely due to the reaction of the

working class organized in the CNT and the UGT. In the words of a leading anarchist intellectual, Franco's rising 'hastened the revolution we all desired but which none had expected so soon'.[1] The most sensational events were in Barcelona, where the anarchists felt that at last the moment had arrived to make their revolution, and where, for several months, it looked as though they were in fact doing this. By the evening of 20th July the anarchist and syndicalist groups of the CNT were in control of the city. They had stormed the barracks during the night; and Francisco Ascaso, who was killed in one of these fierce assaults, became the first notable anarchist hero and martyr of the Civil War. The popular rising was violent and bloody; it was claimed that 500 people had been killed and 3,000 wounded in the battle; and its success was followed by a period of truly revolutionary change. The rich bourgeoisie of Barcelona seemed to have disappeared overnight; churches were burned; prison doors were opened. For the moment the workers' organizations forgot their quarrels; and even the members of the Civil Guard, which in Barcelona remained loyal to the government, were ready to fraternize with their former enemies on the left. Since the majority of the working class in Barcelona were members of the CNT, the revolution inevitably seemed to be a triumph for the anarchists and an opportunity to put into practice their long-cherished beliefs. It was the workers, the anarchist leaders felt, who had suppressed the military revolt; and it was they who would now take control of the city and of Catalonia.

Indeed, the fact was recognized by the Catalan authorities, and Companys, the Catalan nationalist head of the regional government, the *Generalitat*, received the leaders of the CNT as soon as the fighting was over. The two most prominent were the formidable and notorious Durruti and José García Oliver, who, although also a half-educated workman by origin and a man who had served his revolutionary apprenticeship in the violence of the clandestine anarchist movement of the twenties, possessed considerable astuteness and organizing ability, as well as courage and independence. 'We went armed to the teeth,' García Oliver later wrote, 'with rifles, machine-guns and pistols, in shirtsleeves, dirty with powder and smoke. . . . Companys received us standing up, with visible emotion. . . . In substance what he said was the following: "First I must declare that the CNT and the FAI have never been treated as their true importance deserved. You have always been harshly persecuted and I myself with much regret, but forced by political realities, although I formerly was one of you,* often have been obliged to oppose and persecute you. Now you are masters of the city and of Catalonia. . . . You have conquered and everything is in your power; if you do not need me or do not want me as President of Catalonia, tell me now so that I can go and be one more soldier in the struggle against fascism. If, on the other hand, you believe that here in this post . . . I, with the men of my party, my name and my prestige, can be useful in this struggle, which, although it has today ended so well in this city, we do not know when it will end in the rest of Spain, you can count on me and on my loyalty." The CNT and the FAI decided on collaboration and democracy, renouncing revolutionary totalitarianism which would have led to the strangling of the revolution by a trade-union and anarchist dictatorship."[1]

García Oliver, writing afterwards, may well have been justifying his own conduct during these months, but in fact he expressed very clearly the dilemma of the anarchists in the summer of 1936. The whole of previous anarchist theory supposed that, once the revolutionary shock had occurred, the existing state would at once have crumbled, the anarchists would have eliminated their enemies either by violence or persuasion, and so the way would be clear for the construction of the libertarian society. In fact, in July 1936, although the anarchists were masters of the situation in certain places, notably Barcelona, in other areas the revolution was by no means over. The rival workers' organizations, the UGT and the socialists, although a minority in Barcelona, were elsewhere a formidable force, and one whose aim of erecting a centralized socialist society based on the nationalization of industry and its control by the state was fundamentally opposed to that

* In his career as a lawyer Companys had often acted as defence counsel for accused anarchists.

of the anarchists. Even the bourgeoisie, though they may have fled in terror from the rising in Barcelona, or removed their hats and ties in an attempt to pass themselves off as workers, were by no means vanquished. Both in the government of Catalonia and in the central government in Madrid the middle-class republican parties were still in office and many of the organs of government still owed allegiance to them.

Above all, however, the anarchist revolution, like similar attempts before, in Spain itself or in Italy or Russia, was in danger as long as it was not universal. As it became clear that Franco's rising had immediately neither succeeded nor failed but merely started a long civil war, so the problems confronting the anarchist leaders became insuperable. In the early days, following the successes of the left in July, anarchist leaders could still proclaim, as Durruti did, that 'we will make war and revolution at the same time'. But it soon became apparent that not only was this not possible but also, as García Oliver seems to have realized from the moment of that first interview with Companys, making war precluded making revolution.

However, even if the CNT was not in a position to carry through a general revolution in the summer of 1936, it was able to carry out many measures which anarchists regarded as an essential part of the new society, and its strength in many of the areas not yet under Franco's control was such that CNT support was essential if the government was to wage war at all. Accordingly, for several months the anarchists and syndicalists were left free to run the areas and organizations they controlled in their own way. Certainly in Barcelona all observers were struck by the extent to which a revolution had occurred: and the atmosphere had not visibly changed much when George Orwell arrived in December and described the city so vividly in *Homage to Catalonia*. The unions had simply taken over the factories, sometimes keeping the old managers as technical advisers; public services were run by the workers themselves; the small shopkeepers, the barbers and the bakers were organized in syndicates; the brothels were closed, thus putting into practice a principle which an anarchist periodical had shortly before expressed as follows: 'He who buys a kiss puts himself on the level of the woman who sells it. Hence an anarchist must not purchase kisses. He should merit them.'[1] The essential idea behind these arrangements was that the functions hitherto performed by the capitalist entrepreneurs or by the state should now be performed by committees of the workers themselves. Thus, too, the maintenance of order was the task not of professional police but of patrols organized by a committee of the syndicates.

It was in Barcelona and other parts of Catalonia that these measures were carried farthest, both because of anarchist strength in this area and because the self-government granted to Catalonia in 1932 and the difficulties of communication in the confusion of the early weeks of the war had combined to make Catalonia virtually an independent state. In the countryside of Catalonia attempts were made at establishing collective farms, though it is understandable that in an area of small peasant proprietors or leaseholders[2] these attempts had only limited success. Indeed, the anarchist leaders were repeatedly having to warn the more violent militants against the dangers of forcible collectivization. 'Does anyone believe . . . that through acts of violence an interest in or a desire for socialism can be wakened in the minds of our peasantry?' Juan Peiró, always one of the most realistic of the CNT leaders, asked. 'Or perhaps that by terrorizing it in this fashion it can be won over to the revolutionary spirit prevailing in the towns and cities?'[3] Certainly some of Peiró's comrades, notably Durruti, did seem to believe it. However, even when collectivization was not attempted, the middlemen dealing in agricultural produce were abolished and supply committees took over the task of distribution.

In Andalusia, the traditional home of rural anarchism, the villagers seized on the possibilities of revolution with more enthusiasm than the peasants of Catalonia. Unfortunately, however, the village communes did not last long, for much of Andalusia was conquered by Franco's troops within the first months of the war. Before this happened, however, there were many villages where, as in past insurrections, the Civil Guard were disarmed and imprisoned or murdered, the archives were burnt and the *reparto* proclaimed. Franz Borkenau, an extremely intelligent Austrian political writer and journalist, visited the village of Castro del Río, near Córdoba, in September 1936. He found that the estates were now worked by the labourers under the direction of anarchist committees; money had been abolished, and the members of the village commune received such necessaries as were available direct from the village store. There was a kind of fierce puritanism, so typical of one sort of anarchism. 'I tried', Borkenau wrote in his diary, 'in vain to get a drink, either of coffee or wine or lemonade. The village bar had been closed as nefarious commerce. I had a look at the stores. They were so low as to foretell approaching starvation. But the inhabitants seemed to be proud of this state of things. They were pleased, as they told us, that coffee drinking had come to an end; they seemed to regard the abolition of useless things as a moral improvement. What few commodities they needed from outside, mainly clothes, they hoped to get by direct exchange of their surplus in olives (for which, however, no arrangement had yet been made). Their hatred of the upper class was far less economic than moral. They did not want to get the good living of those they had expropriated, but to get rid of their luxuries, which to them seemed to be so many vices.'[1] Castro del Río was not untypical of the villages where libertarian communes were established, although it had long been known as an important anarchist centre. Most of them did not last long. Castro del Río itself was overrun after a hard struggle not long after Borkenau's visit. Elsewhere, if they escaped Franco they were rarely able to maintain their original purity of intention. As in the past, their only hope of survival lay in a general triumph of the anarchist revolution, and this was once again denied them.

It was when the sphere of activities controlled by the anarchists was directly involved in the war that difficulties arose. Libertarian communism could work temporarily in a remote area if the inhabitants were prepared to accept the austerity involved, but it was harder to run a factory on anarchist lines if in order to function it needed raw materials from sources outside anarchist control, which had to be transported by trains or trucks in the hands of a rival organization. Many of the factories which the CNT had taken over seemed to function well, at any rate for a time; Borkenau was impressed, for example, by a bus factory in Barcelona, although he noted that it was more concerned with repairing old vehicles than with producing new ones. However, as stocks became scarce and as the war went on and the policy of Britain and France prevented the government from obtaining supplies from abroad, the inconvenience and inefficiency of an economy run by independent committees became increasingly apparent, and the demand for centralization was accepted even by some of the CNT leaders themselves.

If the difficulties of putting anarchist principles into practice in a society that not only had not completed its revolution but was also fighting a savage war soon became clear in the economic field, they were even more evident in the army. As soon as the war started, the members of the various political and syndical organizations at once formed themselves into militia groups, each separate from the other, with its own flag, its own equipment, such as it was, and, above all, its own command. The anarchist position was clear enough: 'We cannot be uniformed soldiers. We want to be militiamen of Liberty. To the front, certainly. But to the barricades as soldiers not subject to the Popular Forces, certainly not!'[1] In the first enthusiasm the lack of discipline and of organization in the anarchist columns was made up for by fitful revolutionary fervour; but as the war on the Aragón front slowed down to a stalemate and to monotonous and squalid trench warfare (well evoked by George Orwell, who was fighting alongside the anarchists as a member of the dissident communist POUM militia) the disadvantages of this sort of military autonomy began to be obvious. However, some of the anarchist military leaders were able to achieve considerable personal reputations. Durruti, for example, formed the most famous anarchist column and set out from Barcelona in an unsuccessful attempt to recapture Saragossa. In the areas occupied by his forces he tried, like Makhno in Russia before him, to put into practice his belief that war and revolution were inseparable (and strengthened his reputation for violence and terrorism as a result). If the anarchist advance involved bringing ruin and destruction to the villages which they occupied, this could only bring the social revolution nearer. 'I do not expect help from any government in the world,' he told a correspondent of the *Montreal Star*. And, as for ruins: 'We have always lived in slums and holes in the wall. . . . We can also build. It is we who built the palaces and cities here in Spain and in America and everywhere. We, the workers, can build cities to take their place. And better ones – we are not in the least afraid of ruins. We are going to inherit the earth. The bourgeoisie may blast and ruin their world before they leave the stage of history. But we carry a new world in our hearts.'[1]

When the situation in Madrid became critical in November 1936, Durruti was persuaded to bring his column, some 3,000 strong, from the Aragón front to help in the defence of the capital. He was mistrustful of collaboration with the other forces in Madrid, where anarchist influence was much less strong than in Barcelona, and insisted on being given an independent sector of the front. His vanity soon received a bitter blow, for on their first day in their new position his men refused to go into action in the face of Franco's guns; and although Durruti angrily demanded a chance to redeem this disgrace, it was to the communist-dominated International Brigades – deeply distrusted by all good anarchists – that most of the merit of saving Madrid was due. Durruti did not indeed have the opportunity to show his gifts as a commander in the field again, for on 21st November he was killed during a lull on the front by a bullet which many believed to have been fired not by one of Franco's snipers but by one of Durruti's enemies – perhaps a communist, perhaps an anarchist extremist discontented with the new CNT/FAI policy of collaboration with the government. The death of Durruti deprived the anarchists of one of their most famous and most ruthless legendary heroes, and his funeral in Barcelona provided that city with the last of its great demonstrations of anarchist power, with 200,000 supporters in the streets – an occasion perhaps reminiscent of that in Moscow twenty-four years before, when Kropotkin's funeral had given the Russian anarchists a last opportunity of parading their strength before the communists finally closed in on them. Within a month of Durruti's death the Soviet newspaper *Pravda* was already claiming that 'So far as Catalonia is concerned, the cleaning up of Trotskyists and anarchists has begun, and it will be carried out with the same energy as in the USSR.'[1]

The claim was, in fact, premature. The anarchists were never completely 'cleaned up' and their forces continued to play a role until the end of the war. After Durruti's death there was still one anarchist commander, Cipriano Mera, who continued an effective military career in a senior position, even though he had come to accept a degree of organization and discipline which would probably have been too much for Durruti. As he himself said in December 1937: 'The blood of my brothers shed in the struggle made me change my views. I understood then that if we were not to be definitely defeated, we had to construct our own army . . . a disciplined and capable army organized for the defence of the workers. Henceforth I did not hesitate to urge upon all combatants the necessity of submitting to new military principles.'[2]

Everywhere the specifically anarchist character of the columns organized by the CNT and FAI diminished as the necessities of war demanded greater discipline and more central control. The so-called 'Iron Column', which had been formed in Valencia largely from people released from jail at the moment of the revolution in July and therefore doubtless containing a certain number of common criminals as well as idealistic anarchists, was sent to the Teruel front, and by March 1937 was forced to turn itself into a conventionally organized brigade simply because this was the only way by which it could obtain supplies. It was this problem of equipment and raw materials which, above all, led to the decline of the anarchists. The revolutionary idea of an anarchist militia supplied by anarchist-run factories inevitably broke down when faced with a general shortage of basic supplies; and it was, of course, the fact that during the Civil War the government was only able to obtain supplies from the Soviet Union that contributed largely to the increased influence of the communists and the eclipse and suppression of their rivals. There is no doubt that the communist demand for central control and discipline was justified in the interests of military efficiency; and a situation in which rival armed groups were trying to steal each other's equipment – as when in March 1937 the communists succeeded in stealing twelve tanks from an anarchist depot in Barcelona by producing a forged order from the anarchist commissioner[1] – was clearly intolerable.

The tragedy of the anarchist leaders was that the more concessions they made so as to help create a unified war effort by the republic, the less influence they had over the course of events which they had hoped to control. When Durruti and García Oliver had called on Companys in July 1936, Companys had recognized the fact that the collaboration of the CNT was essential in an emergency which, at that stage, no one had expected to develop into a full-scale, full-length war. At the beginning of the war the CNT leaders were determined to retain their independence and to stand by their principles, by refusing to take part in government or to become involved in politics. 'Perhaps many wonder', their Madrid newspaper wrote in September 1936, 'how it is that the CNT, one of the principal forces preparing for the victory of the people at the front and in the rear . . . does not form part of the government. Undoubtedly, if the CNT were inspired by political ideas, the number of its seats in the government would have to be at least as large as that of the UGT and the socialists. However, the CNT once again affirms its unshakeable adhesion to its anti-authoritarian postulates and believes that the libertarian transformation of society can only take place as a result of the abolition of the state and the control of the economy by the working class.'[2] However, just as in France during the First World War, the syndicalist leaders had found themselves obliged to recognize the existence of the state and collaborate with the government, so, within a few weeks, the Spanish anarchists of the CNT and FAI found themselves faced with the spectacle of four of their most respected leaders actually becoming ministers in the government of the despised republic. By the end of September the anarchists already had a representative in the government of Catalonia in charge of economic affairs. As the crisis of the war deepened, the parties of the left tended temporarily to forget their differences and to draw together in the hope of defeating Franco. Thus, towards the end of October, as the threat to Madrid grew, the CNT in Barcelona sacrificed some of its doctrinal purity in order to agree on a programme which both it and the UGT could support. This involved the acceptance of a unified military command and military discipline, as well as the admission that conscription was necessary (as Makhno had found in the Russian Civil War) to maintain recruitment for the army. It also put an end to expropriation of small proprietors and owners of small businesses, showing how far the CNT's leaders were prepared to go in regarding their own revolution as temporarily suspended, even if some of their supporters – especially the Anarchist Youth Movement – were still strongly opposed to such compromises.

By the end of October 1936 the situation looked very gloomy for the republic. Franco's troops were closing in on Madrid and the fall of the capital seemed near. In this atmosphere of emergency the anarchists finally overcame their last hesitations and agreed to join the central government. In Catalonia the anarchists had salved their consciences by referring to the *Generalitat* as a regional defence council, but in joining the central government even this pretence had to be abandoned. The same paper which six weeks before had declared the CNT's unshakeable adhesion to its postulates was now writing: 'In order to win the war and save the people of the world, it [the CNT] is ready to collaborate with anyone in a directive organ, whether this be called a council or a government.'[1] The reasons for joining the government were sound practical ones, and the four CNT leaders who accepted posts as ministers displayed both courage and common sense in attempting at this critical moment to contribute to unity on the republican side and to have a say in the actual running of the war. They were among the most respected people in the movement. Juan Peiró was a glassworker with a long experience of syndicalist organization; he had, as we have seen, originally stood for a firm rejection of any syndicalist involvement in politics and had opposed Pestaña's

willingness to collaborate with the politicians of the left. However, the experiences of Primo de Rivera's régime and of the
early days of the republic had made him abandon his former
intransigence and, as the leading signatory of the Manifesto of
the Thirty, he had upheld the necessity of discipline and organization as against the reliance on uncoordinated, spontaneous
revolutionary fervour of the true anarchists. Although his breach
with the CNT had been healed just before the Civil War began,
he still represented the most moderate element in the CNT and,
as Minister of Industry, was opposed to violent collectivization
and was closer in view, perhaps, to the leaders of the French
syndicalist movement than to his anarchist colleagues of the
FAI. The Ministry of Commerce and Industry had been split
so as to provide two ministerial posts instead of one, and Peiró's
colleague as Minister of Commerce was another moderate syndicalist, Juan López Sánchez, a leader of the important Valencia
federation of the CNT. The other two anarchist members of the
government represented the more militant wing of the movement
and were leading members of the FAI. One was García Oliver,
now thirty-five years old and, after Durruti, the acknowledged
leader of the militant anarchists of Catalonia, who had been at
the head of the armed insurrection in January 1933. He became
Minister of Justice and, after performing a real anarchist gesture
and destroying the records of convicts in Spanish prisons, he
surprised many of his associates by being an efficient and practical
minister who tried to introduce reforms into the legal and judicial
system, such as abolishing fees which made recourse to the courts
impossible for the poor, as well as setting up special Popular
Tribunals to deal with offences against the republic arising out of
the war, and labour camps in which those condemned by these
tribunals could, in theory, be employed on useful work.

The other anarchist minister was a representative of the purest
intellectual anarchism, Federica Montseny. She came from a
family of anarchist intellectuals in Barcelona, and her father was
a well-known propagandist and writer who wrote under the
name of Federico Urales. She was a successful and impassioned
speaker whose sincerity, integrity and intellectual clarity com-

manded great respect. As Minister of Health in a wartime government she had little opportunity for anarchist reforms in her own department, though she did issue a decree legalizing abortion. Her role – apart from providing the example, unheard of in Spain, of a woman in a ministerial post – seems to have been to reassure the anarchist militants about the participation in the government of their leaders, since Federica Montseny's known devotion to anarchist principles and her personal honesty seemed to suggest that any course she followed must be an honourable and reasonable one.

Certainly the decision to accept office and thus to seem to break all the principles on which their lives had been based was a hard one for all the CNT/FAI ministers and perhaps especially for Federica Montseny, the one true intellectual among them. In June 1937, after the fall of the government of which she had been a member, she described in moving terms her personal predicament: 'Daughter of a family of old anarchists, descendant of a whole dynasty, so to speak, of anti-authoritarians, with my activity and a life of struggle in permanent defence of ideas inherited from my own parents, my entry into the government . . . necessarily meant more than merely an appointment as a Minister. For us who had struggled constantly against the state, who had always said that the state could achieve absolutely nothing, that the words Government and Authority meant the negation of any possibility of liberty for individuals and peoples, our incorporation as an organization and as individuals into a government project meant either an act of historical audacity of fundamental importance or a theoretical and tactical correction of a whole structure and a whole chapter of history. . . . Accustomed to other activities, accustomed to work in the syndicates, to action, to propaganda, to the continuous silent labour of a movement which was created and formed in opposition and which worked in opposition, with a dose of goodwill, of enthusiasm, of respect and generosity which other movements lacked, for us entry into the government was bound also to mean the painful step towards an experience which was to be instructive for us. What reservations, what doubts, what inner anguish

I had personally to overcome before accepting this task! For others it could be their goal, it could be the satisfaction of all their ambitions. For me it was simply a breach with all my work, with all my life, with all my past linked to the life of my parents. It was bound to represent for me a tremendous effort which cost me many tears. And I accepted. And I accepted conquering myself. . . . So I entered the government and so we left for Madrid.'[1]*

This painful decision was the logical result of the attitude which the anarchists had adopted after the rising in Barcelona on 19th and 20th July, when they agreed to collaborate with President Companys and the Catalán government. They had realized that, in Barcelona itself, there was nothing to stop them taking over completely, carrying through their revolution and imposing the anarchist society. But the anarchist leaders were too sensible to see that this course, in the conditions of civil war and with the revolution only triumphant in limited areas, could not last long, and that for the moment they would have to work with other movements – notably the socialists and the UGT – if they were to survive at all, let alone achieve their revolutionary goals. At the same time, they were very conscious of what had happened to the anarchists in the Russian Revolution and were afraid that, if they remained aloof from the political parties that still controlled the government, their influence would be undermined by their socialist and communist rivals. Moreover, in the crisis produced by the threat to Madrid, some sort of coordinated effort was necessary if Franco was to be stopped from winning an immediate victory in which the anarchists would not only lose all they had gained but would also suffer reprisals that might well break the whole movement permanently. The anarchist ministers hoped that their presence in the government would make cooperation with other revolutionary and republican movements easier; they also hoped naturally enough that, with the formidable force of the CNT behind them, they would be

---

* She did not stay long in Madrid, for soon after the formation of the new government it was decided, in the face of anarchist opposition, to evacuate the government to Valencia.

able to influence the policies and institutions of the republic in the direction in which the anarchists wanted them to go.

They were to be disappointed on both counts. During the six months the anarchists were in the government, relations with the socialists and communists deteriorated to the point of civil war, while the whole structure of committees, which seemed to the anarchists the natural way to organize the war, had been replaced by orthodox socialist measures of centralization and government or municipal control. The main reason for this was the growing influence of the communists and their determination to crush any rival movement. Their power grew partly because the Soviet Union was the only source of foreign aid to the republic; and consequently the communists, the agents through whom this aid became available, assumed an importance out of all proportion to their original popular support in Spain. At the same time the socialist leaders still hoped that by presenting a respectable non-revolutionary image to the outside world they might persuade France and Britain to give up the policy of non-intervention and provide them with some of the materials they so desperately needed. So, as Largo Caballero, the socialist leader and Prime Minister, explained to his anarchist colleagues, nothing must be done to affect French and British capital investments in Spain. Thus both the pressure which the communists and socialists were exerting to make the unity (and uniformity) of the Popular Front a reality, and the desire of Largo Caballero and the other leading members of the government to play down the revolutionary aspect of their policies, meant that the anarchist ministers – a minority in the government – had no alternative except either to accept compromises which went against all their principles or to resign and call out their supporters to demonstrate against the government at a time when winning the war seemed more important than anything else. They accepted the compromises; and thus they were forced to see the anarchist successes of the early weeks of the war gradually undone. The militia columns were converted into orthodox brigades, with discipline, permanent officers and centralized commands. The extreme anarchism of the libertarian communes gave way to state requisitioning. When the villages were not, like Castro del Río, overrun by Franco's troops, the pure anarchism of the first outbreaks could not stand up against the resistance of the small peasants and tenant farmers who were quite ready to increase the size of their own holdings at the expense of the landlords but who were not at all prepared to give up to a collective the small piece of land they already owned themselves. The anarchists of the FAI had uncompromising views about this: 'We cannot consent to small holdings,' one of their papers wrote, 'because private property in land always creates a bourgeois mentality, calculating and egotistical, which we wish to uproot for ever.'[1] And when they were forced to admit failure the anarchists recognized the reason: 'What we have been up against most is the backward mentality of the majority of small owners. Just imagine what it meant to the peasant proprietor, accustomed to his small plot of land, his donkey, his wretched hut, his petty harvest . . . to have to give up this burden which he has carried with him from time immemorial, and say, "Take them, comrades. My humble belongings are for everyone. We are all equal. A new life has begun for us." '[2] Not only were the small peasants and shopkeepers unready to make this sacrifice, but also the government, whose socialist or republican members often relied on the support of just those classes, was reluctant to ask it of them.

As the military and economic programme of the anarchists was either eaten away by the brutal necessities of war or the stubborn facts of human nature, so, too, their insistence on decentralization and administration by committee was largely overcome. All that the moderate syndicalists, like Peiró or López Sánchez, now hoped for was a federal republic with some measure of workers' control in industry; but as the war went on and the economic and military situation grew worse, and the communists increased their influence in the government, even this was to be denied them. The predictions of those more extreme members of the FAI who had opposed entry into the government, and the forebodings of foreign anarchists like the veteran French publicist Sebastien Faure, a survivor from the heroic age of French anarchism, who visited Spain at the beginning of the war, seemed to be justified. Many other foreign sympathizers were equally intransigent. There was an Italian group fighting in Durruti's column, which lost some of its members to the Italian battalion of the International Brigade, but of which the remaining members were especially refractory, refusing any kind of co-operation with regular military forces and, on one occasion, walking out on the eve of a battle, though redeeming themselves from charges of cowardice by later taking part on their own terms.[1] There was, too, in the Spanish movement itself a considerable minority which shared these views and was prepared to express them violently, if necessary. The revolutionary prestige of García Oliver and Federica Montseny was sufficient to overcome much opposition; but it was not inexhaustible. During the early months of 1937 in Catalonia relations between anarchists and the communist-led PSUC (*Partido socialista unificado de Cataluña*) grew worse: there were quarrels in Barcelona over the question of food control, when the socialists abolished rationing in the city and did away with the committees which the anarchists had originally set up. Elsewhere there were similar disputes; there were quarrels in Valencia over the arrangements for marketing the orange crop, when one orange-growing village revolted against the government because they claimed they were not getting a fair price from the syndicalist committee which sold their crops. During February 1937 the anarchist columns on the Aragón front were short of arms and the FAI threatened to instruct its ministers to resign if this apparent discrimination did not stop. A month later the anarchist members of the Catalán *Generalitat* actually did resign after the republicans and socialists had insisted on creating a unified police force and on dissolving the revolutionary patrols. The anarchists finally agreed to rejoin after the CNT members of the central government had appealed to them to preserve the solidarity of the Popular Front, but throughout April 1937 the situation in Barcelona was growing more tense and the FAI extremists were becoming increasingly critical both of their leaders and of their socialist and communist rivals. In Catalonia, too, the other revolutionary and dissident party, the POUM, was moving towards open conflict with the

communists, who were determined to suppress it. At the end of
April all these hostilities broke into open war. While the anarchist
newspaper *Solidaridad Obrera* published an open attack on the
communists, the murderers on both sides started their work. On
25th April the communist youth leader was found assassinated:
two days later three anarchists were killed, including the mayor of
the frontier town of Puigcerda, who tried to bring the frontier
guard under anarchist control. The socialist press replied with an
attack on the '*incontrolados*' of the FAI – who represented a threat
always likely to alarm the inhabitants of Barcelona with memories
not only of the previous July but also of the bloody gang-fights
twenty or so years before. When the First of May came – the traditional moment to assert the solidarity of the working class against
their oppressors – it was decided not to hold any demonstrations
for fear that they would develop into a violent clash between the
differing factions. In Valencia the leaders of the anarchists and
socialists were appealing for unity; but in Barcelona the situation
was explosive.

On 3rd May the fighting began. How or why it started is still
extremely obscure. The communists and socialists claimed that it
was begun by the dissidents on the left – the POUM and the
anarchists. The anarchists attributed it to communist provocation. There is also some evidence that Franco's agents in Barcelona were working to set the rival working-class organizations
against each other. But in any case suspicions and tempers were
sufficiently aroused for any incident, however provoked, to lead
easily to large-scale fighting. In the event it was in the *Telefónica*
– the main communications centre of the city – that the fighting
started. The telephone building was controlled by a joint committee of the CNT, the UGT and a government representative,
and the trouble began with the arrival of the socialist chief of
police to investigate suspicions that the CNT were tapping lines
for their own purposes. The first fights were, in fact, from storey
to storey of the building. However, the whole city was soon
divided, with the traditionally anarchist quarters outside the
centre of the city at open war with the areas controlled by the
government forces and their UGT supporters. The Catalan

government was persuaded by the CNT to withdraw the police from the *Telefónica*, but refused to call for the resignation of the police chief and of the Minister of the Interior, whom the CNT held responsible for starting the trouble.* On the next day, García Oliver and Federica Montseny, the two most respected anarchist leaders, arrived from Valencia by car, and with great courage went into the streets of Barcelona, using all their personal influence and prestige to persuade their followers to stop shooting. Although on 5th May a truce was temporarily established, on the next day fighting broke out again and for two days the internecine war raged in the city. With the Durruti column at Lérida ready to march on Barcelona, the conflict threatened to spread. The government in Valencia, after an initial reluctance to exacerbate the situation, decided to restore order by force; and 4,000 men were dispatched to Barcelona. Once again, the anarchists found that local strength was not enough if a central government was still in existence, and they were obliged to give in. By 8th May the CNT leaders were calling for the dismantling of the barricades and a return to normality, and the rank and file had no choice but to obey them.

Some 400 people had been killed and 1,000 wounded in the fighting. One of the victims who had been murdered in the street was Camillo Berneri, a leading Italian intellectual anarchist. But the consequences to the anarchist movement in Spain were far graver than the loss of many individual militants. The Barcelona fighting was followed directly by the fall of the government of Largo Caballero, and its replacement by an administration in which the influence of the communists was still further increased. The anarchist ministers, although they had often been severely critical of Largo Caballero, supported him at this point, especially as one of the demands of the communists and of those socialists who opposed Largo Caballero was the disciplining of the dissident parties on the left. Thus the anarchist ministers resigned when Largo Caballero fell. The ill-fated if unavoidable experiment of anarchist participation in government was at an

* Both of these men had been anarchists, so the feelings on both sides may have been particularly bitter.

end. Although the new government declared the POUM illegal
and arrested many of its members, the CNT as a whole was still
too powerful to be dissolved, though it was not strong enough
to prevent the dissolution of the committee which it had set up to
control the government of the province of Aragón. The language
of the government decree appointing a governor-general in place
of the Council of Aragón shows how completely, even if justifi-
ably, the reversal of anarchist principles was being enforced: 'The
moral and material necessities of the war demand imperiously
the concentration of the authority of the state. . . . The division
and subdivision of power and authority has on more than one
occasion dissipated effective action. . . .'[1] It was true enough;
and again, in the midst of a war which they still supported, there
was nothing for the anarchists to do except bow to the decision.

From June 1937 until the end of the war the role of the CNT
and FAI was very much less important than it had been; and,
although some of the extreme anarchists declared anew their
hostility to all authority, the majority of the FAI and CNT
became more like members of an ordinary political party or
trade-union movement than they had ever been. The FAI,
indeed, was in a particularly difficult position. Either it had to
revert to its original role as an extremist group providing a
conspiratorial network to keep the CNT on a revolutionary path,
or it had to merge itself into the CNT and adopt, in the special
situation of the civil war, openly political and propagandist aims.
At the start of the war the FAI had hoped to fulfil its original
role: 'Our duty is to maintain an organization which represents
those ideas which embody a magnificent corpus of doctrine which
we have with so much determination preserved and enriched by
practice.' And, as the syndicates were, by the necessities of war,
obliged to cooperate with political groups, there was all the more
need for the FAI to be 'a motor producing the quantity of
fabulous energy needed to move the syndicates in the direction
which most conforms to the longings of Humanity for renovation
and emancipation'.[2]

It was an ideal which the anarchists had been forced to
abandon by 1938. The failure of the anarchist revolution, the

powerlessness of the anarchist ministers and the threat of repression after the Barcelona fighting, all revealed that the anarchists were as far from realizing their dreams as ever. The CNT was becoming more and more a syndicalist organization playing its part in the running of the war in conjunction with the government and the UGT. When a socialist leader welcomed an agreement between the CNT and UGT with the words, 'Bakunin and Marx embrace over this document of the CNT',[1] it was the principles of Bakunin that had had to be sacrificed. In the spring of 1938, when it looked as though Franco's victory was near, a CNT representative again joined the government; and it was a sign of how much the influence of the CNT had declined that it was now obliged to accept a single post instead of the four it had previously held; nor is there much to suggest that its representative, Segundo Blanco, exercised much influence on the conduct of the war.

In October 1938 a national congress attended by representatives of the CNT, the FAI and the anarchist youth movement (as well as by Emma Goldman) debated the first principles of anarchism once again. What was notable was that the uncompromising libertarians were now in a minority and that the majority were prepared to revise their beliefs and accept the sad facts of twentieth-century life. As one speaker put it: 'We must jettison our literary and philosophical baggage to be able to obtain hegemony tomorrow. It is our comrades' refusal to accept militarism from the start which is responsible for the restricted position we are now in.'[2] But in any case, although new plans for the organization of the movement were drawn up and a belief in the old goals of decentralization and workers' control were reiterated, the anarchists, like everyone else on the republican side, were powerless to avoid defeat. At the last minute, in March 1939, Cipriano Mera, one of the few anarchist commanders who had retained both his military position and his prestige, made a desperate effort to avert total defeat and annihilation by using his influence to support Colonel Casado's attempt to secure some sort of negotiated peace in spite of the government's expressed intention of fighting to the last. This, too, was in vain, and the anarchists suffered very heavy penalties in the vast reprisals with which Franco celebrated his victory. Some died in a last gesture of resistance; some escaped into exile.* Others were less fortunate still and, like Juan Peiró, were handed back by Pétain to Franco in 1940. But the greatest number, if they escaped immediate death, were imprisoned in Spain; some of them may still remain in jail.

The anarchist tradition in Spain is certainly not dead; but it is impossible to say how important a part it may still play or what form it will take, and it may well be that the anarchists will not recover the ground lost to the communists during the Civil War. But perhaps its historical role is best summed up by the leading recent historian of the movement, José Peirats: 'There may be a certain disproportion between the force expended by the Spanish working-class movement and the results obtained. . . . What is beyond any criticism and what is beyond any consideration of effectiveness is the depth of generous idealism, of honesty and the spirit of struggle and sacrifice of the Spanish libertarians.'[1]

* Federica Montseny is in France, still courageously and indefatigably organizing Spanish workers there; García Oliver is in Mexico.

CHAPTER X

Conclusion

'Give flowers to the rebels failed.' So runs the first line of an Italian anarchist poem which Vanzetti sat translating in his prison cell. And, as one looks at the repeated failures of anarchism in action, culminating in the tragedy of the Spanish Civil War, one is tempted to strike the same elegiac note. The contradictions and inconsistencies of anarchist theory, the difficulty, if not the impossibility, of putting it into practice all seem illustrated by the experiences of the past hundred and fifty years. Nevertheless, anarchism is a doctrine that has attracted a number of people in each generation, and its ideas still have an appeal, though perhaps more as a personal ethical creed than as a social revolutionary force. Most of the people who have become anarchists were not self-torturing neurotics – though some of the terrorists undoubtedly were – but people who regarded anarchism as a practical revolutionary ideal and a realizable hope. The philosophical anarchists – a Godwin and even a Proudhon or a Kropotkin – may have come to think that their criticism of existing society was more theoretical than practical and that the system of social values they sought to inculcate was not immediately realizable; but they certainly believed that it might be realized one day. The mass of poor people who, from the 1880s on, accepted anarchism as a basis for action, did so, however, because the total revolution which the anarchists promised seemed to offer an immediate hope of success, and indeed seemed to be the only possibility of improving their desperate condition.

Anarchism is necessarily a creed of all or nothing, and consequently it has had less success in countries where there is still a hope of winning something out of the existing system. When a trade union can successfully negotiate higher wages or better

conditions of work, and when political parties are able to introduce measures of reform and to remedy grievances, then the
extreme solution of a total revolution seems less desirable. To
this extent, Bakunin's belief that the true revolutionaries are
those with nothing to lose has been justified. However, anarchism
in action has always come up against the fact that, for better or
for worse, all the nations of the west – even Russia and Spain,
where anarchism seemed to have the best prospects of success –
have decided on political action and a centralized government as
the means of obtaining the society they want. 'The government
of man' is no nearer being replaced by 'the administration of
things' than it was when the utopian socialists put forward the
idea in the first half of the last century. The political party, so
abhorred by all good anarchists, has become the characteristic
organ of twentieth-century government, so that even the dictatorships of the twentieth century have used the single party as a
means of exercising their tyranny instead of practising the un-
disguised autocracy of earlier periods. Thus, in practice, the
anarchists have deliberately dissociated themselves from what the
majority of people in the twentieth century have regarded as
essential for political and social progress. While their criticism of
traditional ideas of state sovereignty, representative government
and political reform may have often been valid, and the warnings
they have repeatedly issued about the dangers of sacrificing
liberty in the supposed interests of the revolution have often
been justified, the anarchists have failed to suggest just how their
alternative system can be made to work. They have never, that
is to say, envisaged any intermediate stage between existing
society and the total revolution of their dreams.

In another respect, too, the anarchists have shown themselves
opposed to the dominating trends of contemporary economic
organization. Mass production and consumption, and large-scale
industry under a centralized direction, whether capitalist or
socialist, have, whatever one may think about them, become the
characteristic forms of western society and of the newly emergent
industrial countries elsewhere. It is hard to see how these could
be adapted to anarchist ideas about production and exchange;

and therefore the anarchists who have envisaged the total destruction of existing society as a preliminary to the erection of a new order are doubtless right. However, the ambivalent attitude of the anarchists towards technological progress has left a corresponding ambivalence in their views of the future society. Although, as we have seen, Godwin and Kropotkin welcomed new inventions which would relieve men of unpleasant and squalid tasks – refuse disposal has always been one of the great problems confronting utopian thinkers – nevertheless, the basic assumptions of anarchism are all contrary to the development of large-scale industry and of mass production and consumption. When it comes to the point, the anarchists are all agreed that in the new society man will live in extreme simplicity and frugality and will be quite happy to do without the technical achievements of the industrial age. For this reason, much anarchist thinking seems to be based on a romantic, backward-looking vision of an idealized past society of artisans and peasants, and on a total rejection of the realities of twentieth-century social and economic organization. While some syndicalist ideals and a degree of workers' control of industry may mitigate some of the inhumanity of large factories, a total destruction of the contemporary structure of industry is scarcely imaginable without violent cataclysm. However, in certain emergency situations such as existed in Russia in 1917 and in Catalonia in 1936, when the governmental and economic machinery has been disrupted or destroyed by war, there might still exist a chance of putting anarchist ideas into practice and of starting to rebuild from nothing a new society on anarchist principles. Perhaps the anarchist revolution could only take place after the total disruption of the means of government, communications, production and exchange by, say, a nuclear war; and perhaps, after all, the terrorists were right, and only a bomb on a larger scale than any they ever envisaged could prepare the way for the true social revolution.

However, in countries where industrial development has not yet conditioned the whole social structure as it has in Europe and North America, the ideals of the anarchists might still seem to be within reach. In India, Gandhi himself and subsequent social reformers such as Jayaprakash Narayan and Vinoba Bhave have dreamed of basing Indian society on (in Gandhi's words) 'self-sufficient, self-governing village republics'.[1] Perhaps even in India the development of a centralized industrial community has gone too far to be stopped, and Jayaprakash Narayan has realized that the changes he proposes also involve the abandonment of India's western-style parliamentary democracy. Indeed, his attack on liberal parliamentary institutions and his demand for 'self-governing, self-sufficient, agro-industrial, urbo-rural local communities'[1] is closely reminiscent of Proudhon. And, like Proudhon, Mr Narayan is perhaps too optimistic when he thinks that the rejection of liberal institutions will lead to a better form of government. He writes that 'The evidence from Cairo to Djakarta indicates that Asian peoples are having second thoughts, and are seeking to find better forms than parliamentary democracy to express and embody their democratic aspirations.'[2] What is sad is that the evidence hardly suggests that these new forms have anything in common with Mr Narayan's admirable Proudhonian ideals. Indeed, if the Indians, with a long tradition of village communities and with the example and teaching of Gandhi, the only twentieth-century statesman with the moral sophistication to make a revolution that was ethical as well as social and political, have not succeeded in starting a social revolution on the lines advocated by Mr Narayan, it is hard to see who else is likely to do so.

However, if the anarchists have failed to make their revolution and seem even further from doing so today than ever, they have all the same provided a continuous criticism of prevailing views and have occasionally made us think again about our political and social presuppositions. They have consistently pointed out the dangers of making the wrong kind of revolution, and their warnings over the last hundred years that Marxism would lead to dictatorship and to the replacement of the old tyrannies by a new one have been proved all too right. Whatever they may have thought they were doing, the anarchists have, in fact, produced a revolutionary ideal which corresponds exactly to Sorel's myth – 'not a description of things but an expression of will'. It is by their ruthless and extreme assertion of an uncompromising set of beliefs that the anarchists have set an example and issued a challenge. Like all puritans, they have succeeded in making us just a little uneasy about the kind of life we lead.

Clemenceau once said: 'I am sorry for anyone who has not been an anarchist at twenty'; and it is obvious that the ardent and irrepressible optimism of anarchist doctrines will always have an appeal to the young in revolt against the social and moral conceptions of their elders. Yet it is not so much the enthusiasm of youth that has made the anarchist leaders impressive, but rather, in the case of men like Kropotkin or Malatesta, the consistency and devotion with which, in spite of disappointments and in face, it may be thought, of overwhelming contrary evidence, they have maintained into old age their beliefs unchanged and their hopes undimmed. The strength of anarchism has lain in the characters of those who have practised it; and it is as an austere personal moral and social code that it will continue to attract people who want a total alternative to the values of contemporary society and politics and whose temperaments respond to the appeal of ideas carried to their logical conclusions, regardless of the practical difficulties involved.

There is also another sense in which anarchism, quite apart from its success or failure as a social revolutionary movement, will always find some converts. Certain types of anarchists provide examples of a *'jusqu'au boutisme'*, an extreme degree of individualist self-assertion, which rejects all conventions and all restrictions. These anarchists practise in their everyday lives the Nietzschean *Umwertung aller Werte*, the overturning of all accepted values. The bohemians of the 1890s are echoed by the beat generation of the 1950s in their protest against the stuffiness and conformity of the bourgeois society in which they have grown up. And, while this sort of revolt often ends in futility and sometimes in personal disaster, it can also produce a revolutionary art which effectively challenges convention and tradition and is truly anarchist in its disruptive effect. The Dada painters and writers, for example, produced an art which, by attacking the idea of art itself, enabled them, as they thought, to escape from values of any kind. Their successors, the surrealists, again asserted their right to complete freedom. As one of their historians put it: 'Surrealism has nothing in common with a religious movement. Yet it is the only thing capable of giving man what all religions had provided for him: total liberty of the human being in a liberated world.'[1] This desire to assert total individual freedom from all restraints and conventions has its dangers: it can become both trivial and silly. As a leading surrealist, André Breton, remarked: '*Il n'y a rien avec quoi il soit si dangereux de prendre des libertés comme avec la liberté.*'[2] A state of permanent rejection of all rules is the most exacting way of life possible, and individualist anarchism, like social anarchism, demands a devotion and austerity which few who practise it attain. (It is not entirely surprising, for instance, that some of the leading surrealists have preferred to turn to the ready-made discipline of the communists rather than to the self-imposed freedom of their original beliefs.) However, just as the revolutionary anarchist thinkers provided a vision of an alternative social order and a challenge to all our accepted political and economic conventions, so the individualist anarchists and the artists whose work has reflected their beliefs have provided a series of salutary shocks to our moral and aesthetic beliefs. The idea of a 'morality without obligations or sanctions' is as attractive as that of a society without government or governed; and, in one form or another, each will have its disciples in every generation.

NOTES

CHAPTER I: HERESY AND REASON

Page 17   1   Notably Professor Norman Cohn in his admirable *Pursuit of the Millennium* (London 1957).

Page 18   1   Quoted in Georg Adler, *Geschichte des Sozialismus und Kommunismus von Plato bis zum Gegenwart*. Teil I (Leipzig 1899), p. 98.

           2   Cohn, op. cit., p. 36.

Page 20   1   loc. cit.

           2   Cohn, op. cit., p. 89.

           3   loc. cit.

Page 21   1   Emmanuel Aegerter, *Les Hérésies du Moyen Age* (Paris 1939), p. 42.

           2   See, e.g., Arno Beust, *Die Katharer* (Stuttgart 1953).

Page 24   1   Cohn. op. cit., p. 267.

Page 28   1   Quoted Maxime Leroy, *Histoire des Idées Sociales en France*, vol. I, *De Montesquieu à Robespierre* (Paris 1946), p. 239.

           2   Quoted Alain Sergent and Claude Harmel, *Histoire de l'Anarchie* (Paris 1949), p. 35.

Page 29   1   Morelly, *Code de la Nature ou le véritable esprit de ses lois, 1755*, ed. E. Dolléans (Paris 1910), p. 48.

Page 30   1   J. J. Rousseau, *Emile* (New Ed., Paris 1951), p. 6.

Page 31   1   H. N. Brailsford, *Shelley, Godwin and their Circle* (London 1913), p. 80. For Godwin's life, see George Woodcock, *William Godwin* (London 1946).

           2   H. N. Brailsford, op. cit., p. 88.

Page 32   1   William Godwin, *An Enquiry Concerning Political Justice* (1st ed., London 1793), 2 vols., vol. I, pp. 233–4.

           2   Ibid.. vol. I, p. 11.

           3   Ibid., vol. I, p. 31.

Page 33   1   Ibid., vol. II, p. 866.

           2   Ibid., vol. I, p. 9.

           3   Ibid., vol. II, p. 788.

Page 34   1   Ibid., vol. II, p. 845.

           2   Ibid., vol. II, p. 858.

           3   Ibid., vol. II, p. 844.

           4   Ibid., vol. II, pp. 846–47.

Page 35   1   Ibid., vol. II, p. 842.

           2   Ibid., vol. II, p. 852.

           3   Ibid., vol. II, p. 853.

           4   Ibid., vol. II, pp. 853–4.

           5   Ibid., vol. II, p. 851.

Page 36   1   Ibid., vol. I, p. 269.

           2   Ibid., vol. II, p. 558.

           3   Ibid., vol. II, p. 564.

           4   Ibid., vol. II, p. 564–5.

Page 37   1   Ibid., vol. I, pp. 215.

           2   Ibid., vol. II, p. 734.

           3   H. S. Salt, Introduction to *Godwin's Political Justice* (a reprint of Part VIII of the *Enquiry*) (London 1890), p. 29.

Page 38   1   H. N. Brailsford, op. cit., pp. 91–92.

CHAPTER II: THE MYTH OF THE REVOLUTION

Page 40   1   See Chapters V and VI below.
           2   P. A. Kropotkin, *The Great French Revolution* (Eng. tr. New York
               1909), pp. 581–2.
Page 42   1   Robespierre, 2 June 1793, quoted Albert Soboul, *Les Sans-Culottes
               parisiens en l'An II* (Paris 1958), p. 419.
           2   A. Soboul, op. cit., p. 461.
           3   A. Soboul, op. cit., p. 411.
Page 43   1   Quoted A. Soboul, op. cit., p. 459.
           2   Quoted A. Sergent and C. Harmel, op. cit., p. 59.
           3   Ibid., p. 82.
Page 44   1   A. Soboul, op. cit., p. 211.
           2   *L'Ami du Peuple*, no. 647, quoted P. Kropotkin, *The Great French
               Revolution*, pp. 265–6.
           3   *Chronique de Paris*, 3 October 1792, quoted A. Soboul, op. cit., p. 655.
Page 45   1   Quoted Maxime Leroy, *Histoire des idées sociales en France*, vol. I: *De
               Montesquieu à Robespierre* (Paris 1946), p. 282.
           2   Advielle, *Histoire de Gracchus Babeuf et du Babouvisme* I. 30, quoted
               Maxime Leroy, *Histoire des idées sociales en France*, vol. II. *De Babeuf à
               Tocqueville* (Paris 1950), p. 57. The best account in English is David
               Thomson, *The Babeuf Plot* (London 1947).
Page 46   1   M. Leroy, op. cit., vol. II, pp. 69–70.
           2   Ibid., p. 73.
           3   Quoted ibid., p. 76.
Page 47   1   Abbé de Barmel, *Mémoires pour servir à l'histoire du Jacobinisme, de
               l'impiété et de l'anarchie* (London 1797), quoted M. Leroy, op. cit.,
               vol. I, p. 346.
           2   On Buonarroti, see esp. A. Galante Garroni, *Buonarroti e Babeuf*
               (Turin 1948) and *Filippo Buonarroti è i Rivoluzionari dell' Ottocento*
               (Turin 1954). Also, in English, Elizabeth L. Eisenstein, *Filippo
               Michele Buonarroti* (Cambridge, Mass. 1959).
Page 48   1   E. Eisenstein, op. cit., p. 69.
           2   Armando Saitta, *Filippo Buonarroti* (Rome 1951), vol. I, p. 3, quoted
               Eisenstein, op. cit., p. 10.
           3   Quoted E. Eisenstein, op. cit., p. 149.
Page 49   1   Quoted M. Leroy, op. cit., vol. II, p. 47.
Page 50   1   F. Engels, *Die Entwicklung des Sozialismus von der Utopie zur Wissen-
               schaft*, quoted Karl Mannheim, *Ideology and Utopia* (Cheap ed.,
               London 1960), p. 220.
Page 51   1   Quoted Charles Gide, *Selections from the Works of Fourier*, tr. Julia
               Frankton (London 1901), p. 22.
Page 52   1   Quoted George Woodcock, *Pierre-Joseph Proudhon* (London 1956),
               p. 13.
           2   J. A. Langlois, *Notice sur Proudhon* in Proudhon, *Correspondence*, vol.
               I (Paris, 1874), p. xxii. See also A. Cuvillier, *Introduction* to P. J.
               Proudhon, *De la création de l'ordre dans l'humanité* (Oeuvres complètes,
               new ed., Paris 1927), pp. 21 ff.
           3   H. de Saint-Simon, *On Social Organization* in *Henri Comte de Saint-
               Simon: Selected Writings*, ed. and tr. F. M. H. Markham (Oxford
               1952), p. 78. For an excellent discussion of Saint-Simon's life and
               doctrines, see Frank E. Manuel, *The New World of Henri Saint-Simon*
               (Cambridge, Mass. 1956).

Page 53 1 Quoted E. Dolléans, *Proudhon* (Paris 1948), p. 41.
      2 E. H. Carr, *Michael Bakunin* (London 1937), p. 62.
Page 55 1 Wilhelm Weitling, *Evangelium eines armen Sünders* (Bern 1845), p. 17.
      2 Quoted Carl Wittke, *The Utopian Communist* (Baton Rouge 1950), p. 39.
Page 56 1 Wilhelm Weitling, *Garantien der Harmonie und Freiheit* (Jubilee ed. Berlin 1908), p. 247.
      2 Ibid.
      3 For this somewhat obscure episode, see *Die Kommunisten in der Schweiz nach den bei Weitling vorgefundenen Papieren* (Zurich 1843). This is the report drawn up by order of the Zurich authorities by Bluntschli, later a famous professor of jurisprudence, at the time of Weitling's arrest. See also Wittke, op. cit., pp. 35–44.
      4 W. Weitling, *Garantien*, p. 236.

CHAPTER III: REASON AND REVOLUTION: PROUDHON

Page 61 1 P. J. Proudhon, *La révolution sociale démontrée par le coup d'état du deux Décembre* (Oeuvres complètes, nouvelle éd., Paris 1938), p. 126.
      2 P. J. Proudhon, *Mémoires sur ma vie* (written 1841), p. 5, printed in *Carnets de P. J. Proudhon*, vol. I (Paris 1960). For Proudhon's life see George Woodcock, *Pierre-Joseph Proudhon* (London 1956); Edouard Dolléans, *Proudhon* (Paris 1948); Daniel Halévy, *La jeunesse de Proudhon* (Paris 1948). For an excellent discussion of certain aspects of Proudhon's thought, see H. de Lubac, *Proudhon et le Christianisme* (Paris 1945), Eng. tr. *The Unmarxian Socialist* (London 1948).
Page 62 1 P. J. Proudhon, *Carnets*, vol. I, p. 3.
Page 63 1 *Système des Contradictions Economiques* (New ed., 2 vols., Paris 1923), vol. II, p. 310.
Page 64 1 P. J. Proudhon, *Système des Contradictions Economiques ou Philosophie de la Misère* (New ed., Paris 1923), vol. II, p. 361.
      2 P. J. Proudhon, *Qu'est-ce que la Propriété?* (Paris 1840), p. 87.
Page 65 1 E. Dolléans: *Proudhon*, p. 173.
      2 Quoted Pierre Haubtmann, *Marx et Proudhon* (Paris 1947), p. 27.
Page 66 1 P. Haubtmann, op. cit., pp. 63–64. See also G. Woodcock, *Proudhon* pp. 92–93.
      2 Quoted E. Dolléans, *Proudhon*, p. 99.
Page 67 1 P. J. Proudhon, *Système des contradictions économiques*, vol. I, p. 356.
      2 Ibid., vol. I, p. 372.
Page 68 1 Ibid., vol. II, p. 252.
      2 P. J. Proudhon, *Carnets*, vol. I, p. 169.
Page 69 1 Proudhon to Marx, 17 May 1840, quoted in P. J. Proudhon, *Oeuvres Complètes: Programme Révolutionnaire* (Paris 1938), p. 292.
      2 See, e.g., *Carnets*, vol. II, pp. 26, 173.
      3 Proudhon to Rolland, 3 June 1861, quoted E. Dolléans, op. cit., pp. 384–5.
Page 70 1 Quoted Woodcock, *Proudhon*, pp. 106–7.
      2 *Carnets*, 15 June 1858, quoted E. Dolléans, op. cit., p. 318.
      3 *Carnets*, vol. I, p. 226.
      4 *Qu'est-ce que la Propriété?* pp. 169–70.
Page 71 1 *Qu'est-ce que la Propriéte?* pp. 242–3.
      2 To Alfred Darimon, 14 February 1850, quoted E. Dolléans, *Proudhon*, p. 207.

Page 72   1   Quoted E. H. Carr, *Michael Bakunin* (London 1937), p. 130.
          2   *Les confessions d'un révolutionnaire pour servir à l'histoire de la Révolution de Février* (1849) (New ed., Paris 1929), p. 65.
Page 74   1   *La révolution sociale démontrée par le coup d'état du Deux Décembre* (New ed., Paris 1938), p. 288.
          2   Ibid., p. 290.
Page 75   1   *L'idée générale de la Révolution au 19e siècle* (New ed., Paris 1924), p. 302.
          2   *De la justice dans la révolution et dans l'église* (1st ed., Paris 1858), 3 vols.
          3   *De la justice*, vol. I, p. 151.
          4   Ibid., vol. I, p. 423.
Page 76   1   Ibid., vol. I, p. 486.
          2   To Pierre Leroux, 13 December 1849, quoted E. Dolléans, *Proudhon*, p. 221.
Page 77   1   *De la justice*, vol. I, p. 575.
          2   P. J. Proudhon, *Contradictions politiques* (New ed., Paris 1952), p. 235.
Page 79   1   *L'idée générale de la Révolution au 19e siècle* (New ed., Paris 1929) p. 344.
Page 80   1   Alain Sergent and Claude Harmel, *Histoire de l'anarchie* (Paris 1949), p. 301.
          2   *De la capacité politique des classes ouvrières* (2nd ed., Paris 1865).
Page 81   1   *De la capacité politique*, p. 80.
          2   See Georges Duveau, *La vie ouvrière en France sous le Second Empire* (Paris 1946).
          3   G. Duveau, op. cit., p. 230.

CHAPTER IV: BAKUNIN AND THE GREAT SCHISM

Page 84   1   For Bakunin's life see E. H. Carr, *Michael Bakunin* (London 1937).
          2   E. H. Carr, op. cit., p. 38.
          3   E. H. Carr, op. cit., pp. 8–9.
Page 85   1   E. H. Carr, op. cit., p. 12.
          2   E. H. Carr, op. cit., p. 130.
Page 86   1   *Appeal to the Slavs*, quoted E. H. Carr, op. cit., p. 173.
Page 87   1   Quoted ibid.
          2   E. H. Carr, op. cit., p. 378.
Page 89   1   Quoted E. H. Carr, op. cit., p. 242.
Page 90   1   On the relations between Bakunin and Mazzini, see N. Rosselli, *Mazzini e Bakunin* (Turin 1927); see also Richard Hostetter, *The Italian Socialist Movement. I. Origins (1860–1882)* (Princeton, N.J., 1958), and Arthur Lehning, *Michel Bakounine et l'Italie*. Textes établies et annotées (Leiden 1961).
Page 91   1   Quoted Sergent and Harmel, *Histoire de l'Anarchie*, p. 413.
Page 92   1   M. Bakunin, *Oeuvres*, vol. V, p. 180.
          2   M. Bakunin, *Statism and Anarchy*, quoted Venturi, *Il Populismo russo*, 2 vols. (Turin 1952), vol. II, p. 710 (Eng. ed. *Roots of Revolution* [London 1959]).
          3   *M. Bakunin, Oeuvres*, vol. IV, p. 32.
Page 93   1   M. Bakunin, *Oeuvres*, vol. VI (Paris 1913), p. 399.
          2   M. Bakunin, *Statism and Anarchy*, quoted F. Venturi, op. cit., vol. II, p. 708.
          3   M. Bakunin, *Oeuvres*, vol. V, p. 107.
          4   M. Bakunin, *Oeuvres*, vol. V, p. 252.
          5   Bakunin to James Guillaume, 13 April 1869, quoted F. Venturi, op. cit., vol. I, p. 595.

Page 94   1   Quoted F. Venturi, op. cit., vol. I, p. 592.
Page 95   1   Quoted F. Venturi, op. cit., vol. I, p. 601.
           2   Quoted E. H. Carr, op. cit., pp. 379–80.
Page 96   1   Quoted F. Venturi, op. cit., vol. I, pp. 605, 607.
           2   Quoted E. H. Carr, op. cit., p. 393.
Page 97   1   M. Bakunin, Lecture in Val de Saint-Imier, 1871, *Oeuvres*, vol. V,
               pp. 325–6.
Page 98   1   Vyrubov, quoted E. H. Carr, op. cit., p. 329.
Page 99   1   Quoted E. H. Carr, op. cit., p. 338.
           2   Quoted E. H. Carr, op. cit., p. 344.
           3   Bakunin, *Oeuvres*, vol. IV, p. viii.
Page 100   1   Marx to F. Bolté, 23 November 1871, Karl Marx and Frederick
               Engels, *Selected Works*, (London 1950), vol. II, p. 422.
           2   M. Bakunin, *Aux frères de l'Alliance en Espagne* (1872), quoted Max
               Nettlau: *Bakunin und die Internationale in Italien bis zum Herbst 1872* in
               Archiv für die Geschichte des Sozialismus und der Arbeiterbewegung, vol. II
               (1911–12), pp. 283–4.
Page 101   1   Marx to Kugelmann, 23 August 1866, quoted J. L. Puech, *Le
               Proudhonisme dans l'Association Internationale des Travailleurs* (Paris
               1907), p. 112.
           2   Quoted ibid., pp. 135–6.
Page 102   1   Bakunin to Marx, 22 December 1868, *Neue Zeit*, 1900–1, pp. 6–7.
           2   E. H. Carr, op. cit., p. 352.
Page 103   1   Franz Mehring, *Karl Marx* (Leipzig 1918), p. 424.
           2   M. Bakunin, article in *L'Egalité* 1869, *Oeuvres*, vol. V., p. 151.
Page 104   1   E. H. Carr, op. cit., p. 366.
           2   Marx to Laura Lafargue, quoted Mehring, op. cit., p. 427.
           3   F. Mehring, op. cit., p. 497.
Page 105   1   M. Bakunin, *Oeuvres*, vol. II, pp. xlix–l.
           2   To Herzen, 28 October 1869, *Oeuvres*, vol. V, pp. 233–4.
Page 106   1   Resolution IX of the London Conference. For an excellent discussion
               of the significance of the conference and of the decline of the Inter-
               national, see Miklos Molnar, *Le Déclin de la Première Internationale:
               La Conférence de Londres de 1871* (Geneva 1963).
           2   *Les Prétendues Scissions dans l'Internationale*, Circulaire Privée du Con-
               seil Général de L'Association Internationale des Travailleurs
               (Geneva 1872), p. 37. This and other documents have been con-
               veniently reprinted in Jacques Freymond (ed.) *La Première Inter-
               nationale, Recueil de Documents* (Geneva 1962, 2 vols.).
Page 107   1   M. Bakunin, *Oeuvres*, vol. II, p. l.
Page 108   1   J. Guillaume, *L'Internationale: Documents Souvenirs 1864–1878* (4 vols.,
               Paris 1905–10), vol. I, pp. 74–75.
           2   Quoted M. Nettlau, *Bakunin und die Internationale in Italien*, pp. 283–4.
           3   M. Bakunin, *Ai miei amici d'Italia . . .* quoted M. Nettlau, *Bakumin
               e l'Internazionale in Italia* (Geneva 1928), p. 253.
Page 109   1   Ibid., p. 320.
           2   J. Guillaume, op. cit., vol. II, pp. 160–1.
Page 110   1   M. Bakunin, *L'Empire Knouto-Germanique et la Révolution Sociale* (1871),
               Oeuvres, vol. II, p. 297.
           2   F. Engels (Jan.–Feb. 1873) in *Almenacco Repubblicano 1874*, quoted
               Karl Marx and Frederick Engels, *Selected Works*, vol. I (London 1950).
Page 111   1   Max Nettlau, *Miguel Bakunin, la Internacional y la Alianza en España
               1868–1873* (Buenos Aires 1925), p. 20.

Page 112   1   Anselmo Lorenzo, *El Proletariado Militante* (Mexico City n.d.), p. 19.
Page 113   1   M. Nettlau, *M. Bakunin, La Internacional y la Alianza en España*, p. 53.
          2   M. Bakunin, *Oeuvres*, vol. II, p. 272.
          3   Bakunin to Elisée Reclus, 15 February 1875, quoted James Guillaume, op. cit., vol. III, p. 284.
Page 114   1   *Le Père Duchêne*, no. 8 du 30 ventose an 79, quoted Charles Thomann, *Le Mouvement Anarchiste dans les montagnes neuchâteloises et le Jura bernois* (La Chaux-de-Fonds 1947), p. 52.
          2   F. Venturi, op. cit., vol. II, p. 699.

CHAPTER V: TERRORISM AND PROPAGANDA BY THE DEED

Page 118   1   For the Lazzaretti, see E. J. Hobsbawm, *Primitive Rebels* (Manchester 1959).
Page 119   1   Carlo Monticelli, *A. Costa e l'Internazionale*, quoted Armando Borghi *Errico Malatesta* (Milan 1947), p. 48.
          2   George Woodcock, *Anarchism* (New York 1962), p. 344.
Page 120   1   A. Costa, *Bagliori di socialismo* (Florence 1900), quoted Hostetter, op. cit., p. 146.
          2   See the discussion in Hostetter, op. cit., pp. 252–3.
Page 121   1   Cessarelli to Cipriani, April 1881, quoted Hostetter, op. cit., p. 377.
Page 122   1   This account is mainly based on Dr Hostetter's researches, op. cit., pp. 381 ff; see also Nettlau, *Malatesta*, pp. 107–9.
Page 123   1   A. Costa, *Open letter from a group of Internationalists to G. Nicotera*, Jan. 1877, quoted Hostetter, p. 376.
          2   A. Borghi, *Malatesta*, p. 63.
Page 124   1   Emilio Covelli in *La Plebe*, 27 July 1879, quoted Hostetter, op. cit., p. 409.
Page 125   1   Sergent and Harmel, *Histoire de l'anarchie*, p. 443.
          2   For Kropotkin's life, see George Woodcock and Ivan Avakumovic, *The Anarchist Prince* (London 1950); also Kropotkin's own *Memoirs of a Revolutionist*.
Page 127   1   F. Venturi, op. cit., vol. II, p. 790.
          2   Kropotkin gives a dramatic account in his own *Memoirs*; also G. Woodcock and I. Avakumovic, who have assembled further details, op. cit., pp. 140–4.
          3   *Le Révolté*, Dec. 1880, quoted Jean Maitron, *Histoire du mouvement anarchiste en France* (1880–1914) (Paris 1951), p. 70.
Page 128   1   G. Woodcock and I. Avakumovic, op. cit., p. 343.
          2   James's knowledge was derived from a *fait divers* in the newspaper; see Lionel Trilling, *The Liberal Imagination* (Paperback ed., New York 1953), pp. 65–96. Conrad probably knew both Kropotkin and Stepniak through their English friends Edward Garnett and his family; see Jocelyn Baines, *Joseph Conrad* (London 1959), pp. 370–1.
Page 129   1   Gaetano Natale, *Giolitti e gli Italiani* (Milan 1949), pp. 467–70.
Page 130   1   *Le Droit Social*, 12 March 1888, quoted Maitron, op. cit., p. 150.
Page 131   1   Maitron, op. cit., p. 194.
          2   Ibid.
Page 132   1   Maitron, op. cit., p. 213.
Page 133   1   Maitron, op. cit., p. 169.
Page 134   1   The most recent attempt to reconstruct his career is that in André Salmon, *La terreur noire* (Paris 1959), pp. 141–256, a vivid, if over-imaginative account. See also Maitron, op. cit., pp. 195–212.

Page 136 1 Maitron, op. cit., p. 205 fn. 4.

2 Quoted Eugenia W. Herbert, *The Artist and Social Reform: France and Belgium 1885–1900* (New Haven 1961), p. 119.

3 *The Letters of Oscar Wilde*, ed. Rupert Hart-Davis (London 1962), p. 768.

Page 137 1 A. Salmon, op. cit., p. 343.

Page 138 1 Emile Henry's speech to the jury is printed in full in Maitron, op. cit., pp. 529–34.

Page 139 1 For Most's life, see Rudolf Rocker, *Johann Most* (Berlin 1924).

Page 140 1 R. Rocker, op. cit., p. 209.

Page 141 1 Henry David, *History of the Haymarket Affair* (New York 1936), p. 292.

Page 142 1 H. David, op. cit., pp. 121–2; Louis Adamic, *Dynamite* (London 1931), p. 47.

2 H. David, op. cit., p. 194.

Page 143 1 H. David, op. cit., p. 208;

2 L. Adamic, op. cit., p. 79.

3 H. David, op. cit., p. 339; L. Adamic, op. cit., p. 79.

4 H. David, op. cit., p. 463.

Page 144 1 For Emma Goldman's life, see her own *Living My Life* (2 vols., New York 1932), and Richard Drinnon, *Rebel in Paradise* (Chicago 1961).

Page 146 1 *Le Journal*, 19 February 1894, quoted Maitron, op. cit., p. 227.

2 R. Rocker, op. cit., p. 301.

3 Max Nettlau, *Elisée Reclus; Anarchist und Gelehrter* (Berlin 1928), p. 248.

4 M. Nettlau, *Elisée Reclus*, p. 241.

CHAPTER VI: SAINTS AND REBELS

Page 150 1 Quoted L. Levy, *Comment ils sont devenus Socialistes* (Paris 1932), p. 21.

Page 151 1 G. Brandes, Preface to P. Kropotkin, *Memoirs of a Revolutionist* (London 1899), vol. I, pp. xiii–xiv.

2 P. Kropotkin, *Memoirs of a Revolutionist*, p. 139.

Page 152 1 Woodcock and Avakumovic, op. cit., p. 381.

2 Ibid., p. 380.

3 Ibid., p. 360.

Page 153 1 Introduction to L. Tolstoy, *La guerre et le service obligatoire* (Brussels 1896).

2 P. Kropotkin to Mrs Dryhurst, 1893, quoted Woodcock and Avakumovic, op. cit., p 248.

3 P. Kropotkin, *The Great French Revolution* (New York 1909), p. 535.

Page 154 1 Quoted Woodcock and Avakumovic, op. cit., p. 351.

2 Ibid., p. 353.

Page 155 1 P. Kropotkin, *Law and Authority*, reprinted in *Kropotkin's Revolutionary Pamphlets*, ed. G. Roger N. Baldwin (New York 1927), pp. 205–6.

2 P. Kropotkin, *Mutual Aid: A Factor of Evolution* (London 1902), p. 34.

Page 156 1 P. Kropotkin, *Ethics: Origin and Development* (Eng. ed., New York 1924), p. 22.

2 P. Kropotkin, *Anarchist Communism* (1887) in *Kropotkin's Revolutionary Pamphlets*, p. 47.

Page 157 1 M. Guyau, *Esquisse d'une morale ans obligation ni sanction* (Paris 1885), p. 29.

2 Ibid., p. 252.

3 Ibid., p. 246.

4 P. Kropotkin, *La conquête du pain* (Paris 1892), p. 60.

Page 158 1 Ibid., pp. 20–21.
           2 P. Kropotkin, *Anarchist Communism*, p. 60.

Page 159 1 Ibid., p. 59.
           2 *The Times*, 21 July 1960.
           3 P. Kropotkin, *La conquête du pain*, p. 81.

Page 160 1 P. Kropotkin, *Anarchist Communism*, p. 71.
           2 P. Kropotkin, *La conquête du pain*, p. 159.

Page 161 1 P. Kropotkin, *Modern Science and Anarchism* in *Kropotkin's Revolutionary Pamphlets*, p. 157.
           2 P. Kropotkin, *Fields, Factories and Workshops* (London 1899), p. 272.
           3 Woodcock and Avakumovic, op. cit., p. 302.

Page 162 1 Oscar Wilde, *De Profundis* (London 1950), p. 112.

Page 163 1 Saverio Merlino, *Necessità e Basi di una Intesa* (Brussels 1892), reprinted in Saverio Merlino, *Concezione critica del Socialismo Libertario*, ed. Aldo Venturini and Pier Carlo Masini (Florence 1957), p. 99.
           2 P.-J. Proudhon, *Du principe de l'art et de sa destination sociale* (Paris 1865), p. 43.

Page 164 1 Ibid., p. 46.
           2 Ibid., pp. 367–8.

Page 165 1 Courbet to Wey, 26 November 1849, quoted Gerstle Mack, *Gustave Courbet* (London 1951), pp. 69–70.
           2 P.-J. Proudhon, *Du principe de l'art*, pp. 236–7, quoted Mack, op. cit., p. 70.
           3 Quoted Mack, op. cit., p. 71.
           4 J. Guillaume, *L'Internationale*, vol. III, p. 295.

Page 166 1 *L'Avant-Garde*, 12 January 1878, quoted Charles Thomann, *Le mouvement anarchiste dans les montagnes neuchâteloises et le Jura bernois* (La Chaux-de-Fonds 1947), p. 123.
           2 *Le Courier du Dimanche*, 29 December 1861, quoted Mack, op. cit., p. 102.
           3 1861, quoted Mack, op. cit., p. 89.
           4 See Benedict Nicolson, *The Anarchism of Camille Pissarro* in *The Arts*, no. 2, (London 1947), pp. 43–51.

Page 167 1 Quoted Eugenia W. Herbert, *The Artist and Social Reform: France and Belgium 1885–1898* (New Haven, Connecticut 1961), p. 189.
           2 Quoted John Rewald, *Post-Impressionism from Van Gogh to Gauguin* (New York 1956), p. 155.

Page 168 1 Robert L. and Eugenia W. Herbert, *Artists and Anarchism: Unpublished Letters of Pissarro, Signac and Others. I.* (*The Burlington Magazine*, vol. CII, no. 692, November 1960, p. 479).

Page 169 1 John Rewald, *Félix Fénéon* (Gazette des Beaux-Arts, 6e series, vols. xxxi–xxxii, 1947–48), vol. II, p. 110.

Page 170 1 Maurice Barrès, *L'ennemi des lois* (New ed., Paris 1910), p. 302.
           2 *Les Temps Nouveaux*, March 1896, quoted Eugenia Herbert, op. cit., p. 83.

Page 171 1 Emma Goldman, *Living My Life* (London 1932, 2 vols.), vol. I, p. 194.
           2 Max Stirner, *Der Einzige und sein Eigentum* (3rd ed., Leipzig 1901). p. 8.
           3 M. Stirner, op. cit., p. 379.

Page 172 1 Quoted Laura Fermi, *Mussolini* (Chicago 1961), p. 70.
           2 Quoted Maitron, op. cit., p. 379.

Page 173 1 Victor Serge, *Mémoires d'un révolutionnaire* (Paris 1951), pp. 20–21.

CHAPTER VII: THE REVOLUTION THAT FAILED

Page 174   1   Leonard Schapiro, *The Origin of the Communist Autocracy* (London 1955), p. 182.

2   Errico Malatesta in *Studi Sociali*, 15 April 1931; reprinted in E. Malatesta, *Scritti scelti*, ed. C. Zaccaria and G. Berneri (Naples 1947), p. 326.

3   Armando Borghi, *Errico Malatesta* (Milan 1947), p. 95.

Page 175   1   See Enzo Santarelli, *L'azione di Errico Malatesta e i moti di 1898 ad Ancona* in *Movimento Operaio*, 1954, pp. 248–72.

2   *Questione Sociale*, 14 June 1899, quoted Borghi, *Malatesta*, pp. 126–7.

Page 177   1   Rudolf Rocker, *The London Years* (London 1956), p. 208.

Page 178   1   Gaudens Megaro, *Mussolini dal mito al realtá* (Milan 1947), p. 245 (Eng. ed., *Mussolini in the Making*, 1938).

2   Max Nettlau, *Errico Malatesta; la vida de un anarquista* (Buenos Aires 1923), p. 193.

Page 180   1   E. Malatesta, *Scritti scelti*, p. 170.

2   Quoted Woodcock and Avakumovic, op. cit., p. 391.

Page 181   1   Ibid., pp. 425–6.

Page 182   1   Ibid., p. 430.

Page 183   1   Voline (V. M. Eichenbaum), *Nineteen-Seventeen: The Russian Revolution Betrayed* (Eng. tr. London 1954), p. 76.

Page 184   1   Alexander Berkman, *The Bolshevik Myth* (London 1925), pp. 90–91.

2   For Makhno's career, see the excellent account based on the available Russian sources, in David Footman, *Civil War in Russia* (London 1961), pp. 245–303.

Page 185   1   D. Footman, op. cit., pp. 253–4.

2   Ibid., p. 271.

Page 186   1   Ibid., p. 280.

2   Ibid., p. 284.

Page 187   1   Ibid., p. 289.

Page 188   1   Quoted ibid., p. 289.

Page 189   1   Emma Goldman, *My Disillusionment in Russia* (London 1925), p. 69.

Page 190   1   Emma Goldman, *Living My Life* (London 1932), vol. II, p. 577.

Page 191   1   See G. Katkov, *The Kronstadt Rising* in *St Antony's Papers*, no. 6 (London 1959).

2   Quoted Voline, op. cit., p. 154.

3   A. Berkman, *The Bolshevik Myth* (London 1925), p. 319.

Page 192   1   See James Joll, *The Second International* (London 1955), Ch. III.

CHAPTER VIII: ANARCHISTS AND SYNDICALISTS

Page 195   1   *La Révolte*, March 1891, quoted Maitron, op. cit., p. 240.

2   *Les Temps Nouveaux*, August 1900, quoted ibid., p. 382.

3   M. Bakunin, *Oeuvres*, vol. V, p. 182.

Page 196   1   *Bulletin de la Fédération Jurassienne*, 1 November 1774, quoted J. Maitron, op. cit., p. 261.

2   Quoted J. Maitron, op. cit., p. 261.

Page 198   1   Maurice Pelloutier, *Fernand Pelloutier: sa vie, son oeuvre (1867–1901)* (Paris 1911), p. 5.

2   Ibid., p. 62.

Page 199   1   F. Pelloutier, *L'Anarchisme et les syndicats ouvriers* in *Les Temps Nouveaux*, November 1895, quoted J. Maitron, op. cit., p. 251.

Page 199   2   Quoted J. Maitron, *Le syndicalisme revolutionnaire: Paul Delesalle* (Paris 1952), p. 24.

           3   Quoted J. Maitron, *Histoire du mouvement anarchiste*, p. 252.

Page 201   1   Figures based on the 1906 census as given in Bernard Georges and Denise Tintant, *Léon Jouhaux: Cinquante ans de syndicalisme*, vol. I (Paris 1962), p. 11.

           2   Quoted J. Maitron, *Delesalle*, p. 81.

Page 202   1   Quoted E. Dolléans, *Histoire du mouvement ouvrier*, vol. II (2nd ed., Paris 1946), p. 117.

           2   J. Maitron, *Delesalle*, p. 111.

Page 203   1   The translation of these passages from the *Charte d'Amiens* is that given in G. D. H. Cole, *The Second International* (vol. III of *A History of Socialist Thought* (London 1956), Part I, p. 371).

           2   Amédée Dunois in *Congrès anarchiste tenu à Amsterdam 24–31 août 1907. Compte rendu analytique* . . . (Paris 1908), p. 14.

Page 204   1   *Compte rendu*, pp. 36–38.

           2   Ibid., p. 62.

           3   Ibid., p. 70.

           4   Ibid., p. 46.

Page 205   1   Ibid., p. 85.

           2   Ibid., p. 83.

Page 206   1   Jean Variot, *Propos de Georges Sorel* (Paris 1935), pp. 54–57.

Page 207   1   J. Variot, op. cit., p. 65.

Page 208   1   G. Sorel, *Matériaux d'une théorie du prolétariat* (Paris 1918), p. 58.

           2   G. Sorel, *Réflexions sur la violence* (3rd ed., Paris 1912), p. 205.

           3   G. Sorel, Preface to F. Pelloutier, *Histoire des Bourses du Travail* (Paris 1902).

           4   G. Sorel, *La décomposition du Marxisme* (Paris 1907), pp. 53–54.

Page 209   1   G. Sorel, *Matériaux d'une théorie du prolétariat*, p. 268; see Richard Humphreys, *Georges Sorel: Prophet Without Honor* (Cambridge, Mass. 1951), p. 18.

           2   G. Sorel, *Réflexions*, p. 120.

Page 210   1   G. Sorel, *De église et de l'état*, pp. 31–32.

           2   G. Sorel, *Réflexions*, p. 46.

           3   Ibid., p. 180.

Page 211   1   G. Sorel, *Matériaux*, p. 199.

           2   For a general discussion of the various aspects of Sorel's thought, see Richard Humphreys, *Georges Sorel: Prophet Without Honor* (Cambridge, Mass. 1951); H. Stuart Hughes, *Consciousness and Society* (London 1959); Irving Louis Horowitz, *Radicalism and the Revolt Against Reason: The Theories of Georges Sorel* (London 1961).

Page 212   1   Wyndham Lewis, *The Art of Being Ruled* (London 1926), p. 128.

           2   Daniel Halévy, *Péguy et les Cahiers de la Quinzaine* (Paris 1941), p. 108.

Page 213   1   E. Dolléans, *Histoire du mouvement ouvrier*, vol. II, p. 127.

           2   L. Jouhaux gave these figures in a lecture at Brussels in December 1911. See Dolléans, op. cit., p. 189 fn. 1.

Page 214   1   Quoted E. Dolléans, op. cit., p. 155.

           2   Bernard Georges and Denise Tintant, op. cit., vol. I, p. 3.

Page 215   1   Quoted B. Georges and D. Tintant, op. cit., vol. I, p. 320.

Page 216   1   Ibid., pp. 388–9.

Page 218   1   P. E. Brissenden, *The IWW: A Study of American Syndicalism* (2nd ed. New York 1920), p. 66.

Page 219   1   P. E. Brissenden, op. cit., p. 92.

Page 219　2　Thomas Hagerty, quoted Ira Kipnis, *The American Socialist Movement 1897–1912* (New York 1952), p. 192.

Page 220　1　Ibid.

　　　　　2　Brissenden, op. cit., pp. 138–9.

　　　　　3　*The Industrial Worker*, 23 April 1910, quoted Brissenden, op. cit., p. 271.

Page 221　1　*Mother Earth*, October 1913, quoted Brissenden, op. cit., p. 318.

Page 222　1　See Marjorie Ruth Clark, *Organized Labour in Mexico* (Chapel Hill, NC 1934).

Page 223　1　*Beatrice Webb's Diaries, 1912–1924*, ed. Margaret Cole (London 1952), p. 7.

　　　　　2　See Fanny F. Simon, *Anarchism and Anarcho-Syndicalism in South America* in *The Hispanic American Historical Review*, vol. xxvi (1946), pp. 38–59.

CHAPTER IX: ANARCHISTS IN ACTION: SPAIN

Page 225　1　See, e.g., Joaquín Maurín, *Hacia la segunda revolucion* (Barcelona 1935).

Page 226　1　R. Mella, quoted J. Díaz del Moral, *Historia de las Agitaciones Campesinas Andaluzas–Córdoba* (Madrid 1929), p. 90.

　　　　　2　For Pi y Margall's ideas and career, see Alastair Hennessy, *The Federal Republic in Spain* (London 1962).

　　　　　3　Casimiro Martí, *Origenes del Anarquismo en Barcelona* (Barcelona 1959), p. 37.

Page 228　1　Anselmo Lorenzo, *El Proletariado Militante* (Mexico n.d.), p. 164.

Page 229　1　For an account of the events at Alcoy, see Rafael Coloma, *La Revolución Internacionalista Alcoyana de 1873* (Alicante 1959).

Page 231　1　Gerald Brenan, *The Spanish Labyrinth* (Paperback ed., London 1960), p. 156.

　　　　　2　See Rudolf Rocker, *Fermin Salvochea* (Ediciones Tierra y Libertad, 1945); there is also a vivid fictional account in Blasco Ibañez' novel *La Bodega*, in which the character of Fernando Salvatierra is based on Salvochea.

Page 233　1　See Sol Ferrer, *La Vie et l'oeuvre de Francisco Ferrer* (Paris 1962).

Page 234　1　Quoted Yvonne Turin, *L'Education et l'Ecole en Espagne de 1874 à 1902* (Paris 1959), p. 315.

　　　　　2　Y. Turin, op. cit., p. 317.

Page 236　1　Federica Montseny, *Anselmo Lorenzo: el hombre y la obra* (Toulouse n.d.), p. 36.

Page 237　1　S. Ferrer, op. cit., p. 231.

Page 239　1　See Palmiro Marbo, *Origen, Desarollo y Trascendencia del Sindicalismo* (Mexico 1919).

Page 240　1　J. Díaz del Moral, op. cit., p. 61.

　　　　　2　J. Díaz del Moral, op. cit., p. 305.

　　　　　3　See J. Díaz del Moral, op. cit., pp. 264 ff.

Page 241　1　J. Díaz del Moral, op. cit., p. 227.

Page 243　1　Quoted Manuel Buenacasa, *El Movimiento Obrero Español: 1886–1926* (Barcelona 1928), pp. 133–7.

Page 244　1　J. Peirats, *La CNT en la Revolución Española* (3 vols., Toulouse 1951), vol. I, p. 7.

Page 246　1　J. Peirats, op. cit., vol. I, pp. 42–43.

Page 247　1　J. Peirats, op. cit., vol. I, pp. 46–47.

Page 248   1   G. Brenan, *The Spanish Labyrinth*, p. 250.
            2   J. Peirats, op. cit., vol. I, p. 51.
Page 249   1   Ibid., p. 53.
            2   See the interesting account based on a study of Casas Viejas itself in
                E. J. Hobsbawm, *Primitive Rebels*, pp. 84 ff.; see also Peirats, op. cit.,
                vol. I, pp. 55 ff.
Page 252   1   For a good account of anarchist attitudes in this period, see Edward
                Conze, *Spain Today* (London 1936).
Page 253   1   The main speeches and resolutions of this congress are given in
                J. Peirats, op. cit., vol. I, pp. 109 ff.
Page 254   1   Federica Montseny in *Solidaridad Obrera*, 22 December 1936, quoted
                Burnett Bolloten, *The Grand Camouflage* (London 1961), p. 20.
Page 255   1   J. Peirats, op. cit., vol. I, pp. 162–3.
Page 257   1   *Revista Blanca*, 8 June 1934, quoted Burnett Bolloten, op. cit., p. 65
                fn. 21.
            2   For the special position of the *Rabassaires*, as whose spokesman
                Companys had made his reputation, see Brenan, op. cit., pp. 276 ff.
            3   Quoted B. Bolloten, op. cit., p. 74.
Page 258   1   Franz Borkenau, *The Spanish Cockpit* (London 1937), p. 167; cf. the
                similar account of the commune at Alcora in the province of Castel-
                lón, in H. E. Kaminski, *Ceux de Barcelone* (Paris 1937), pp. 113 ff.
Page 259   1   Hugh Thomas, *The Spanish Civil War* (London 1961), p. 189.
Page 260   1   *Montreal Star*, 30 October 1936, quoted H. Thomas, op. cit., p. 289.
Page 261   1   *Pravda*, 17 December 1936, quoted H. Thomas, op. cit., p. 363.
            2   *CNT*, 20 September 1937, quoted B. Bolloten, op. cit., p. 251.
Page 262   1   See J. Peirats, op. cit., vol. II, pp. 172 ff.
            2   *CNT*, 5 September 1936, quoted B. Bolloten, op. cit., pp. 155–6.
Page 263   1   *CNT*, 23 October 1936, quoted B. Bolloten, op. cit., p. 158.
Page 266   1   Quoted J. Peirats, op. cit., vol. II, pp. 270–2.
Page 268   1   *Tierra y Libertad*, 16 January 1937, quoted B. Bolloten, op. cit., p. 57.
            2   *CNT* secretary to Peasants' Federation of Castile in *Juventud Libre*,
                10 July 1937, quoted B. Bolloten, op. cit., p. 70.
Page 269   1   On the Italian anarchists in Spain, see *Un trentennio di Attività
                Anarchica* (Forlí, n.d.), pp. 192–201.
Page 272   1   J. Peirats, op. cit., vol. II, p. 360.
            2   FAI Circular no. 3, October 1936, quoted J. Peirats, op. cit., vol.
                II, p. 319.
Page 273   1   Luis Araquistain, quoted J. Peirats, op. cit., vol. III, p. 53.
            2   J. Peirats, op. cit., vol. III, p. 304.
Page 274   1   J. Peirats, op. cit., vol. I, p. x.

CHAPTER X: CONCLUSION

Page 278   1   Jayaprakash Narayan, *A Plea for Reconstruction of Indian Polity*
                (Wardha 1959), p. 63.
            2   Ibid., p. 36.
Page 280   1   Maurice Nadeau, *Histoire du surréalisme* (Paris 1945), p. 268.
            2   Quoted Peter Heintz, *Anarchismus und Gegenwart* (Zurich 1951). I
                am grateful to Professor Juan Marichal of Harvard University for
                drawing my attention to this interesting essay.

SUGGESTIONS FOR FURTHER READING

A short selection of books in English is given below. There is a fuller list in George Woodcock, *Anarchism* (New York 1962; London 1963), a work which is a valuable and comprehensive history of the anarchist movement.

General

Norman Cohn, *The Pursuit of the Millennium* (London 1957).

G. D. H. Cole, *History of Socialist Thought* (4 vols., London 1953–8).

Alexander Gray, *The Socialist Tradition: Moses to Lenin* (London 1946).

J. L. Talmon, *The Origins of Totalitarian Democracy* (London 1952); *Political Messianism* (London 1960).

George Woodcock, *Anarchism* (London 1963).

Biographies, memoirs and critical studies

Godwin

H. N. Brailsford, *Shelley, Godwin and their Circle* (London 1913).
David Fleisher, *William Godwin: A Study in Liberalism* (London 1951).
George Woodcock, *William Godwin* (London 1936).

Weitling

Carl Wittke, *The Utopian Communist* (Baton Rouge 1950).

Proudhon

D. W. Brogan, *Proudhon* (London 1936).
J. Hampden Jackson, *Marx, Proudhon and European Socialism* (London 1957).
H. de Lubac, *The Unmarxian Socialist* (London 1948).
George Woodcock, *Pierre-Joseph Proudhon* (London 1956).

Bakunin and Marx

I. Berlin, *Karl Marx* (New ed., London 1952).
E. H. Carr, *Michael Bakunin* (London 1937); *Karl Marx* (London 1934).
Franz Mehring, *Karl Marx* (Eng. tr., New York 1935).

Kropotkin

P. Kropotkin, *Memoirs of a Revolutionist* (London 1899).
George Woodcock and Ivan Avakumovic, *The Anarchist Prince* (London 1950).

Emma Goldman

Emma Goldman, *Living My Life* (2 vols., London 1931); *My Disillusionment in Russia* (London 1923).
Richard Drinnon, *Rebel in Paradise* (Chicago 1961).
Alexander Berkman, *Prison Memoirs of an Anarchist* (New York 1912); *The Bolshevik Myth* (New York 1925).

Georges Sorel

> Richard Humphreys, *Georges Sorel: Prophet without Honor* (Cambridge, Mass. 1951).
>
> Irving Louis Horowitz, *Radicalism and the Revolt against Reason: the Theories of Georges Sorel* (London 1961).
>
> H. Stuart Hughes, *Consciousness and Society* (London 1961).

Rudolph Rocker

> Rudolph Rocker, *The London Years* (London 1956).

Miscellaneous special studies

Louis Adamic, *Dynamite: Class Violence in America* (London 1931).

Burnett Bolloten, *The Grand Camouflage* (London 1961).

Franz Borkenau, *The Spanish Cockpit* (London 1937).

Gerald Brenan, *The Spanish Labyrinth* (New ed., London 1960).

P. E. Brissenden, *The IWW: A Study of American Syndicalism* (New York 1960).

E. H. Carr, *The Romantic Exiles* (London 1933); *Studies in Revolution* (London 1950).

David Footman, *Civil War in Russia* (London 1961).

Eugenia W. Herbert, *The Artist and Social Reform: France and Belgium 1885–1900* (New Haven 1961).

E. J. Hobsbawm, *Primitive Rebels* (Manchester 1959).

Richard Hostetter, *The Italian Socialist Movement*, vol. I, *Origins (1860–1882)* (Princeton 1958).

James Joll, *The Second International 1889–1914* (London 1955).

Ira Kipnis, *The American Socialist Movement 1897–1919* (New York 1952).

Hugh Thomas, *The Spanish Civil War* (London 1961).

Franco Venturi, *Roots of Revolution* (London 1959) [English translation of *Il Populismo Russo* (2 vols., Turin 1953).]

Voline, *Nineteen-seventeen: The Russian Revolution Betrayed* (London 1954) [English abridged edition of *Le Révolution Inconnue* (Paris n.d.)].

INDEX

Other
Universal Library Titles
IN HISTORY

THE RUSSIAN REVOLUTION
by WILLIAM HENRY CHAMBERLIN

Volume I: 1917–1918
  From the Overthrow of the Czar to the Assumption
  of Power by the Bolsheviks

Volume II: 1918–1921
  From the Civil War to the Consolidation of Power

Unequaled as an authoritative and vigorous account of the most far-reaching revolution of modern times, Chamberlin's panoramic history covers the crucial years between the fall of the Czar and the end of the Civil War. Volume I is essentially concerned with the dramatic year of revolution, 1917, that culminated in the seizure of power by the Bolsheviks. Volume II is given over to the bloody period of Civil War, counter-revolutionary activity and foreign intervention which swept Russia in the next several years and which ended in the final victory of the Soviets.

"Chamberlin's monumental history . . . represents a definitive work on which his successors will find it difficult to improve."

—V. M. DEAN

UL 188	$2.65
UL 189	$2.65

STUDIES IN REVOLUTION
by E. H. Carr

The distinguished historian, E. H. Carr, traces in these pages the ideological origins of the European revolutionary movement. Starting with Saint-Simon—the French aristocrat turned revolutionary theorist—Carr goes on to discuss the major revolutionary thinkers of the nineteenth and twentieth centuries, including Marx, Proudhon, Herzen, Plekhanov, Lenin, and Stalin. Professor Carr's sharply drawn political portraits and incisive historical analysis provide a comprehensive and dramatic introduction to the men and ideas that helped reshape Europe's history in the past hundred years.

UL 171 $1.65

ALEXANDER HERZEN AND THE BIRTH OF RUSSIAN SOCIALISM
by Martin Malia

Called by *The New York Times* "the best book on Herzen available in English," this is the exciting account of the call for revolution and overthrow of the Czar as it developed throughout Russia in the nineteenth century. In external form a history of the evolution of Herzen's thought, Professor Malia's book is, at the same time, an exploration into the spiritual, intellectual, and political history of his age and a revealing study in the relationship of ideology to political and social alienation.

UL 176 $2.65

A SELECTED LIST OF TITLES IN THE
Universal Library

History and Political Science

Literature, Criticism, Drama, and Poetry

Psychology

Titles of General Interest